Microsoft® Official Academic Course

Mobile Development
Fundamentals, Exam 98-373

WILEY

VP & PUBLISHER	Don Fowley
EDITOR	Bryan Gambrel
DIRECTOR OF SALES	Mitchell Beaton
EXECUTIVE MARKETING MANAGER	Chris Ruel
MICROSOFT PRODUCT MANAGER	Rob Linsky of Microsoft Learning
EDITORIAL PROGRAM ASSISTANT	Jennifer Lartz
ASSISTANT MARKETING MANAGER	Debbie Martin
SENIOR PRODUCTION MANAGER	Janis Soo
ASSOCIATE PRODUCTION MANAGER	Joel Balbin
CREATIVE DIRECTOR	Harry Nolan
COVER DESIGNER	Georgina Smith
TECHNOLOGY AND MEDIA	Tom Kulesa/Wendy Ashenberg

Cover photo: © Peter Cade/Getty Images, Inc.

This book was set in Garamond by Aptara, Inc. and printed and bound by Bind-Rite Robbinsville.
The cover was printed by Bind-Rite Robbinsville.

ISBN 978-1-118-35992-1

Printed in the United States of America

10 9 8 7 6 5 4 3 2 1

www.wiley.com/college/microsoft *or*
call the MOAC Toll-Free Number: 1+(888) 764-7001 (U.S. & Canada only)

Foreword from the Publisher

Wiley's publishing vision for the Microsoft Official Academic Course series is to provide students and instructors with the skills and knowledge they need to use Microsoft technology effectively in all aspects of their personal and professional lives. Quality instruction is required to help both educators and students get the most from Microsoft's software tools and to become more productive. Thus our mission is to make our instructional programs trusted educational companions for life.

To accomplish this mission, Wiley and Microsoft have partnered to develop the highest quality educational programs for Information Workers, IT Professionals, and Developers. Materials created by this partnership carry the brand name "Microsoft Official Academic Course," assuring instructors and students alike that the content of these textbooks is fully endorsed by Microsoft, and that they provide the highest quality information and instruction on Microsoft products. The Microsoft Official Academic Course textbooks are "Official" in still one more way—they are the officially sanctioned courseware for Microsoft IT Academy members.

The Microsoft Official Academic Course series focuses on *workforce development*. These programs are aimed at those students seeking to enter the workforce, change jobs, or embark on new careers as information workers, IT professionals, and developers. Microsoft Official Academic Course programs address their needs by emphasizing authentic workplace scenarios with an abundance of projects, exercises, cases, and assessments.

The Microsoft Official Academic Courses are mapped to Microsoft's extensive research and job-task analysis, the same research and analysis used to create the Microsoft Technology Associate (MTA) and Microsoft Certified Solutions Developer (MCSD) exams. The textbooks focus on real skills for real jobs. As students work through the projects and exercises in the textbooks they enhance their level of knowledge and their ability to apply the latest Microsoft technology to everyday tasks. These students also gain resume-building credentials that can assist them in finding a job, keeping their current job, or in furthering their education.

The concept of life-long learning is today an utmost necessity. Job roles, and even whole job categories, are changing so quickly that none of us can stay competitive and productive without continuously updating our skills and capabilities. The Microsoft Official Academic Course offerings, and their focus on Microsoft certification exam preparation, provide a means for people to acquire and effectively update their skills and knowledge. Wiley supports students in this endeavor through the development and distribution of these courses as Microsoft's official academic publisher.

Today educational publishing requires attention to providing quality print and robust electronic content. By integrating Microsoft Official Academic Course products, *WileyPLUS*, and Microsoft certifications, we are better able to deliver efficient learning solutions for students and teachers alike.

Joseph Heider

General Manager and Senior Vice President

Preface

Welcome to the Microsoft Official Academic Course (MOAC) program for Mobile Development Fundamentals. MOAC represents the collaboration between Microsoft Learning and John Wiley & Sons, Inc. publishing company. Microsoft and Wiley teamed up to produce a series of textbooks that deliver compelling and innovative teaching solutions to instructors and superior learning experiences for students. Infused and informed by in-depth knowledge from the creators of Microsoft products, and crafted by a publisher known worldwide for the pedagogical quality of its products, these textbooks maximize skills transfer in minimum time. Students are challenged to reach their potential by using their new technical skills as highly productive members of the workforce.

Because this knowledge base comes directly from Microsoft, creator of the Microsoft Certified Solutions Developer (MCSD) and Microsoft Technology Associate (MTA) exams (www.microsoft.com/learning/certification), you are sure to receive the topical coverage that is most relevant to students' personal and professional success. Microsoft's direct participation not only assures you that MOAC textbook content is accurate and current; it also means that students will receive the best instruction possible to enable their success on certification exams and in the workplace.

▪ The Microsoft Official Academic Course Program

The *Microsoft Official Academic Course* series is a complete program for instructors and institutions to prepare and deliver great courses on Microsoft software technologies. With MOAC, we recognize that, because of the rapid pace of change in the technology and curriculum developed by Microsoft, there is an ongoing set of needs beyond classroom instruction tools for an instructor to be ready to teach the course. The MOAC program endeavors to provide solutions for all these needs in a systematic manner in order to ensure a successful and rewarding course experience for both instructor and student—technical and curriculum training for instructor readiness with new software releases; the software itself for student use at home for building hands-on skills, assessment, and validation of skill development; and a great set of tools for delivering instruction in the classroom and lab. All are important to the smooth delivery of an interesting course on Microsoft software, and all are provided with the MOAC program. We think about the model below as a gauge for ensuring that we completely support you in your goal of teaching a great course. As you evaluate your instructional materials options, you may wish to use the model for comparison purposes with available products.

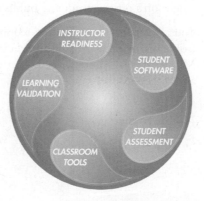

Pedagogical Features

The MOAC textbook for Mobile Development Fundamentals is designed to cover all the learning objectives for that MTA exam 98-373, which is referred to as its "objective domain." The Microsoft Technology Associate (MTA) exam objectives are highlighted throughout the textbook. Many pedagogical features have been developed specifically for *Microsoft Official Academic Course* programs.

Presenting the extensive procedural information and technical concepts woven throughout the textbook raises challenges for the student and instructor alike. The Illustrated Book Tour that follows provides a guide to the rich features contributing to *Microsoft Official Academic Course* program's pedagogical plan. Following is a list of key features in each lesson designed to prepare students for success as they continue in their IT education, on the certification exams, and in the workplace:

- Each lesson begins with an **Exam Objective Matrix**. More than a standard list of learning objectives, the Exam Objective Matrix correlates each software skill covered in the lesson to the specific exam objective domain.

- Concise and frequent **Step-by-Step** instructions teach students new features and provide an opportunity for hands-on practice. Numbered steps give detailed, step-by-step instructions to help students learn software skills.

- **Illustrations:** Screen images provide visual feedback as students work through the exercises. The images reinforce key concepts, provide visual clues about the steps, and allow students to check their progress.

- **Key Terms:** Important technical vocabulary is listed with definitions at the beginning of the lesson. When these terms are used later in the lesson, they appear in bold italic type and are defined. The Glossary contains all of the key terms and their definitions.

- Engaging point-of-use **Reader Aids**, located throughout the lessons, tell students why this topic is relevant (*The Bottom Line*), and provide students with helpful hints (*Take Note*). Reader Aids also provide additional relevant or background information that adds value to the lesson.

- **Certification Ready** features throughout the text signal students where a specific certification objective is covered. They provide students with a chance to check their understanding of that particular MTA objective and, if necessary, review the section of the lesson where it is covered. MOAC offers complete preparation for MTA certification.

- **End-of-Lesson Questions:** The Knowledge Assessment section provides a variety of multiple-choice, true-false, matching, and fill-in-the-blank questions.

- **End-of-Lesson Exercises:** Competency Assessment case scenarios and Proficiency Assessment case scenarios are projects that test students' ability to apply what they've learned in the lesson.

■ Lesson Features

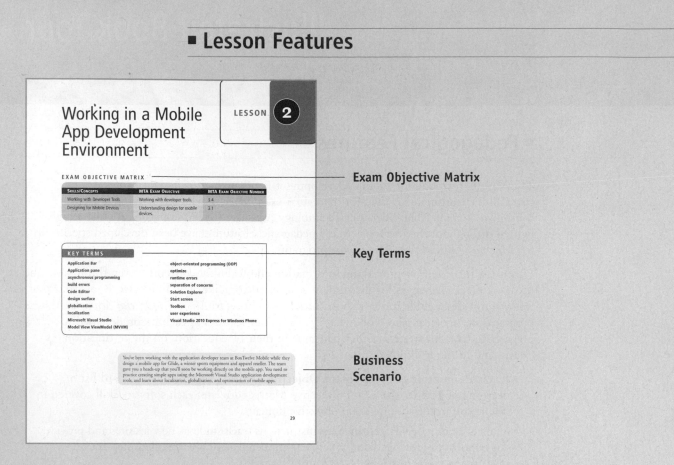

Exam Objective Matrix

Key Terms

Business Scenario

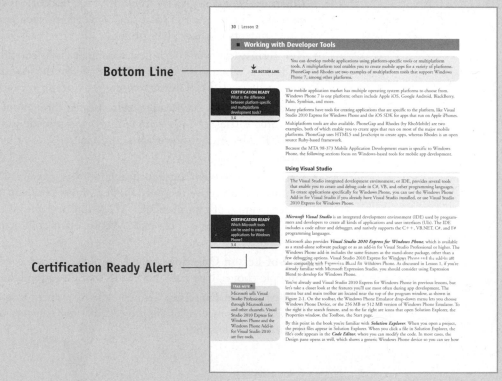

Bottom Line

Certification Ready Alert

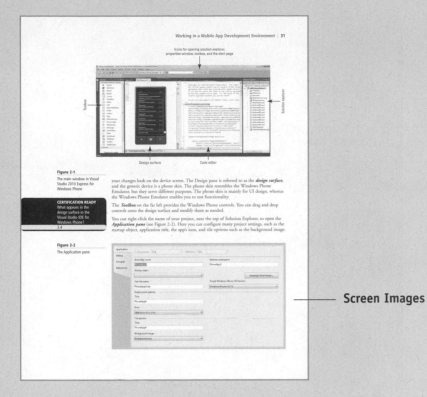

Screen Images

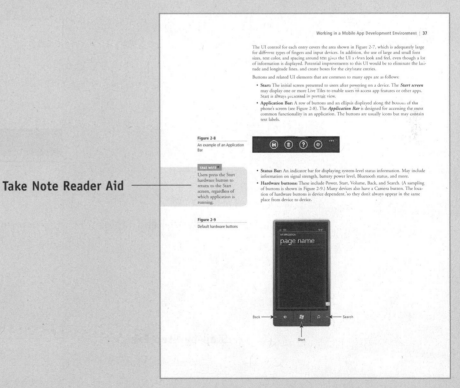

Take Note Reader Aid

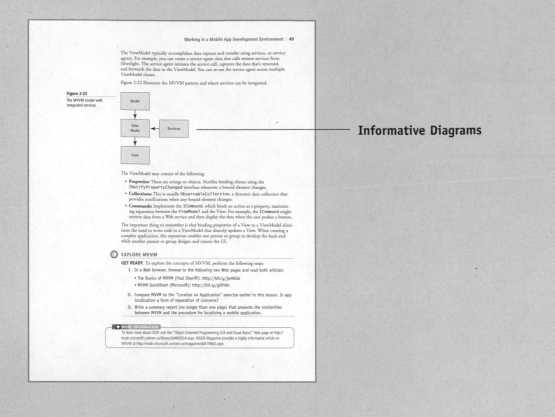

Informative Diagrams

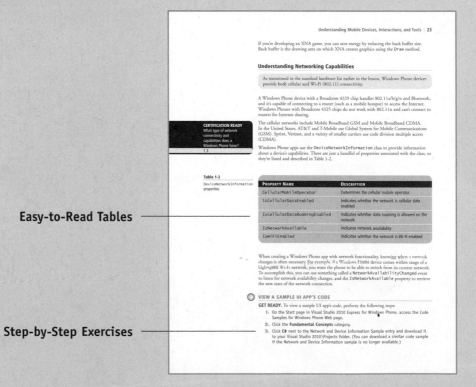

Easy-to-Read Tables

Step-by-Step Exercises

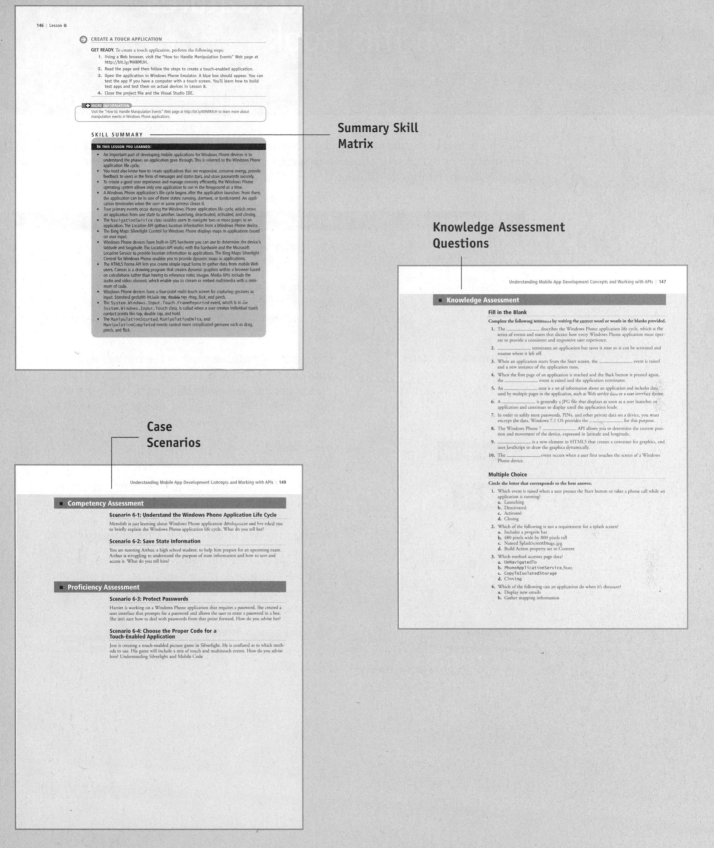

Summary Skill Matrix

Knowledge Assessment Questions

Case Scenarios

Conventions and Features Used in This Book

This book uses particular fonts, symbols, and heading conventions to highlight important information or to call your attention to special steps. For more information about the features in each lesson, refer to the Illustrated Book Tour section.

CONVENTION	MEANING
↓ **THE BOTTOM LINE**	This feature provides a brief summary of the material to be covered in the section that follows.
CLOSE	Words in all capital letters indicate instructions for opening, saving, or closing files or programs. They also point out items you should check or actions you should take.
CERTIFICATION READY	This feature signals the point in the text where a specific certification objective is covered. It provides you with a chance to check your understanding of that particular MTA objective and, if necessary, review the section of the lesson where it is covered.
TAKE NOTE*	Reader aids appear in shaded boxes found in your text. *Take Note* provides helpful hints related to particular tasks or topics.
X REF	These notes provide pointers to information discussed elsewhere in the textbook or describe interesting features of ASP.NET or Windows Phone 7 that are not directly addressed in the current topic or exercise.
Alt + Tab	A plus sign (+) between two key names means that you must press both keys at the same time. Keys that you are instructed to press in an exercise will appear in the font shown here.
Example	Key terms appear in bold italic.

www.wiley.com/college/microsoft *or*
call the MOAC Toll-Free Number: 1+(888) 764-7001 (U.S. & Canada only)

Instructor Support Program

The *Microsoft Official Academic Course* programs are accompanied by a rich array of resources that incorporate the extensive textbook visuals to form a pedagogically cohesive package. These resources provide all the materials instructors need to deploy and deliver their courses. Resources available online for download include:

- **DreamSpark Premium** is designed to provide the easiest and most inexpensive developer tools, products, and technologies available to faculty and students in labs, classrooms, and on student PCs. A free 3-year membership is available to qualified MOAC adopters.

  Note: Microsoft Visual Studio and ASP.NET can be downloaded from DreamSpark Premium for use by students in this course.

- The **Instructor Guide** contains Solutions to all the textbook exercises and Syllabi for various term lengths. The Instructor Guides also includes chapter summaries and lecture notes. The Instructor's Guide is available from the Book Companion site (http://www.wiley.com/college/microsoft).

- The **Test Bank** contains hundreds of questions in multiple-choice, true-false, short answer, and essay formats, and is available to download from the Instructor's Book Companion site (www.wiley.com/college/microsoft). A complete answer key is provided.

- A complete set of **PowerPoint presentations and images** are available on the Instructor's Book Companion site (http://www.wiley.com/college/microsoft) to enhance classroom presentations. Approximately 50 PowerPoint slides are provided for each lesson. Tailored to the text's topical coverage and Skills Matrix, these presentations are designed to convey key concepts addressed in the text. All images from the text are on the Instructor's Book Companion site (http://www.wiley.com/college/microsoft). You can incorporate them into your PowerPoint presentations, or create your own overhead transparencies and handouts. By using these visuals in class discussions, you can help focus students' attention on key elements of technologies covered and help them understand how to use it effectively in the workplace.

Wiley Faculty Network

- When it comes to improving the classroom experience, there is no better source of ideas and inspiration than your fellow colleagues. The **Wiley Faculty Network** connects teachers with technology, facilitates the exchange of best practices, and helps to enhance instructional efficiency and effectiveness. Faculty Network activities include technology training and tutorials, virtual seminars, peer-to-peer exchanges of experiences and ideas, personal consulting, and sharing of resources. For details visit www.WhereFacultyConnect.com.

DREAMSPARK PREMIUM—FREE 3-YEAR MEMBERSHIP AVAILABLE TO QUALIFIED ADOPTERS!

DreamSpark Premium is designed to provide the easiest and most inexpensive way for universities to make the latest Microsoft developer tools, products, and technologies available in labs, classrooms, and on student PCs. DreamSpark Premium is an annual membership program for departments teaching Science, Technology, Engineering, and Mathematics (STEM) courses. The membership provides a complete solution to keep academic labs, faculty, and students on the leading edge of technology.

Software available in the DreamSpark Premium program is provided at no charge to adopting departments through the Wiley and Microsoft publishing partnership.

And tools that professors can use to engage and inspire today's technology students.

Contact your Wiley rep for details.

For more information about the DreamSpark Premium program, go to:

https://www.dreamspark.com/

Note: Microsoft Visual Studio and ASP.NET can be downloaded from DreamSpark Premium for use by students in this course.

■ Important Web Addresses and Phone Numbers

To locate the Wiley Higher Education Rep in your area, go to http://www.wiley.com/ college and click on the "*Who's My Rep?*" link at the top of the page, or call the MOAC Toll Free Number: 1 + (888) 764-7001 (U.S. & Canada only).

To learn more about becoming certified and exam availability, visit www.microsoft.com/ learning/mcp/mcp.

■ Additional Resources

Book Companion Web Site (www.wiley.com/college/microsoft)

The students' book companion site for the MOAC series includes any resources, exercise files, and Web links that will be used in conjunction with this course.

Wiley Desktop Editions

Wiley MOAC Desktop Editions are innovative, electronic versions of printed textbooks. Students buy the desktop version for up to 40% off the U.S. price of the printed text, and get the added value of permanence and portability. Wiley Desktop Editions provide students with numerous additional benefits that are not available with other e-text solutions.

Wiley Desktop Editions are NOT subscriptions; students download the Wiley Desktop Edition to their computer desktops. Students own the content they buy to keep for as long as they want. Once a Wiley Desktop Edition is downloaded to the computer desktop, students have instant access to all of the content without being online. Students can also print out the sections they prefer to read in hard copy. Students also have access to fully integrated resources within their Wiley Desktop Edition. From highlighting their e-text to taking and sharing notes, students can easily personalize their Wiley Desktop Edition as they are reading or following along in class.

■ About the Microsoft Technology Associate (MTA) Certification

Preparing Tomorrow's Technology Workforce

Technology plays a role in virtually every business around the world. Possessing the fundamental knowledge of how technology works and understanding its impact on today's academic and workplace environment is increasingly important—particularly for students interested in exploring professions involving technology. That's why Microsoft created the Microsoft Technology Associate (MTA) certification—a new entry-level credential that validates fundamental technology knowledge among students seeking to build a career in technology.

The Microsoft Technology Associate (MTA) certification is the ideal and preferred path to Microsoft's world-renowned technology certification programs, such as Microsoft Certified Solutions Developer (MCSD). MTA is positioned to become the premier credential for individuals seeking to explore and pursue a career in technology, or augment related pursuits such as business or any other field where technology is pervasive.

MTA Candidate Profile

The MTA certification program is designed specifically for secondary and post-secondary students interested in exploring academic and career options in a technology field. It offers students a certification in basic IT and development. As the new recommended entry point for Microsoft technology certifications, MTA is designed especially for students new to IT and software development. It is available exclusively in educational settings and easily integrates into the curricula of existing computer classes.

MTA Empowers Educators and Motivates Students

MTA provides a new standard for measuring and validating fundamental technology knowledge right in the classroom while keeping your budget and teaching resources intact. MTA helps institutions stand out as innovative providers of high-demand industry credentials and is easily deployed with a simple, convenient, and affordable suite of entry-level technology certification exams. MTA enables students to explore career paths in technology without requiring a big investment of time and resources, while providing a career foundation and the confidence to succeed in advanced studies and future vocational endeavors.

In addition to giving students an entry-level Microsoft certification, MTA is designed to be a stepping stone to other, more advanced Microsoft technology certifications, like the Microsoft Certified Solutions Developer (MCSD) certification.

Delivering MTA Exams: The MTA Campus License

Implementing a new certification program in your classroom has never been so easy with the MTA Campus License. Through the purchase of an annual MTA Campus License, there's no more need for ad hoc budget requests and recurrent purchases of exam vouchers. Now you can budget for one low cost for the entire year, and then administer MTA exams to your students and other faculty across your entire campus where and when you want.

The MTA Campus License provides a convenient and affordable suite of entry-level technology certifications designed to empower educators and motivate students as they build a foundation for their careers.

The MTA Campus License is administered by Certiport, Microsoft's exclusive MTA exam provider.

To learn more about becoming a Microsoft Technology Associate and exam availability, visit www.microsoft.com/learning/mta.

▪ Activate Your FREE MTA Practice Test!

Your purchase of this book entitles you to a free MTA practice test from GMetrix (a $30 value). Please go to www.gmetrix.com/mtatests and use the following validation code to redeem your free test: **MTA98-373-FFDB5DA19E61**.

The **GMetrix Skills Management System** provides everything you need to practice for the Microsoft Technology Associate (MTA) Certification.

Overview of Test features:

- Practice tests map to the Microsoft Technology Associate (MTA) exam objectives
- GMetrix MTA practice tests simulate the actual MTA testing environment
- 50+ questions per test covering all objectives
- Progress at own pace, save test to resume later, return to skipped questions
- Detailed, printable score report highlighting areas requiring further review

To get the most from your MTA preparation, take advantage of your free GMetrix MTA Practice Test today!

For technical support issues on installation or code activation, please email support@gmetrix.com.

Acknowledgments

■ MOAC MTA Technology Fundamentals Reviewers

We'd like to thank the many reviewers who pored over the manuscript and provided invaluable feedback in the service of quality instructional materials:

Yuke Wang, University of Texas at Dallas

Palaniappan Vairavan, Bellevue College

Harold "Buz" Lamson, ITT Technical Institute

Colin Archibald, Valencia Community College

Catherine Bradfield, DeVry University Online

Robert Nelson, Blinn College

Kalpana Viswanathan, Bellevue College

Bob Becker, Vatterott College

Carol Torkko, Bellevue College

Bharat Kandel, Missouri Tech

Linda Cohen, Forsyth Technical Community College

Candice Lambert, Metro Technology Centers

Susan Mahon, Collin College

Mark Aruda, Hillsborough Community College

Claude Russo, Brevard Community College

Heith Hennel, Valencia College

Adrian Genesir, Western Governors University

Zeshan Sattar, Zenos

Douglas Tabbutt, Blackhawk Technical College

David Koppy, Baker College

Sharon Moran, Hillsborough Community College

Keith Hoell, Briarcliffe College and Queens College—CUNY

Mark Hufnagel, Lee County School District

Rachelle Hall, Glendale Community College

Scott Elliott, Christie Digital Systems, Inc.

Gralan Gilliam, Kaplan

Steve Strom, Butler Community College

John Crowley, Bucks County Community College

Margaret Leary, Northern Virginia Community College

Sue Miner, Lehigh Carbon Community College

Gary Rollinson, Cabrillo College

Al Kelly, University of Advancing Technology

Katherine James, Seneca College

David Kidd, Western Governors University

Bob Treichel, Lake Havasu Unified School District & Mohave Community College

Brief Contents

Contents

Understanding Mobile Devices, Interactions, and Tools

EXAM OBJECTIVE MATRIX

SKILLS/CONCEPTS	MTA EXAM OBJECTIVE	MTA EXAM OBJECTIVE NUMBER
Introduction to Mobile App Development for Windows Phone Devices		
Understanding Mobile Device Tools	Understanding mobile device tools.	1.1
Understanding the Physical Capabilities of Mobile Devices	Understanding the physical capabilities of the mobile device.	1.2
Planning for Physical Interactions with the Mobile Device	Planning for physical interactions with the mobile device.	1.3

KEY TERMS

.NET Framework

Accelerometer sensor

App Hub

application capabilities

application manifest

application programming interface (API)

backward-compatible

class

Compass sensor

framework

gesture

Gyroscope sensor

mobile app

Motion API

opting in

sensor

Silverlight for Windows Phone

software development kit (SDK)

touch event

Windows Phone

Windows Phone Marketplace

Windows Phone Software Development Kit (SDK)

XNA framework

You are an entry-level application developer at BoxTwelve Mobile. Your manager has asked you to work with the development team to create Windows Phone apps for a new client that sells winter sports equipment and apparel. Your goal is to learn about Windows Phone app development tools and device essentials to be ready to assist the developers when work begins next week.

■ Introduction to Mobile App Development for Windows Phone Devices

↓ THE BOTTOM LINE

A mobile app is a software program designed to run on a mobile device, like a Windows Phone. To create apps for Windows Phone, you use one of two development platforms: Microsoft Silverlight for Windows Phone or the XNA framework.

The mobile device scene has exploded in the last few years, with thousands of applications (apps) available to run on a variety of mobile devices like smartphones. A *mobile app* is simply a small software program designed to run on a mobile device, and many mobile apps are actually Web-based programs that help you connect to the Internet and interact with a Web site. Apps generally come with crisp, clean user interfaces (UIs) that are fun, easy to use, and functional.

Anyone who has purchased a smartphone knows there are many choices, from Windows Phones to iPhones to Android devices and more. This book is an introduction to Windows Phones and will help you prepare for the Microsoft Technology Associate (MTA) 98-373 certification exam.

The term *Windows Phone* refers to a device or the operating system that runs on the device. Currently, device versions are Windows Phone 7 and Windows Phone 7.5. Each uses a slightly different operating system version, as shown in Table 1-1.

Table 1-1

Windows Phone devices and operating systems

DEVICE RELEASE	OPERATING SYSTEM VERSION
Windows Phone 7	Windows Phone OS 7.0
Windows Phone 7.5	Windows Phone OS 7.1

Applications created for Windows Phone OS 7.0 run on both Windows Phone 7 and Windows Phone 7.5 devices. However, applications developed for Windows Phone OS 7.1 are not *backward-compatible*, which means they don't work on devices running a previous version of the operating system, which in this case is Windows Phone OS 7.0. To reach the widest audience, developers create apps that run on both operating systems.

TAKE NOTE*

Although the MTA 98-373 exam is geared toward Windows Phone OS 7.x as of this writing, the Microsoft Windows Phone 8 operating system, associated developer tools, and supported devices will be available when this book is in print. According to Microsoft, Windows Phone 7.x applications run on Windows Phone 8, and Windows Phone 8 developer tools support building applications for Windows Phone 7.x. The new tools let you choose to target Windows Phone 7.x or 8.0 when creating an application. To ensure your application will run on either operating system, build it for Windows Phone 7.x; an app built specifically for Windows Phone 8 will not run in Windows Phone 7.x.

Development Platforms for Windows Phones

Developers can use two platforms to create Windows Phone apps: Silverlight for Windows Phone or the XNA framework. Whereas Silverlight is geared toward data-driven apps and games, the XNA framework is used primarily for game development.

To develop for Windows Phone, the primary platforms used are Microsoft Silverlight for Windows Phone or the XNA framework.

Silverlight for Windows Phone is a development platform that enables you to create all kinds of data-driven apps like news feeds and weather reports, client apps for social media sites like Digg and Facebook, and games. The **XNA framework** is a set of tools provided by Microsoft for game development.

Silverlight combines two languages to create apps: Extensible Application Markup Language (XAML) to create the user interface and a .NET framework language that makes the app run. The **.NET Framework** is a Windows component that includes several programming languages, such as C# and Visual Basic (VB), and provides the code-execution environment. Developers write applications using one of the .NET languages, and the apps execute inside of a runtime environment called the Common Language Runtime.

TAKE NOTE*

In Lesson 5, you'll dive into Silverlight. You'll also be introduced to HTML5, the up-and-coming Web markup language. As you'll see, you can use Silverlight and HTML5 to create Internet apps that run on mobile devices. Regarding Windows Phone 8, keep in mind that HTML5 features are supported by the new operating system but only from within a browser. Applications written in XNA and Silverlight are targeted for Windows Phone 7.x and will run in Windows Phone 8, however, you can't write apps in XNA or Silverlight specifically for Windows Phone 8. You can get the latest details at the Windows Phone Dev Center at http://dev.windowsphone.com/en-us/home.

The XNA framework has historically been used to develop Windows and Xbox 360 applications. If you're creating a game for Windows Phone, especially a 3D game, you'll likely use the XNA framework. Like Silverlight, XNA framework uses either C# or VB code, however, it does not use XAML. Starting with Windows Phone 7.5, you can combine features of Silverlight for Windows Phone and the XNA framework in a Windows Phone app. Doing so lets you create mobile apps and games with a user interface based on XAML and code in C# or VB.

This book focuses mainly on Silverlight for Windows Phone and the C# programming language. You will revisit XNA framework again in Lesson 5.

➕ MORE INFORMATION

If you need help deciding whether to use Silverlight or XNA, visit the "Developing a Windows Phone Application from Start to Finish" Web page at http://bit.ly/hs6gzQ.

Exploring the Development and Marketplace Submission Process

App Hub is a Microsoft portal that developers must join to submit apps to the Windows Phone Marketplace. The general app development lifecycle includes registering at App Hub, planning your app, developing and testing your app, gathering certification requirements, and submitting the app to the Windows Phone Marketplace.

TAKE NOTE*

The App Hub membership fee is waived for Microsoft DreamSpark students. DreamSpark is an international program that gives eligible students free access to commercial developer tools, like Microsoft Visual Studio Professional.

TAKE NOTE*

Although Zune software is used for connecting to a Windows Phone 7 device for app testing purposes, Microsoft will likely replace Zune with another technology for Windows Phone 8 app development.

TAKE NOTE*

Windows Phone app certification should not be confused with MTA certification; the former certifies a program is viable for distribution, the latter certifies an individual understands a technology.

Windows Phone developers start by registering at *App Hub*, a Microsoft portal that gives you access to development tools, sample code, and online help in the form of documentation and forums. You must have a Windows Live ID to register at App Hub.

App Hub offers an annual membership, which is required to be able to submit an app to the *Windows Phone Marketplace*, an online store where users buy apps and download some for free. If you simply register and don't pay for an App Hub membership, you can still use the site and post to the forums but you can't submit apps. To download apps from the Marketplace, you must have a registered Windows Phone device.

To start developing apps, download and install the free Windows Phone Software Development Kit (which you'll learn about shortly), and then plan and develop your app. The kit includes app development programs and utilities for testing your app without the need for a physical device.

Another free software package that mobile app developers use is Zune. The software was designed originally to synchronize media files (mainly music) between a PC and a mobile device. You can also use Zune to download apps from the Marketplace and get updates for your device. Because of the PC-to-device synchronization feature, many developers use Zune to test apps on a physical device during development.

When you're ready to submit an app to the Marketplace, you must decide whether you want to sell the app, make it available as a free download, or make money by displaying ads when your app runs. The submission process also requires you to describe your app, provide artwork for the Marketplace Web site listing, and other tasks. Your app will go through a certification process to ensure it runs properly, is reliable, and is free of malicious content. Upon approval, your app will be published on the Marketplace site and appear in the Windows Phone Marketplace catalog.

The general Windows Phone app development lifecycle, shown in Figure 1-1, is summarized as follows:

- **Register as a Windows Phone developer:** You must register through App Hub.
- **Plan your app:** Decide which type of app you want to create, what it should look like, and the general flow of how it works.
- **Develop and test your app:** Use the free tools provided by Microsoft to create and thoroughly test your app.
- **Gather and verify prerequisites for certification:** All apps must be certified by Microsoft before distribution. Microsoft provides a checklist to help you prepare for certification.
- **Submit your app for certification:** Once you've developed and thoroughly tested a mobile app or game, you can submit it to the Windows Phone Marketplace for certification and approval.

Figure 1-1

The Windows Phone app development lifecycle

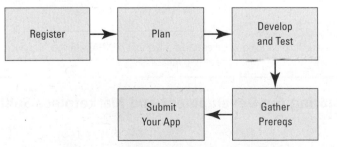

Lesson 8 covers all of the details for testing and distributing Windows Phone apps. As you'll learn throughout the lessons in this book, a good deal of work goes into a well-designed, well-behaved app. So let's start by becoming familiar with the Marketplace and App Hub by working through the next exercise, and then look at the tools you use to develop apps.

⊕ EXPLORE APPS IN THE WINDOWS PHONE MARKETPLACE

GET READY. To find out the kinds of apps available on the Windows Phone Marketplace Web site, perform the following steps:

1. Go to the Windows Phone Marketplace main Web page at **http://www.windowsphone. com/en-US/marketplace**.

2. Browse through the apps and note at least five that appeal to your interests. Make a note of the app name and universal resource locator (URL).

3. If you have a registered Windows Phone, use the device to download a few free apps and see how they work.

4. If you're continuing immediately to the next exercise, leave your Web browser open.

⊕ REGISTER AT APP HUB

GET READY. To register at App Hub, perform the following steps:

1. Go to the App Hub main Web page at **create.msdn.com/en-US/**.

2. Click the sign in link in the upper-right corner. You are prompted to sign in to your Windows Live account. (You can register for a free account if you don't have one.)

3. The App Hub registration process begins. Follow the prompts to select your account type (Company, Individual, or Student), enter personal details, enter profile information, and pay (if joining as a member).

   When entering personal details, you're asked for your publisher name (see Figure 1-2). That's the name that appears as the publisher of your apps in the Marketplace. Consider this carefully because once you select a name, you can't change it. If you decide to publish under a different publisher name, you need to create a new account and pay another membership fee.

Figure 1-2

A portion of the App Hub Personal Details registration page

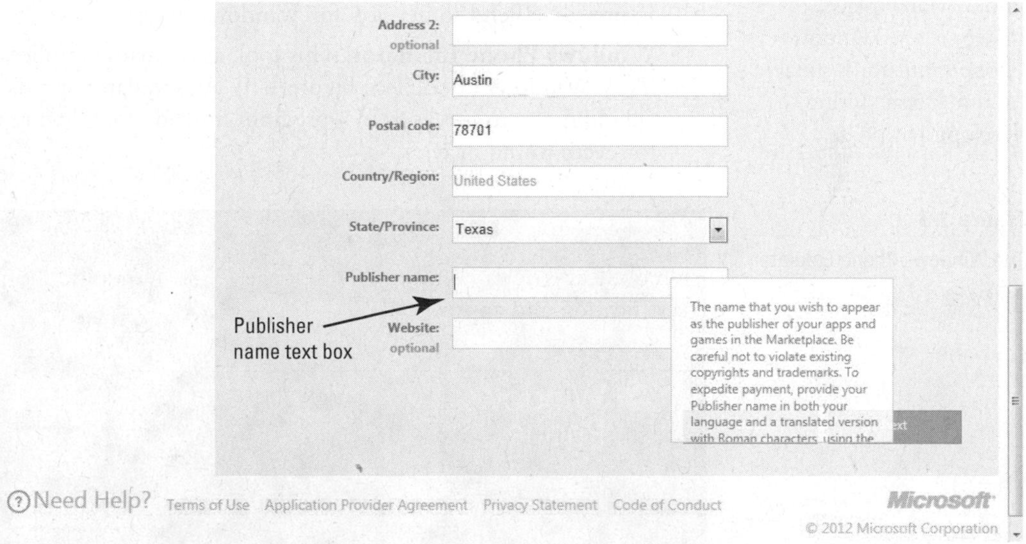

4. When you get to the Membership screen, you can pay to join or just click **Cancel**. You can join later by updating your App Hub account.

5. Your App Hub account is set up and ready to use. Feel free to browse the App Hub site to learn about its features and resources.

6. If you're continuing immediately to the next section, leave your Web browser open.

■ Understanding Mobile Device Tools

THE BOTTOM LINE

Windows Phone development uses a set of tools available in the Windows Phone Software Development Kit, referred to as the SDK. The SDK includes Visual Studio 2010 Express for Windows Phone, Silverlight for Windows Phone, XNA 4.0 Game Studio, Expression Blend for Windows Phone, and Windows Phone Emulator.

CERTIFICATION READY
Which tools are used to create and test Windows Phone apps?
1.1

To develop apps and games for Windows Phone devices, you need to install a suite of tools collectively called the *Windows Phone Software Development Kit (SDK)*. The latest version at this writing is SDK 7.1, which is geared toward Windows Phone 7.0 and Windows Phone 7.5 devices. The Windows Phone SDK is available for download from http://bit.ly/qpof3e.

The primary tools included in the Windows Phone SDK are as follows:

- **Visual Studio 2010 Express for Windows Phone:** This is the main program in which you create apps. When you create a new project (app) in Visual Studio 2010 Express, you choose whether the app will be based on Silverlight for Windows Phone or XNA Game Studio.

- **Silverlight for Windows Phone:** This tool enables you to create Silverlight apps.

- **Windows Phone SDK 7.1 Extensions for XNA 4.0 Game Studio:** This tool enables you to create games using the XNA framework.

- **Expression Blend for Windows Phone:** This is another Microsoft development platform that works with Visual Studio to create apps. If you're already familiar with Microsoft Expression Studio (such as for developing Web apps), you should consider using Expression Blend to develop for Windows Phone.

- **Windows Phone Emulator:** This tool, as the name implies, is software that acts much like a Windows Phone (see Figure 1-3). An emulator speeds up development time by enabling you to test apps in a program instead of deploying the app to a physical device for every round of tests.

TAKE NOTE ✱

You must test your apps on a physical Windows Phone before submitting the app to the Windows Phone Marketplace. However, the Windows Phone Emulator is suitable for quick tests during the development phase.

Figure 1-3

The Windows Phone Emulator

In addition to the tools listed above, the Windows Phone SDK also installs several helper applications, utilities, and assemblies that support one or more of the main tools.

To install the SDK, you must be running Windows Vista x86 or x64 with Service Pack 2 or Windows 7 x86 or x64. All editions except Starter edition will work. Your computer must have at least 4 gigabytes (GB) of free disk space on the drive on which you install the tools, and at least 3 GB of random access memory (RAM). For better performance and to ensure you have plenty of storage space for new projects, a computer with at least 8 GB of RAM and 10 GB or more of free disk space is recommended.

TAKE NOTE*

You'll come across several development terms throughout this lesson, so here's a brief glossary: A *software development kit (SDK)* is a set of installable programs and components that provide a framework. A *framework* is a collection of APIs. An *application programming interface (API)* is a set of software functionalities (data structures, protocols, routines, and so on) released by a software manufacturer to help developers design applications more easily. Assemblies and class libraries provide the data and machine instructions required to implement the functionalities.

INSTALL THE WINDOWS PHONE SDK

TAKE NOTE*

The Windows Phone SDK 7.1.x runs in Windows 7 or Windows Vista with Service Pack 2. As of this writing, the Windows Phone 8 SDK must be installed in the Windows 8 operating system.

GET READY. To install the Windows Phone SDK, perform the following steps:

1. In Windows Explorer, in the Downloads folder, create a subfolder named **Windows Phone Dev Tools**.

2. Using a Web browser, go to the Windows Phone SDK Web page at http://bit.ly/qpof3e. Download the **release notes** and the **installation EXE file**, as shown in Figure 1-4, to your Windows Phone Dev Tools folder.

3. Read the release notes.

4. Double-click the **EXE** file to install the SDK tools and necessary components on your computer.

5. Installing the set of tools can take several minutes to an hour, depending on the speed of your computer. When the installation is complete, click **Exit** as shown in Figure 1-5.

Figure 1-4

The Windows SDK download Web page

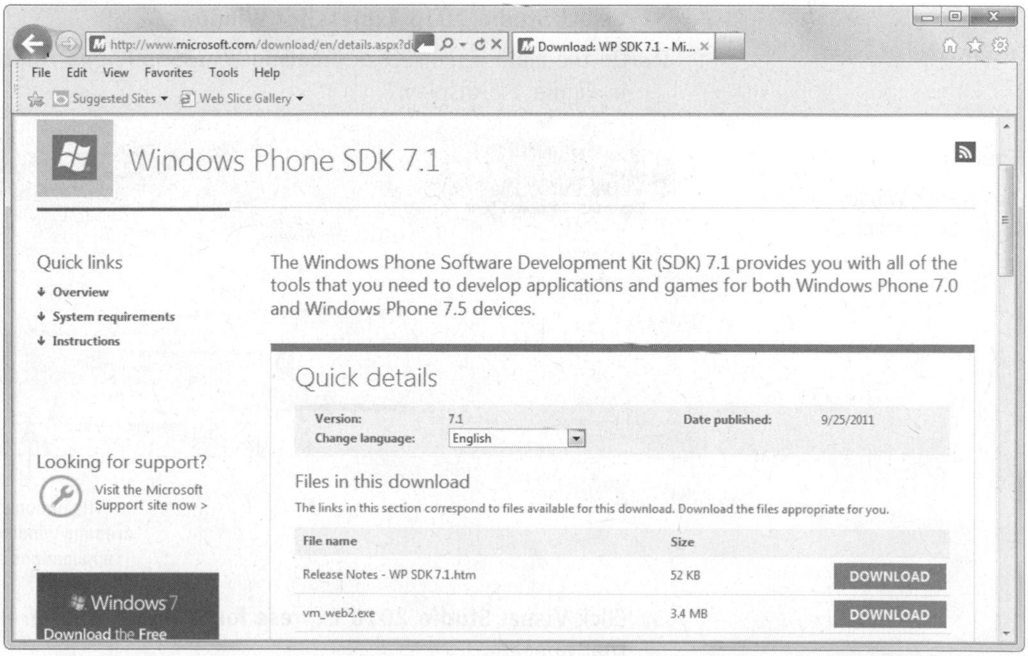

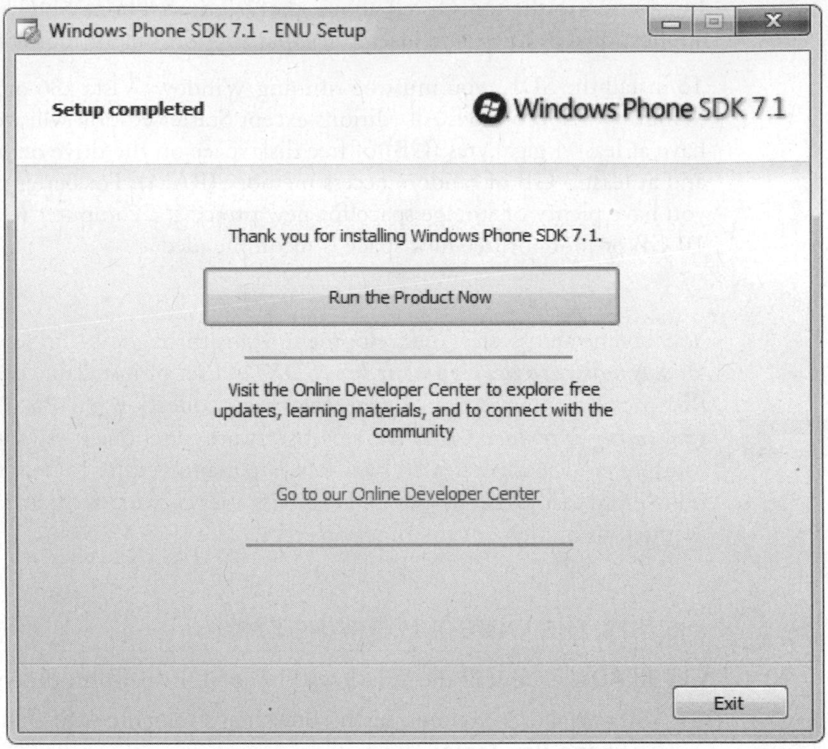

Figure 1-5

The installation is complete

6. Microsoft often makes updates available to its tools and programs. Scroll down the Windows SDK Web page. If you see a link for an update to the SDK, click the link, and then follow the instructions for downloading and installing the update.

7. Restart your computer.

⊙ TAKE A TOUR OF VISUAL STUDIO 2010 EXPRESS FOR WINDOWS PHONE

GET READY. To become familiar with Visual Studio 2010 Express for Windows Phone, perform the following steps:

1. To open the software, click **Start > All Programs > Visual Studio 2010 Express > Visual Studio 2010 Express for Windows**.

2. On the main screen, click **Creating Windows Phone Applications**. The options shown in Figure 1-6 display.

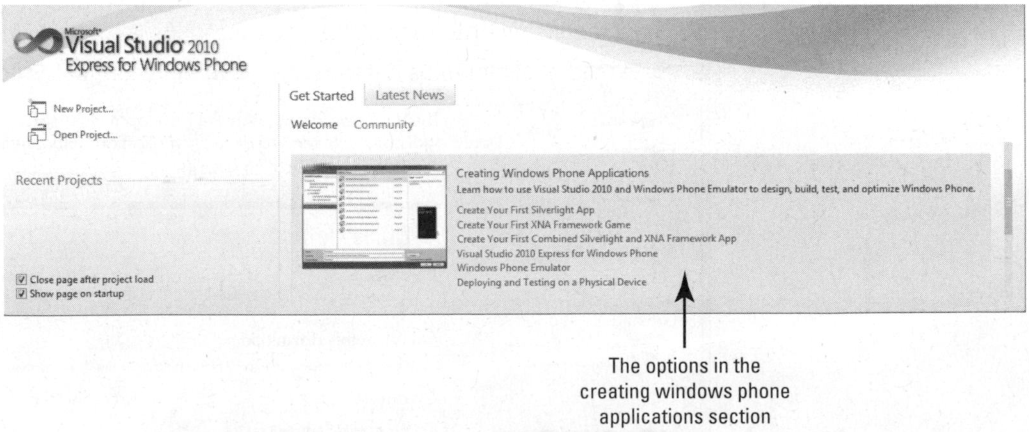

Figure 1-6

The Creating Windows Phone Applications options

The options in the creating windows phone applications section

3. Click **Visual Studio 2010 Express for Windows Phone.** Read through the Web page that appears.

4. When you're done, click the **X** in the tab for the Web browser window to return to the Visual Studio 2010 Express start page.

5. Leave the program open and continue with the next exercise.

➔ DOWNLOAD A CODE SAMPLE

GET READY. To find some sample code to work with until you begin creating your own app, perform the following steps:

1. In Visual Studio 2010 Express for Windows Phone, scroll down the start page and click **Learning Resources**.

2. Click **Code Samples for Windows Phone**. On the Code Samples for Windows Phone Web page that appears, click the **Fundamental Concepts** category.

3. Browse the samples and choose one that looks interesting to you.

4. Click **C#** next to the sample (see Figure 1-7) to download the C# code to your computer. (You can download the VB code if you prefer.)

Figure 1-7

Selecting a code sample

◢ Common Application Development Tasks

The following code samples demonstrate some of the common development tasks when you create a Windows Phone application.

	Download	Settings Sample
☑ CheckBox Setting Times New Roman Arial Comic Sans MS	C# | VB	This sample shows two Settings screens, one where the settings changes take effect immediately and one where the user has to confirm the changes. For more information on adding settings to your application, see How to: Create a Settings Page for Windows Phone. *Updated 9/2011*
highlights: Contains digits only. Press period key to display addit 1 2 4 5	Download C# | VB	**Keyboard Index Sample** You can change the on-screen keyboard to one of 10 built-in options. This technique makes it much faster and easier for users to enter data in your applications. This sample lets you see all 10 options, and explains the highlights of each. For more

5. Save the archive file to your My Documents\Visual Studio 2010\Projects folder.

6. In Windows Explorer, navigate to **My Documents\Visual Studio 2010\Projects**, double-click the ZIP file, and extract the contents.

7. In Visual Studio 2010 Express, close the Code Samples for Windows Phone window by clicking the **X** in the tab.

8. Click **Open project** on the Start page, or select **File > Open Project**.

9. Double-click the code sample's folder in the Projects folder, select the **.sln** file, and click **Open**.

10. Browse the Solution Explorer pane on the right side of the window. Solution Explorer should look similar to Figure 1-8.

11. Click through the items on the menu bar at the top of the Visual Studio 2010 Express window to become familiar with them.

12. Select **File > Close Solution** to close the code sample files, and then close Visual Studio 2010 Express.

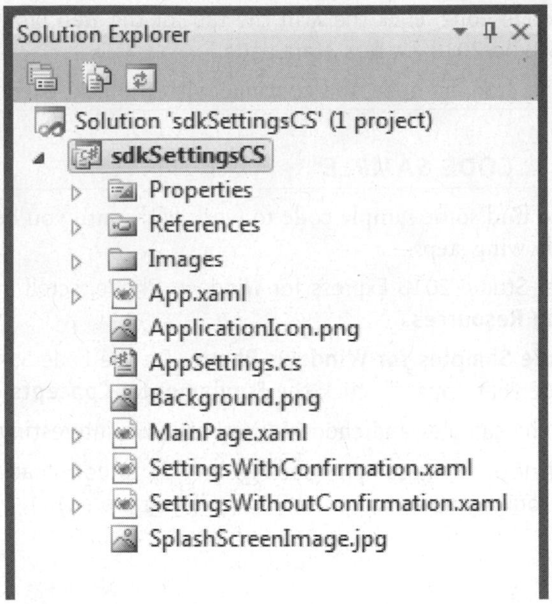

Figure 1-8

The Solution Explorer pane

```
Solution Explorer                    ▼ ⊣ ×
  📋 | 📑 📲
  📦 Solution 'sdkSettingsCS' (1 project)
  ▲  📰 sdkSettingsCS
     ▷  📑 Properties
     ▷  📁 References
     ▷  📁 Images
     ▷  📰 App.xaml
        🖼 ApplicationIcon.png
        📄 AppSettings.cs
        🖼 Background.png
     ▷  📰 MainPage.xaml
     ▷  📰 SettingsWithConfirmation.xaml
     ▷  📰 SettingsWithoutConfirmation.xaml
        🖼 SplashScreenImage.jpg
```

➕ **MORE INFORMATION**

To learn more about the Windows Phone SDK, visit the "Installing the Windows Phone SDK" Web page at http://bit.ly/pMsIay. To understand what's changed in Windows Phone SDK 7.1, go to http://bit.ly/jeUC0b and the "What's New in the Windows Phone SDK 7.1.1 Update" Web page at http://bit.ly/A738GT.

Understanding Windows Phone Application Capabilities and Detection Tools

Application capabilities are features that can be used by a Windows Phone. They may require the user to opt in to use them due to privacy or security concerns. Capabilities are listed in a file called the application manifest, which is required for submission to the Windows Phone Marketplace. You can use the Windows Phone Capability Detection Tool and the Windows Phone Marketplace Test Kit to autodetect app capabilities and update the manifest file.

Windows Phone works under a security model that's based on capabilities. This model requires a user to opt in to capabilities offered by an application. *Application capabilities* are features that can be used by a Windows Phone device. *Opting in* is a way for users to choose features they want to use that might pose privacy or security issues. Application capabilities can include networking, geolocation, a camera, and many more.

TAKE NOTE*

To understand opt in, consider an application that works with Twitter and provides geolocation. When a user (named Mike, for example) tweets on the mobile device, he can tap a link to geolocate the tweet, which displays the location from where Mike posted the tweet. This is the opt-in part—by tapping the link, Mike is opting in, or giving his device permission to use the geolocation service to geotag his tweet.

Developers use a file called the *application manifest* to list an application's capabilities. When you first create a project in an app development tool, the software automatically creates the manifest file, which you may have to modify as you develop and change your app. If you don't specify an application's capabilities accurately, your app might not run as expected. It's also likely to fail the validation process when you submit your app to the Windows Phone Marketplace.

The name of the Windows Phone application manifest file is WMAppManifest.xml. An example of the Capabilities section of the file for a sample app is shown in Figure 1-9.

Figure 1-9

The Capabilities section of an application manifest file

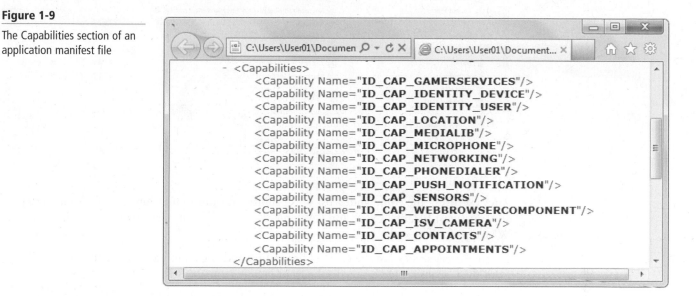

To ensure your manifest is correct when you submit your app, you can use a few tools during development that autodetect capabilities:

- **Windows Phone Capability Detection Tool:** If you develop an app for Windows Phone OS 7.0, you can use the Windows Phone Capability Detection Tool to create a list of required capabilities.
- **Windows Phone Marketplace Test Kit:** If you develop your app for Windows Phone OS 7.1, you can use the Capability Validation test in the Marketplace Test Kit to detect your app's capabilities.

The next two sections address each tool in more detail.

Using the Windows Phone Capability Detection Tool

CERTIFICATION READY
Under which circumstances is the Windows Phone Capability Detection Tool used?
1.1

The Capability Detection Tool targets apps developed for Windows Phone OS 7.0. This tool runs at a command line. To use the tool, open a command-prompt window and navigate to the folder that contains the Windows Phone Capability Detection Tool executable, named CapabilityDetection.exe (see Figure 1-10). The path to the Capability folder is one of the following, depending on whether you are running the x64 or x86 version of Windows:

- Program Files\Microsoft SDKs\Windows Phone\v7.0\Tools\CapDetect
- Program Files (x86)\Microsoft SDKs\Windows Phone\v7.0\Tools\CapDetect

Run the following command, which detects the phone's capabilities required by your app:

```
capabilitydetection <path to Rules.xml> <path to project output folder>
```

The Rules.xml file comes with the Capability Detection Tool and contains rules for determining capabilities required by your app. The project output folder contains your app's assemblies.

After executing the command, a list of capabilities for the application appears. To update your app's manifest file, open your app development tool and then open the manifest file (named WMAppManifest.xml).

Delete the capabilities in the Capabilities section and copy and paste the required capabilities from the Capability Detection Tool output list.

Now let's take a look at the Windows Phone Marketplace Test Kit.

+ MORE INFORMATION

To learn more about the Windows Phone Capability Detection Tool, visit the How to: Determine Application Capabilities Web page at http://bit.ly/alMZ6O.

Using the Windows Phone Marketplace Test Kit

CERTIFICATION READY
What is the purpose of the Windows Phone Marketplace Test Kit?
1.1

The Marketplace Test Kit is a series of tests you can run against an app you developed for Windows Phone OS 7.1 to determine if the app is ready for submission to the Marketplace. Although this tool runs within the app development tool rather than a command line, the Marketplace Test Kit uses a Rules.xml file similar to the Windows Phone Capability Detection Tool. The Capability Validation test within the Marketplace Test Kit lists your app's capabilities.

You can start the tool from within Visual Studio 2010 Express for Windows Phone. After creating a release build of the app you want to test, select the Project menu and then select Open Marketplace Test Kit (see Figure 1-11).

The Marketplace Test Kit window opens. Click Automated Tests on the left, and then click Run Tests, as shown in Figure 1-12. All of the automated tests run on your app, including the Capability Validation test. Respond to any messages that indicate one or more tests failed, if any, and then rerun the test.

The tool lists application capabilities in the Result Details column of the Capability Validation test. Each capability starts with ID_CAP, such as ID_CAP_LOCATION and ID_CAP_PUSH_NOTIFICATION.

The app manifest file should contain only the capabilities listed in the Result Details column. You can edit the manifest file by opening it from the Solution Explorer pane on the right. The file is named WMAppManifest.xml. Just delete any capabilities that aren't listed in the Result Details column.

Figure 1-11

Using the menus to open the Marketplace Test Kit

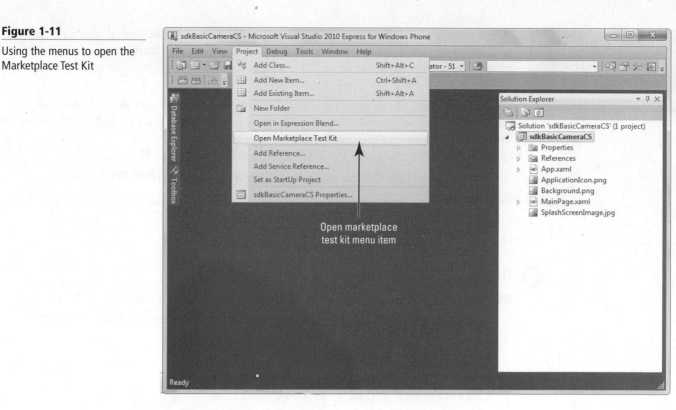

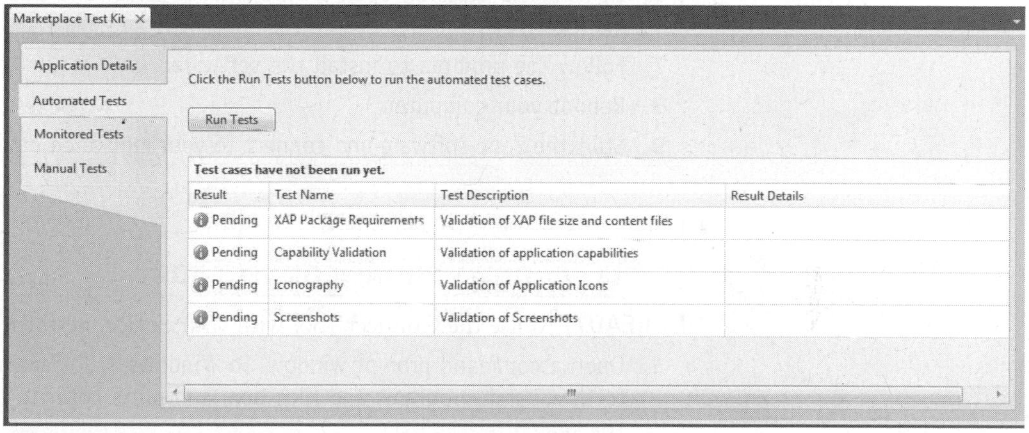

Figure 1-12

Running validation tests using the Marketplace Test Kit

MORE INFORMATION

To learn more about Windows Phone Marketplace Test Kit, visit the How to: Determine Application Capabilities Web page at http://bit.ly/alMZ6O. Details about application manifests for Windows Phone are at http://bit.ly/djd2XG.

Using the Windows Phone Connect Tool

The Windows Phone Connect Tool enables you to connect a Windows Phone device to a computer to test an app on the physical device, instead of the Windows Phone Emulator. To use the Connect Tool you must perform the following steps:

1. Install Zune software.
2. Connect your device to your computer with a serial or USB cable; the device must be registered.

When you connect your device to the computer, the Zune software should start automatically and detect your device. If it doesn't open, use the Windows Start menu to launch the program manually. Close the Zune software after it detects your device—you don't need it to actually run and test your app on the device.

To use the Connect Tool, open a command prompt window, navigate to the folder that contains the WPConnect.exe file, and then execute wpconnect.exe. You can find the file in one of the following folders:

- Program Files\Microsoft SDKs\Windows Phone\v7.1\Tools\WPConnect
- Program Files (x86)\Microsoft SDKs\Windows Phone\v7.1\Tools\WPConnect

Once the Connect Tool software connects with the device, you can use it test your app. You don't have to disconnect when you're finished.

 INSTALL THE ZUNE SOFTWARE

GET READY. To install the Zune software, perform the following steps:

1. In a Web browser, go to http://www.zune.net/en-US/products/windowsphone7/default.htm.
2. Click the **Download software** button.
3. On the resulting Web page, click **Download now**.
4. Save the Zune software to your Downloads folder.
5. Close the Web browser.
6. In Windows Explorer, open the Downloads folder and double-click the **ZuneSetupPkg.exe** file.
7. Follow the prompts to install the software.
8. Reboot your computer.
9. Start the Zune software and connect to your registered device with a serial or USB cable.

USE THE WINDOWS PHONE CONNECT TOOL

GET READY. To use the Connect Tool with your device, perform the following steps:

1. Open a command prompt window. In Windows 7, for example, click **Start**, type **cmd** in the Search programs and files box, and press Enter to launch the **cmd.exe** file from the search results list.
2. Navigate to one of the following folders, whichever is appropriate to your computer:

   • Program Files\Microsoft SDKs\Windows Phone\v7.1\Tools\WPConnect

   • Program Files (x86)\Microsoft SDKs\Windows Phone\v7.1\Tools\WPConnect

3. Type **wpconnect.exe** and press **Enter**.
4. You should receive confirmation that the device is connected.
5. Type **exit** in the command prompt window to close it. Disconnect your device from your computer.

+ MORE INFORMATION

To learn more about the Windows Phone Connect Tool, go to http://bit.ly/aS0wzi.

■ Understanding the Physical Capabilities of Mobile Devices

THE BOTTOM LINE

Every Windows Phone device must meet a minimum set of specifications, such as 256 MB of RAM and a four-point multi-touch screen. Other hardware features are optional. Sensors are used to detect and record orientation and motion of the device. APIs work with sensors and hardware features to deliver functionality to the end user.

Microsoft developed its Windows Phone OS for reliability and usability. Windows Phone devices offer popular hardware features such as cameras, motion sensors, and touch screens, along with connectivity for both cell and Wi-Fi connections.

Identifying Different Built-in Hardware

Every family or series of mobile devices must follow certain specifications to ensure that users get the same quality and experience when using the device. Again, to ensure quality and consistency, developers must follow the specifications when writing apps.

CERTIFICATION READY
What are the standard hardware specifications for a Windows Phone device?
1.2

Windows Phone specification requires standard hardware to be included in every Windows Phone device. The standard hardware is as follows:

- At least 256 megabytes (MB) of random access memory (RAM)
- At least 8 GB of flash storage
- Support for both cellular and Wi-Fi connections
- An 800 × 480 WVGA display, which can show movies in widescreen format
- A four-point multi-touch screen
- A common set of hardware buttons, such as Back, Start, and Search
- Features that include A-GPS and Accelerometer

Optional hardware, which is available on select devices, includes the following:

- Compass
- Gyro
- A primary camera on the back of the device
- A front-facing camera

The rest of this section explains many of these hardware items.

Understanding Device Sensors and the Motion API

Sensors are built in to Windows Phone devices and work with APIs to capture motion and orientation data. The Motion API combines sensor data to communicate with applications. The Accelerometer sensor is required in every Windows Phone device; the Compass and Gyroscope sensors are optional.

A Windows Phone device includes **sensors**, which are hardware features that detect the orientation and motion of the device and use that information as input. For example, as a user holds the device and swings her arm back, and then swings the arm forward as if she's bowling; the device recognizes and records the motion. The **Motion API**, a program that's part of every

Windows Phone, uses combined sensor data to communicate with an application, such as an app that helps a bowler improve her approach (and improve her score!). Windows Phone has many sensor APIs, which are built from the SensorBase<TSensorReading> base class. (A *class* is basically a collection of software routines and events that can be extended.)

The three device sensors available for Windows Phone are as follows:

- **Accelerometer:** The *Accelerometer sensor* detects forces applied to the device, such as movement (up, down, sideways) and gravity.
- **Compass:** The *Compass sensor* determines the device's orientation relative to the Earth's magnetic north pole. This sensor is also referred to as a magnetometer. You can use the Compass sensor along with the appropriate APIs to create apps for geocaching and navigation, for example.
- **Gyroscope:** The *Gyroscope sensor* uses motion (rotational forces) to detect the rotational velocity of the device along its three primary axes. A gyroscope's axes are shown in Figure 1-13.

Figure 1-13

A gyroscope's three axes

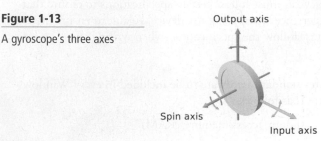

The Accelerometer sensor is required in all Windows Phones, but the Compass and Gyroscope sensors are optional. When designing aps that use the Compass or Gyroscope sensor, you should build in a routine that checks for the presence of the sensor and provide an alternative if the sensor is not available.

Specific APIs retrieve raw data from the Accelerometer, Compass, and Gyroscope sensors, and then the Motion API combines the data from those sensors and crunches the numbers that result into easy-to-use values for the device's attitude and motion. The attitude of a device is the pitch, yaw, and roll. The Motion API also returns values for rotational acceleration and linear acceleration. Experienced developers can use the raw sensor data (the data that the Motion API uses) to make their own calculations and implement custom apps.

The Motion API uses two different sensor configurations:

- **Normal Motion:** Uses the Accelerometer and Compass sensor data
- **Enhanced Motion:** Uses the Accelerometer, Compass, and Gyroscope sensor data

To help prevent incompatibilities between apps and devices, a user who views an application on Windows Phone Marketplace receives a warning if the device doesn't support one or more sensors in the app.

CERTIFICATION READY
What are the three device sensors available in a Windows Phone device?
1.2

CERTIFICATION READY
What is the purpose of the Motion API?
1.2

⊙ VIEW AN APP'S CODE THAT USES SENSORS

GET READY. To view code that works with sensors, perform the following steps:

1. In Visual Studio 2010 Express for Windows Phone, scroll down the start page and click **Learning Resources**.
2. Click **Code Samples for Windows Phone**. On the Code Samples for Windows Phone Web page that appears, click the **Location and Sensors** category.

TAKE NOTE *

You can download the VB code if you prefer, but the following steps and figures were based on C#. You will need to modify the steps slightly to accommodate VB.

3. Click **C#** next to Raw Sensor Data Sample and download it to your Visual Studio 2010\ Projects folder. (You can download a similar code sample if the Raw Sensor Data sample is no longer available.)

4. In Windows Explorer, navigate to **My Documents\Visual Studio 2010\Projects**, double-click the **ZIP** file, and extract the contents.

5. In Visual Studio 2010 Express for Windows Phone, close the Code Samples for Windows Phone window by clicking the **X** in the tab.

6. Click **Open project** on the Start page, or select **File > Open Project**.

7. Double-click the code sample's folder in the Projects folder, select the **.sln** file, and click **Open**.

8. Click the **Find in Files** button on the toolbar. In the Find and Replace dialog box, type **Microsoft.Devices.Sensors** and then click **Find All**. See Figure 1-14.

Figure 1-14

Searching for Microsoft.Devices. Sensors in the code sample

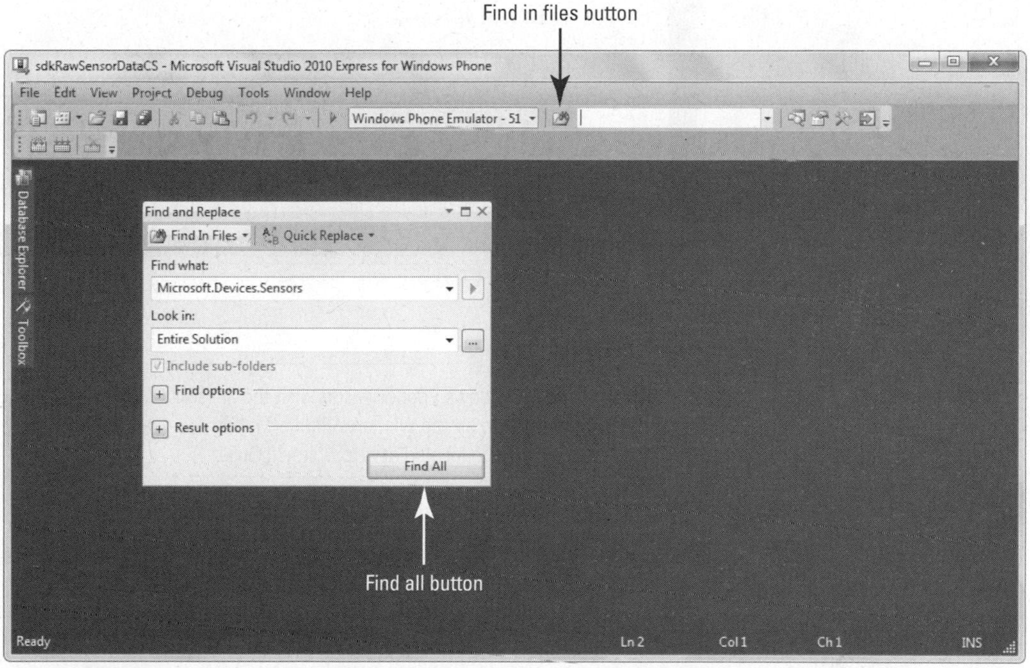

9. The names of files containing sensor code appear in the Find Results window, shown in Figure 1-15. Notice that the first listing indicates the AccelerometerPage.xaml.cs file.

Figure 1-15

The Find Results window

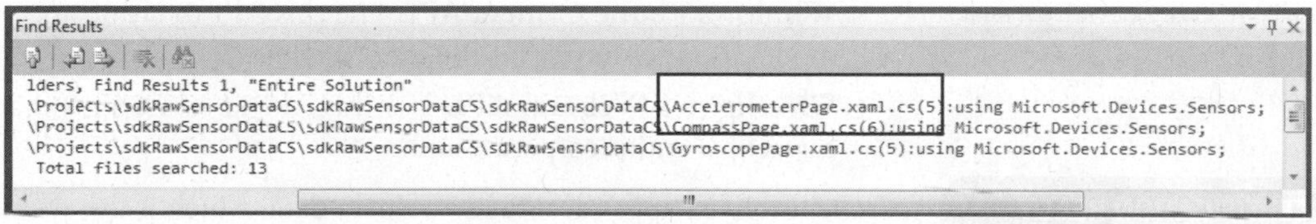

10. Open Solution Explorer, locate the **AccelerometerPage.xaml** entry, click to expand the entry, and then double-click the **AccelerometerPage.xaml.cs** file name.

11. Close Solution Explorer and the Find Results window to free up window space. Browse the code, shown in Figure 1-16, to become familiar with the commands and structure.

12. Close the code sample file and leave Visual Studio 2010 Express open if you continue immediately to the next section.

Figure 1-16

Motion-related code in a
sample file

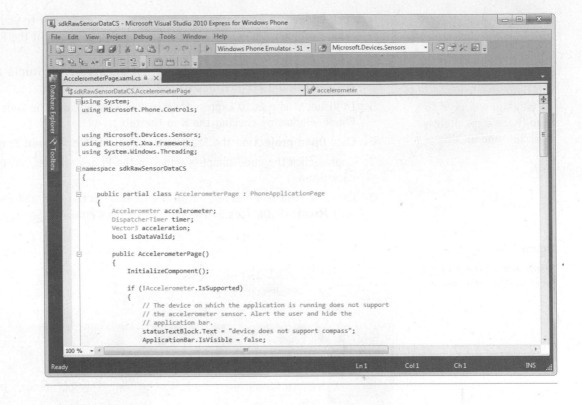

+ MORE INFORMATION

To learn more about Windows Phone sensors, visit the Sensors Overview for Windows Phone Web page at http://bit.
ly/iWkr7V. For information on the Windows Phone Motion API, read the How to: Use the Combined Motion API for
Windows Phone Web page located at http://bit.ly/tLOuSs.

Describing and Defining the Camera Capture and Preview Stream APIs

Windows Phone devices use the Windows Phone camera API and the Silverlight 4 webcam API to produce photos and video.

Nearly every Windows Phone device comes with one or two camera features. The primary
camera is on the back of the device, and it features a 5 megapixel (MP) or greater sensor,
auto-focus, and a flash. Windows Phone 7.5 includes a front-facing camera on the front of
the device. You use two APIs to create camera-based applications:

- **Windows Phone Camera API:** Use this API to create apps that take photos, use flash
  mode, use the shutter button, and the like
- **Silverlight 4 Webcam API:** Use this API to create apps that incorporate video and webcam clips, and incorporate audio

CERTIFICATION READY
Which APIs are used
for camera capture and
preview apps?
1.2

Camera-related apps capture raw camera data, which is live data from the device's camera,
and render it for viewing on the device. To use a primary or front-facing camera in a
Windows Phone app, be sure to include the camera capability (ID_CAP_ISV_CAMERA)
in the application manifest file, which allows the user to opt in and use the camera. Your
camera app won't run without the ID_CAP_ISV_CAMERA capability. For apps designed
specifically for a front-facing camera, also include the front-facing camera capability
(ID_HW_FRONTCAMERA).

As you begin building apps in future lessons, you'll need to be familiar with Windows Phone
classes. Classes related to cameras and photos are defined within the following namespaces,

which are in the Windows Phone class library:

- Microsoft.Devices
- Microsoft.Phone
- System.Windows.Media.Imaging

You can conveniently use the same classes for both the primary camera and the front-facing camera. The PhotoCamera class, which is in the Microsoft.Devices namespace, is the predominant class for photo capture in a Windows Phone 7.5 app. The PhotoCamera class enables the camera shutter, auto-focus, flash, specification of picture resolution, and more.

⊙ VIEW A SAMPLE CAMERA APP'S CODE

GET READY. To view a sample camera app's code, perform the following steps:

1. On the Start page in Visual Studio 2010 Express for Windows Phone, access the Code Samples for Windows Phone Web page. (You've visited this page several times in previous exercises.)

2. Click the **Cameras and Photos** category.

3. Click **C#** next to Basic Camera Sample and download it to your Visual Studio 2010\ Projects folder. (You can download a similar code sample if the Basic Camera sample is no longer available.)

> **TAKE NOTE*** You can download the VB code if you prefer, but the following steps and figures were based on C#. You would need to modify the steps slightly to accommodate VB.

4. Extract the ZIP file in Windows Explorer, and then open the project in Visual Studio 2010 Express for Windows Phone.

5. Open Solution Explorer, expand the **MainPage.xaml** entry, and then double-click the **MainPage.xaml.cs** file.

6. Close Solution Explorer.

7. Browse the code, shown in Figure 1-17, to become familiar with the commands and structure.

Figure 1-17

Camera-related code in a sample file

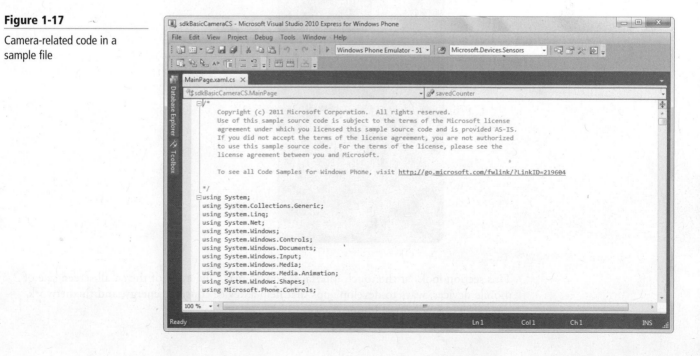

8. Can you find the PhotoCamera class?

9. When you're done, close the code sample file and leave Visual Studio 2010 Express open if you continue immediately to the next section.

 MORE INFORMATION

To learn about camera-related classes, visit the Camera and Photos Class Support for Windows Phone Web page at http://bit.ly/I0jhJ1.

■ Planning for Physical Interactions with the Mobile Device

↓
THE BOTTOM LINE

Windows Phone devices have multi-point touch screens that primarily use finger gestures for input. When designing for a small screen, being able to switch between portrait and landscape orientation is a must. All Windows Phone devices support Wi-Fi and mobile broadband access (GSM or CDMA), and the DeviceNetworkInformation class provides details about network connectivity.

The user interface (UI) style used by Windows Phone OS is called Metro, which includes features like a clean, uncluttered look and feel, use of the full screen, large hubs (graphical buttons), and a focus on lateral scrolling, to name a few. The home screen includes "Live Tiles," which provide links to apps, functions, and user-related items like contacts (see Figure 1-18). Tiles can be rearranged, and some display information about the underlying app, such as the number of e-mail messages in the inbox. Many Tiles require network connectivity to be able to display information, and you can code Tiles and other parts of the UI to take some action in response to a user's touch.

Figure 1-18

An example of a Live Tile

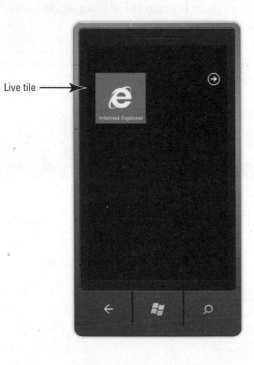

Live tile

This section looks at the touch interface, how to make the most of the small screen size of mobile devices, ways to develop apps that help a device conserve energy, and the network capabilities of Windows Phone devices.

Understanding the Touch Interface

On a Windows Phone, a gesture is a finger movement on the touch screen, which may be a tap, a drag, a press and hold, and so on. You code touch events to perform actions in response to gestures. All Windows Phone devices support four-point multi-touch functionality. The UI is designed for touch devices, and displays a virtual keyboard that appears when typed input is required. Any finger movement is referred to as a *gesture*, which can involve a single finger (one-touch, such as press, tap, press and hold, slide to pan, and so on) or a finger and a thumb (multi-touch, such as a pinch and stretch or a turn to rotate). The action the application takes in response to a gesture is called a *touch event*.

CERTIFICATION READY
What is a touch event?
1.3

Developers use `TouchPanel.GetCapabilities` to determine if the touch panel is available. For example, when `TouchPanelCapabilities.IsConnected` is true, the touch panel is available for reading.

`TouchPanel` also enables you to obtain touch input and to determine the maximum touch count. (The touch count is the number of simultaneous touches that the device can detect.) The `TouchPanelCapabilities.MaximumTouchCount` property determines the number of touch points that the touch panel supports.

The `TouchPanel GetState` method records low-level finger gestures, and the `ReadGesture` method records higher-level gestures. Higher-level gestures include tap, along with drag and pinch.

Accounting for Screen Size/Real Estate when Planning Layout

CERTIFICATION READY
What is a technique for maximizing the readability of small screens?
1.3

Users have gotten used to smartphones that automatically switch from portrait (upright) to landscape (sideways) orientation, and back, by simply rotating the device. The reason for autoswitching is to improve readability of screens, depending on the content being displayed. With many screen sizes less than four inches lengthwise, improving readability for users is a must.

Landscape orientation usually enables a user to more easily read lines of text and longer paragraphs, whereas portrait orientation is handier for using vertical lists and series of buttons. An example of orientation modes is shown in Figure 1-19.

This feature is programmed into applications for Windows Phone using the `Supported-Orientations` property set to `PortraitOrLandscape` either in the XAML or in the code. For example, the syntax is as follows:

```
SupportedOrientations="PortraitOrLandscape"
  Orientation="Portrait">
```

This code uses the `StackPanel` control along with the `ScrollViewer` control to handle both portrait and landscape orientation, as follows:

```
<ScrollViewer x:Name="ContentGrid" Grid.Row="1" VerticalScrollBar
Visibility="Auto">
<!--Background for StackPanel control so you can pan the contents.-->
  <StackPanel Background="Transparent">
<!--Rectangles for demonstrating orientation changes -->
  <Rectangle Width="100" Height="100" Margin="12,0"
HorizontalAlignment="Left" Fill="{StaticResource
PhoneAccentBrush}"/>
```

Figure 1-19

An orientation example

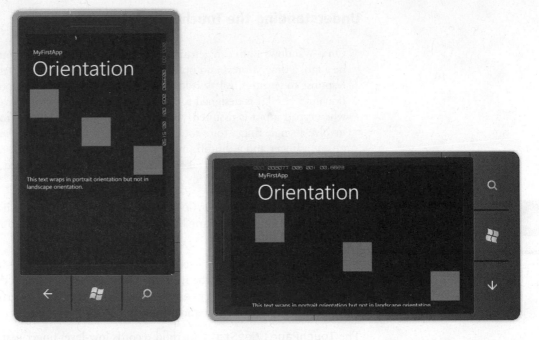

```
  <Rectangle Width="100" Height="100"
HorizontalAlignment="Center"
Fill="{StaticResource PhoneAccentBrush}"/>
  <Rectangle Width="100" Height="100" Margin="12,0"
HorizontalAlignment="Right" Fill="{StaticResource
PhoneAccentBrush}"/>
  <TextBlock Text="This text wraps in portrait orientation but not
in landscape orientation." TextWrapping="Wrap"/>
</StackPanel>
</ScrollViewer>
```

If the app requires one orientation or the other—without switching—use the following syntax (substituting "Landscape" for "Portrait" where applicable):

```
SupportedOrientations="Portrait"
  Orientation="Portrait" >
```

To have more control over a vertical series of elements, like a vertical list of buttons, as the orientation changes, you can use a grid along with the `OrientationChanged` event handler. This allows the user to switch orientation of the device, and the series of buttons maintains proper alignment.

Identifying Ways to Save Energy

Many smartphones and other mobile devices use OLED technology, which stands for organic light emitting diode. Compared to other mobile device screen technologies, OLEDs are brighter, consume less power, and do not require backlighting.

CERTIFICATION READY
How can you save energy by programming for an OLED screen?
1.3

With mobile device screens, the brighter the screen, the more energy the device consumes. Although OLEDs are brighter than other mobile device screen technologies, an OLED screen still consumes less power in comparison. In addition, an OLED display consumes up to 50 percent less power when displaying dark pixels versus light pixels, so creating a UI that uses a dark color scheme can save even more energy. Helping a device to save energy is an important best practice in mobile application development.

If you're developing an XNA game, you can save energy by reducing the back buffer size. Back buffer is the drawing area on which XNA creates graphics using the Draw method.

Understanding Networking Capabilities

As mentioned in the standard hardware list earlier in the lesson, Windows Phone devices provide both cellular and Wi-Fi (802.11) connectivity.

A Windows Phone device with a Broadcom 4329 chip handles 802.11a/b/g/n and Bluetooth, and is capable of connecting to a router (such as a mobile hotspot) to access the Internet. Windows Phones with Broadcom 4325 chips do not work with 802.11n and can't connect to routers for Internet sharing.

The cellular networks include Mobile Broadband GSM and Mobile Broadband CDMA. In the United States, AT&T and T-Mobile use Global System for Mobile Communications (GSM). Sprint, Verizon, and a variety of smaller carriers use code division multiple access (CDMA).

Windows Phone apps use the DeviceNetworkInformation class to provide information about a device's capabilities. There are just a handful of properties associated with the class, so they're listed and described in Table 1-2.

CERTIFICATION READY
What type of network connectivity and capabilities does a Windows Phone have?
1.3

Table 1-2

DeviceNetworkInformation properties

PROPERTY NAME	DESCRIPTION
CellularMobileOperator	Determines the cellular mobile operator
IsCellularDataEnabled	Indicates whether the network is cellular data enabled
IsCellularDataRoamingEnabled	Indicates whether data roaming is allowed on the network
IsNetworkAvailable	Indicates network availability
IsWiFiEnabled	Indicates whether the network is Wi-Fi enabled

When creating a Windows Phone app with network functionality, knowing when a network changes is often necessary. For example, if a Windows Phone device comes within range of a high-speed Wi-Fi network, you want the phone to be able to switch from its current network. To accomplish this, you can use something called a NetworkAvailabilityChanged event to listen for network availability changes, and the IsNetworkAvailable property to retrieve the new state of the network connection.

VIEW A SAMPLE UI APP'S CODE

GET READY. To view a sample UI app's code, perform the following steps:

1. On the Start page in Visual Studio 2010 Express for Windows Phone, access the Code Samples for Windows Phone Web page.

2. Click the **Fundamental Concepts** category.

3. Click **C#** next to the Network and Device Information Sample entry and download it to your Visual Studio 2010\Projects folder. (You can download a similar code sample if the Network and Device Information sample is no longer available.)

TAKE NOTE ✱ You can download the VB code if you prefer, but the following steps and figures were based on C#. You would need to modify the steps slightly to accommodate VB.

4. Extract the Zip file in Windows Explorer, and then open the project in Visual Studio 2010 Express for Windows Phone.

5. Open Solution Explorer and then double-click the **MainPage.xaml** entry.

6. Close Solution Explorer.

7. Browse the code (shown in Figure 1-20) to become familiar with the commands and structure.

Figure 1-20

UI-related code in a sample file

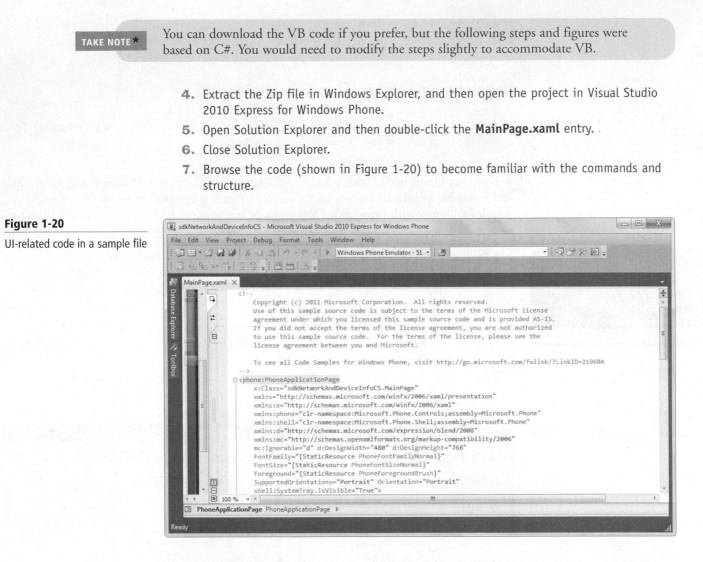

8. When you're done, close the code sample file and then close Visual Studio 2010 Express.

➕ **MORE INFORMATION**

To learn about touch interactions, visit the Working with Touch Input (Windows Phone) Web page at http://bit.ly/HD0Bgz. Information and examples of how to work with orientation on a Windows Phone is at http://bit.ly/IAp8Rk. For more information about Windows Phone network connectivity, read the How to: Determine the Network Capabilities for Windows Phone Web page at http://msdn.microsoft.com/en-us/library/hh202859.aspx.

SKILL SUMMARY

IN THIS LESSON YOU LEARNED:

- A mobile app is a software program designed to run on a mobile device, like a Windows Phone.
- To create apps for Windows Phone, you use one of two development platforms: Microsoft Silverlight for Windows Phone or the XNA framework.
- App Hub is a Microsoft portal that developers must join to submit apps to the Windows Phone Marketplace.

- The general app development lifecycle includes registering at App Hub, planning your app, developing and testing your app, gathering certification requirements, and submitting the app to the Windows Phone Marketplace.
- Windows Phone development uses a set of tools available in the Windows Phone Software Development Kit (SDK).
- The SDK includes Visual Studio 2010 Express for Windows Phone, Silverlight for Windows Phone, Windows Phone SDK 7.1 Extensions for XNA 4.0 Game Studio, Expression Blend for Windows Phone, and Windows Phone Emulator.
- Application capabilities are features that can be used by a Windows Phone. They may require the user to opt in to use them due to privacy or security concerns. Capabilities are listed in a file called the application manifest, which is required for submission to the Windows Phone Marketplace.
- You can use the Windows Phone Capability Detection Tool and the Windows Phone Marketplace Test Kit to autodetect app capabilities and update the manifest file.
- Every Windows Phone device must meet a minimum set of specifications, such as 256 MB of RAM and a four-point multi-touch screen. Other hardware features are optional. Sensors are used to detect and record orientation and motion of the device. APIs work with sensors and hardware features to deliver functionality to the end user.
- Sensors are hardware features built in to Windows Phone devices and that work with APIs to provide data on the orientation and motion of a device.
- Device sensors record data when a Windows Phone device is flipped, moved, or swung, and motion APIs turn orientation and motion into device input.
- The Motion API combines sensor data to communicate with applications. The Accelerometer sensor is required in every Windows Phone device; the Compass and Gyroscope sensors are optional.
- Windows Phone devices use the Windows Phone camera API and the Silverlight 4 webcam API to produce photos and video.
- Windows Phone devices have multi-point touch screens that primarily use finger gestures for input.
- When designing for a small screen, being able to switch between portrait and landscape orientation is a must.
- All Windows Phone devices support Wi-Fi and mobile broadband access (GSM or CDMA), and the `DeviceNetworkInformation` class provides details about network connectivity.

Knowledge Assessment

Fill in the Blank

Complete the following sentences by writing the correct word or words in the blanks provided.

1. Whereas Silverlight is geared toward data-driven apps and games, the XNA framework is used primarily for _____ development.

2. The _____ is a Windows component that includes several programming languages, such as C# and Visual Basic, and it provides the code-execution environment.

3. The _____ is a suite of tools used to develop apps for Windows Phone devices.

4. For security purposes, a user must _____ to certain features of a Windows Phone app.

5. The _____ sensor detects forces applied to the device, such as movement (up, down, sideways) and gravity.

6. The _____ sensor determines the device's orientation relative to the Earth's magnetic north pole.

7. Developers use a file called the _____ to list an application's capabilities.

8. The _____ is an online store where developers distribute their apps.

9. An _____ is a set of software functionalities (data structures, protocols, routines, and so on) released by a software manufacturer to help developers design applications more easily.

10. Regarding a touch screen, any finger movement is referred to as a _____, which can involve a press, tap, or pinch and stretch.

Multiple Choice

Circle the letter that corresponds to the best answer.

1. What is the name of the Windows Phone application manifest file?
   a. WPConnect.xml
   b. WMAppManifest.xml
   c. Rules.xml
   d. WMAppManifest.sln

2. Which of the following is not included in the Windows Phone SDK?
   a. Visual Studio 2010 Express for Windows Phone
   b. Silverlight for Windows Phone
   c. Windows Phone Emulator
   d. Zune software

3. Which command is used by the Windows Phone Capability Detection Tool?
   a. detectfeatures
   b. rulesdetection
   c. capabilitydetection
   d. none of the above

4. You are creating an app for Windows Phone OS 7.0. Which tool can you use to test the application's capabilities?
   a. Windows Phone Capability Detection Tool
   b. Windows Phone Marketplace Test Kit
   c. Windows Phone Marketplace
   d. Silverlight

5. Which API is used to simplify combined motion data?
   a. Accelerator API
   b. Motion API
   c. Gyroscope Motion API
   d. Silverlight API

6. Which sensor is available on all Windows Phone devices?
   a. Accelerometer
   b. Compass
   c. Gyroscope
   d. Camera

7. Which of the following properties is used when programming an app to display content in either portrait or landscape orientation?
   a. LandscapeOrPortrait
   b. OrientationSwitch
   c. ScrollViewer
   d. SupportedOrientations

8. Which API do you use to create apps that take photos, use flash mode, and use the shutter button?
   a. Windows Phone Webcam API
   b. Windows Phone Camera API
   c. CaptureSource
   d. none of the above

9. Which OLED-related technique can you perform to conserve a Windows Phone device's energy?
   a. Disable the camera feature.
   b. Create a UI that uses a dark color scheme.
   c. Create a UI that uses a light color scheme.
   d. Disable the orientation switch feature.

10. Which term best describes the user interface (UI) style used by Windows Phone OS?
    a. Metro
    b. Cosmopolitan
    c. Clean
    d. Windows 7

True / False

Circle T if the statement is true or F if the statement is false.

T   F   **1.** The term Windows Phone refers to a device or the operating system that runs on the device.

T   F   **2.** You use Zune software to test Windows Phone applications directly.

T   F   **3.** To install the Windows Phone SDK, you must be running Windows XP x86 or higher.

T   F   **4.** All Windows Phone devices come with a camera feature.

T   F   **5.** Windows Phone devices provide both cellular and Wi-Fi (802.11) connectivity.

■ Competency Assessment

Scenario 1-1: Understand Windows Phone

Gavin is a colleague at work. He's interested in getting a Windows Phone and possibly trying to create an application. He's been reading about Windows Phone on the Web, but he's confused as to what "Windows Phone" means. Sometimes it seems to be a phone, other times it seems to be an operating system. What do you tell Gavin to clarify the term "Windows Phone?"

Scenario 1-2: Create an Augmented Reality App

Julia wants to develop an augmented reality application for Windows Phone. The app will enable you to hold your Windows Phone device horizontally to display your current location on a map. The map also displays nearby businesses and other amenities. When you hold the device upright and use the camera viewfinder, information about buildings and attractions appear in pop-up balloons. She has asked you to give her tips for how to create the program. What do you tell her?

■ Proficiency Assessment

Scenario 1-3: Create an Application Manifest

Xavier has developed his first app, a tool that acts similarly to a pedometer to record distance when he walks his dogs. Xavier thinks his app will sell well to the general public. He needs to create a list of application capabilities to prepare for submission to the Windows Phone Marketplace but can't figure out how to complete this step. How do you advise Xavier?

Scenario 1-4: Summarize Networking Capabilities

Your manager has asked you to provide a brief summary of the networking capabilities of a Windows Phone device for the development team. She wants to know specifically which cellular networks a Windows Phone can connect to, and any caveats she should know about regarding 802.11 wireless connectivity. What do you include in your report?

Working in a Mobile App Development Environment

EXAM OBJECTIVE MATRIX

SKILLS/CONCEPTS	MTA EXAM OBJECTIVE	MTA EXAM OBJECTIVE NUMBER
Working with Developer Tools	Working with developer tools.	3.4
Designing for Mobile Devices	Understanding design for mobile devices.	3.1

KEY TERMS

Application Bar

Application pane

asynchronous programming

build errors

Code Editor

design surface

globalization

localization

Microsoft Visual Studio

Model View ViewModel (MVVM)

object-oriented programming (OOP)

optimize

runtime errors

separation of concerns

Solution Explorer

Start screen

Toolbox

user experience

Visual Studio 2010 Express for Windows Phone

You've been working with the application developer team at BoxTwelve Mobile while they design a mobile app for Glide, a winter sports equipment and apparel reseller. The team gave you a heads-up that you'll soon be working directly on the mobile app. You need to practice creating simple apps using the Microsoft Visual Studio application development tools, and learn about localization, globalization, and optimization of mobile apps.

■ Working with Developer Tools

↓
__THE BOTTOM LINE__

You can develop mobile applications using platform-specific tools or multiplatform tools. A multiplatform tool enables you to create mobile apps for a variety of platforms. PhoneGap and Rhodes are two examples of multiplatform tools that support Windows Phone 7, among other platforms.

CERTIFICATION READY
What is the difference between platform-specific and multiplatform development tools?
3.4

The mobile application market has multiple operating system platforms to choose from. Windows Phone 7 is one platform; others include Apple iOS, Google Android, BlackBerry, Palm, Symbian, and more.

Many platforms have tools for creating applications that are specific to the platform, like Visual Studio 2010 Express for Windows Phone and the iOS SDK for apps that run on Apple iPhones.

Multiplatform tools are also available. PhoneGap and Rhodes (by RhoMobile) are two examples, both of which enable you to create apps that run on most of the major mobile platforms. PhoneGap uses HTML5 and JavaScript to create apps, whereas Rhodes is an open source Ruby-based framework.

Because the MTA 98-373 Mobile Application Development exam is specific to Windows Phone, the following sections focus on Windows-based tools for mobile app development.

Using Visual Studio

The Visual Studio integrated development environment, or IDE, provides several tools that enable you to create and debug code in C#, VB, and other programming languages. To create applications specifically for Windows Phone, you can use the Windows Phone Add-in for Visual Studio if you already have Visual Studio installed, or use Visual Studio 2010 Express for Windows Phone.

CERTIFICATION READY
Which Microsoft tools can be used to create applications for Windows Phone?
3.4

Microsoft Visual Studio is an integrated development environment (IDE) used by programmers and developers to create all kinds of applications and user interfaces (UIs). The IDE includes a code editor and debugger, and natively supports the C++, VB.NET, C#, and F# programming languages.

Microsoft also provides *Visual Studio 2010 Express for Windows Phone*, which is available as a stand-alone software package or as an add-in for Visual Studio Professional or higher. The Windows Phone add-in includes the same features as the stand-alone package, other than a few debugging options. Visual Studio 2010 Express for Windows Phone and the add-in are also compatible with Expression Blend for Windows Phone. As discussed in Lesson 1, if you're already familiar with Microsoft Expression Studio, you should consider using Expression Blend to develop for Windows Phone.

TAKE NOTE*
Microsoft sells Visual Studio Professional through Microsoft.com and other channels. Visual Studio 2010 Express for Windows Phone and the Windows Phone Add-in for Visual Studio 2010 are free tools.

You've already used Visual Studio 2010 Express for Windows Phone in previous lessons, but let's take a closer look at the features you'll use most often during app development. The menu bar and main toolbar are located near the top of the program window, as shown in Figure 2-1. On the toolbar, the Windows Phone Emulator drop-down menu lets you choose Windows Phone Device, or the 256 MB or 512 MB version of Windows Phone Emulator. To the right is the search feature, and to the far right are icons that open Solution Explorer, the Properties window, the Toolbox, and the Start page.

By this point in the book you're familiar with *Solution Explorer*. When you open a project, the project files appear in Solution Explorer. When you click a file in Solution Explorer, the file's code appears in the *Code Editor*, where you can modify the code. In most cases, the Design pane opens as well, which shows a generic Windows Phone device so you can see how

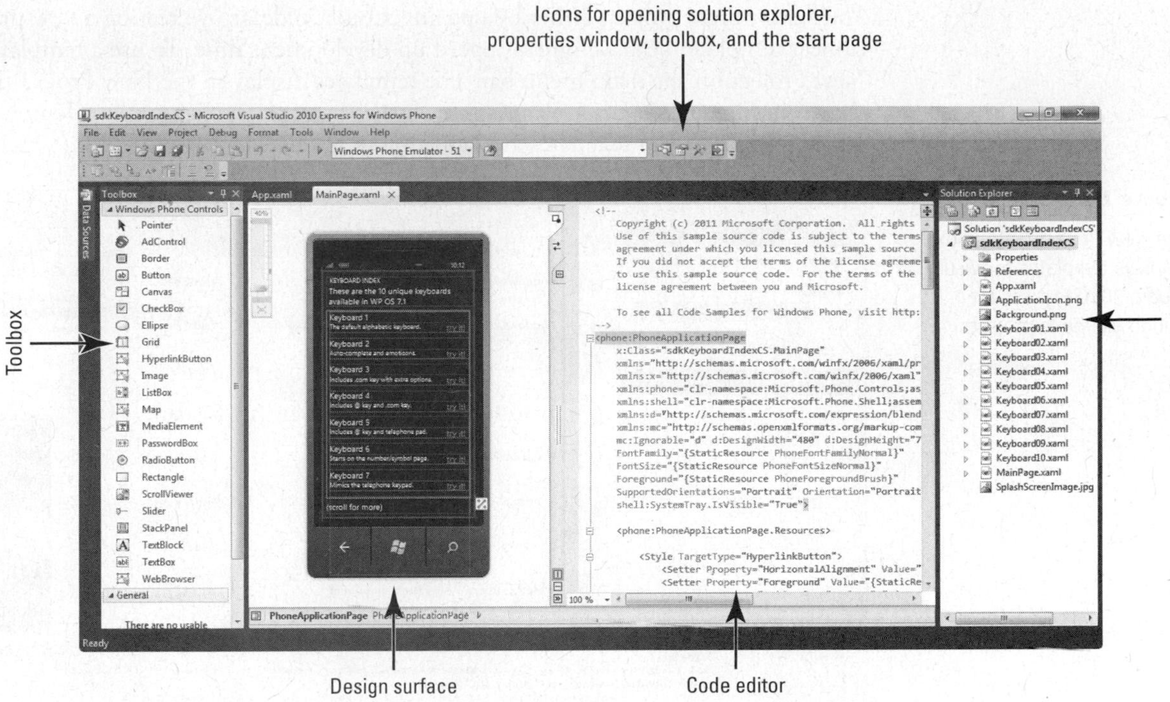

Icons for opening solution explorer,
properties window, toolbox, and the start page

Toolbox

Solution explorer

Design surface

Code editor

Figure 2-1

The main window in Visual Studio 2010 Express for Windows Phone

CERTIFICATION READY
What appears in the design surface in the Visual Studio IDE for Windows Phone?
3.4

your changes look on the device screen. The Design pane is referred to as the *design surface*, and the generic device is a phone skin. The phone skin resembles the Windows Phone Emulator, but they serve different purposes. The phone skin is mainly for UI design, whereas the Windows Phone Emulator enables you to test functionality.

The *Toolbox* on the far left provides the Windows Phone controls. You can drag and drop controls onto the design surface and modify them as needed.

You can right-click the name of your project, near the top of Solution Explorer, to open the *Application pane* (see Figure 2-2). Here you can configure many project settings, such as the startup object, application title, the app's icon, and tile options such as the background image.

Figure 2-2

The Application pane

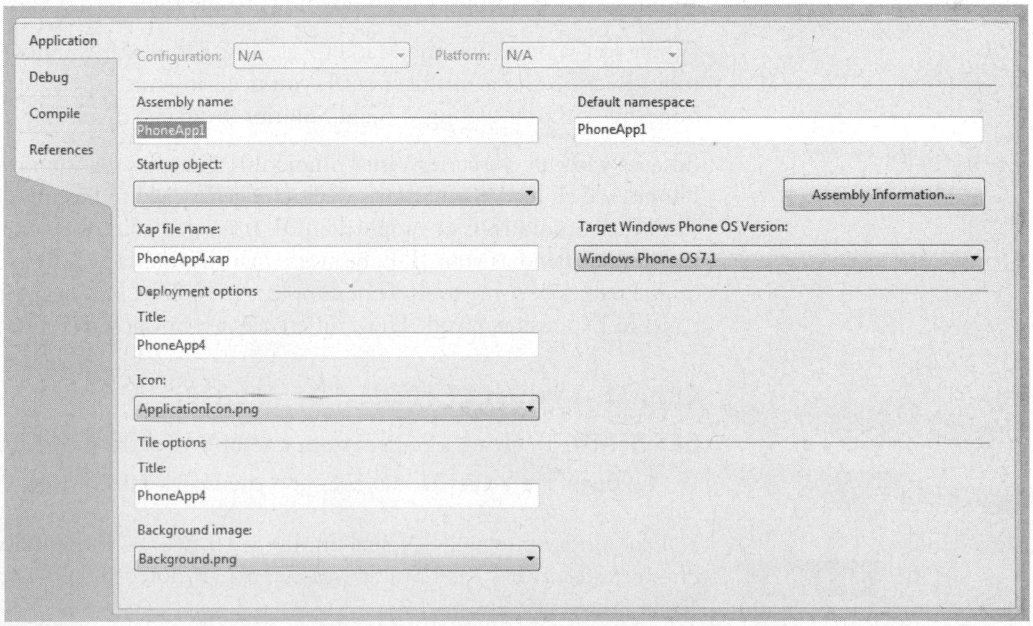

You'll start most projects either by opening sample code or by creating a new project using a project template; both can greatly speed up development time. To use a template, click File > New Project on the main menu bar. The templates display in the New Project dialog box, as shown in Figure 2-3. If you want a more specific template, click Online Templates in the left pane and select from templates available online at Microsoft.com.

Figure 2-3

The New Project dialog box displays templates for Visual Studio 2010 Express for Windows Phone projects

While you're developing an application, you need to check it for errors and its functionality periodically. There are two general types of errors: build and runtime. **Build errors** prevent the code from being compiled. The IDE displays information about build errors to help you correct them. **Runtime errors** are unexpected or incorrect behaviors that occur while an application runs. The IDE doesn't catch runtime errors—you learn about runtime errors while testing an application in an emulator or on a device and must return to the IDE to correct those errors.

In Visual Studio 2010 Express for Windows Phone, when you click the Start Debugging button on the toolbar or press F5, the IDE checks your application for errors and creates a debug build of your application. If no severe build errors are detected, your application opens in the Windows Phone Emulator, as long as you selected an emulator in the Select target for Windows Phone projects drop-down list to the right of the Start Debugging button.

When you want to use the Marketplace Test Kit or the Windows Phone Performance Analysis tool (described later in this lesson), you need to create a release build. You can create a release build by selecting Debug >Build Solution from the menu bar or by pressing F6.

Because you can use either Visual Studio 2010 Express for Windows Phone or the Windows Phone Add-in for Visual Studio, we'll refer generically to the app development environment as the Visual Studio IDE or simply the IDE from this point forward. If you prefer to use Microsoft Expression Blend as your IDE, be aware that the interface differs somewhat from Visual Studio as do the names of some tools. For example, the Toolbox in Visual Studio is equivalent to the Assets panel in Expression Blend. Those differences are not pointed out in the exercises in this book.

⊕ CREATE A PROJECT FROM A TEMPLATE

GET READY. To create a project from a template, perform the following steps:

1. Open the Visual Studio IDE, and then click **File > New Project**.

You should have installed Visual Studio 2010 Express for Windows Phone or the Windows Phone Add-in for Visual Studio in Lesson 1. If not, see the "Understanding Mobile Device Tools" section in Lesson 1.

2. In the Installed Templates section of the left pane, select **Silverlight for Windows Phone** in C#, as shown in Figure 2-4. Note: The app created in this exercise is used in other exercises as well, and the examples later in this lesson use C# code.

Figure 2-4

Selecting a template

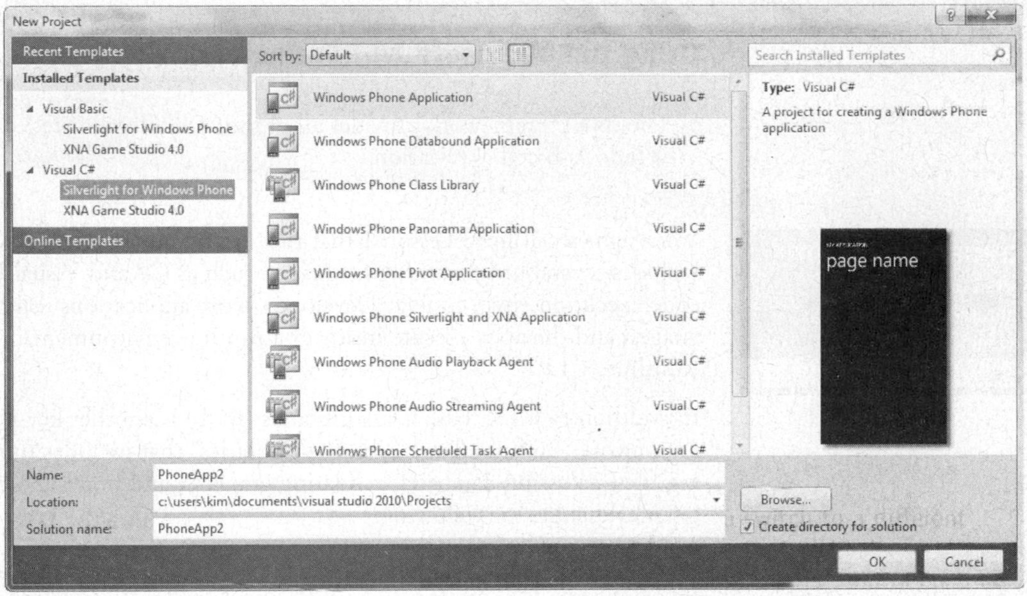

3. Click **Windows Phone Application** in the middle pane.

4. In the Name text box (in the lower part of the window), type a name for the project, such as **MyFirstApp**. Click **OK**.

5. A dialog box displays, prompting you to select the target Windows Phone operating system (OS) version. Select the OS from the drop-down menu shown in Figure 2-5 and then click **OK**.

Figure 2-5

Selecting a Windows Phone version

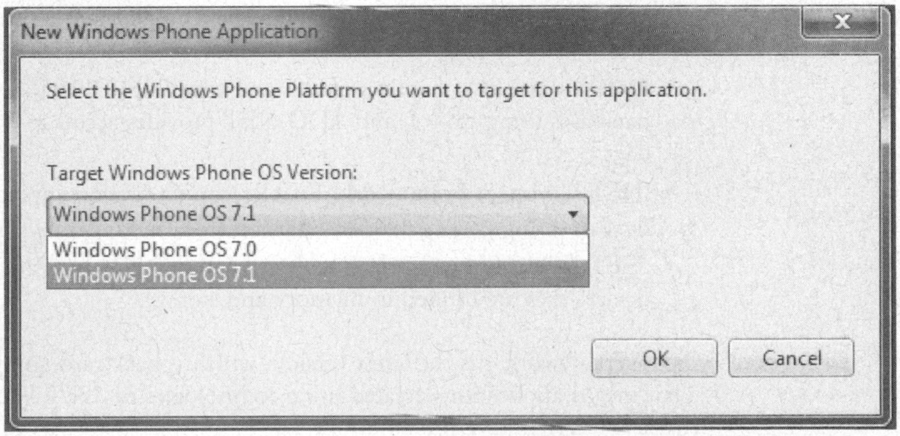

6. A new project window opens. The Solution Explorer pane may or may not be visible. If it is not visible, click its icon on the toolbar to open the pane.

   Notice that the Code Editor displays code for the file that's selected by default, and the Windows Phone skin appears in Design view.

7. You have created the foundation for an application. At this point you would begin adding controls to the UI and functionality to the app. You've got more to learn first, so select **File > Exit** to close the file and the Visual Studio IDE.

➕ **MORE** INFORMATION

For more information about the Visual Studio IDE, go to http://msdn.microsoft.com/en-us/library/ff630878 (v=vs.92).aspx.

Using the Microsoft .NET Framework

The .NET Framework provides all of the technologies needed to create, test, and run Windows-based applications.

CERTIFICATION READY
What are Base Class Libraries in the .NET Framework?
3.4

You might recall from Lesson 1 that the .NET Framework is a Windows component that includes several programming languages, such as C# and Visual Basic, and provides the code-execution environment. Developers write applications using one of the .NET languages, and the apps execute inside of a runtime environment called the Common Language Runtime (CLR).

In addition to CLR, Base Class Libraries (BCL) is another key feature of the .NET Framework. BCL is a large "library of libraries" that includes functions for reading and writing files, accessing databases, rendering graphics, and much more. Other .NET Framework 4 features include the following:

- **ADO.NET:** A set of classes that provides access to data services such as SQL Server and XML.
- **ASP.NET:** A framework that enables you to create Web applications and interfaces.
- **Windows Presentation Foundation (WPF):** Enables you to create stunning user interfaces that may include 2D graphics, 3D graphics, multimedia, and documents.
- **Windows Workflow Foundation (WF):** Enables you to execute long-running processes as workflows (sets of programming steps) within .NET applications.
- **Windows Communication Foundation (WCF):** Enables you to build and access Web services.
- **Windows Forms:** A graphical application programming interface (API) that gives you access to Microsoft Windows-like features.
- **Data access:** Data Services creates and consumes OData, Entity Framework accesses databases using LINQ, and ADO.NET provides access to SQL Server and XML data.
- **.NET Compact Framework:** Enables you to develop applications for Windows CE devices.
- **.NET Micro Framework:** Enables you to develop applications for all kinds of mobile devices that are limited in memory and storage.

.NET Framework 4 is the latest version, which is backward-compatible with earlier versions. That means applications created using technologies in .NET Framework 2 or 3, for example, run seamlessly in .NET Framework 4.

⊙ EXPLORE .NET TECHNOLOGIES

GET READY. To learn more about .NET technologies, perform the following steps:

1. In a Web browser, go to the **.NET Framework Developer Center** at http://msdn.microsoft.com/en-us/netframework/aa496123. The main page is shown in Figure 2-6. You should already have .NET Framework installed, as part of the Windows Phone SDK installation.

Figure 2-6

The .NET Framework Developer
Center main Web page

2. Bookmark the page, or create a Mobile App Development resource list in Notepad and add the .NET Framework Developer Center Web address to your list.

3. Scroll down and click the links to browse detailed information about each of the .NET Framework technologies.

4. Return to the main .NET Framework Developer Center Web page and click through each of the links in the More .NET Framework Resources section. Be sure to bookmark or note pages that you'll want to return to in the future.

5. If you want to sign up for the MSDN Flash newsletter, click the **Subscribe** link and follow the prompts. You'll be able to pick specific programming languages, .NET technologies, and other topics that are of particular interest to you. Microsoft emails the MSDN Flash newsletter every other week.

6. When you're finished, close the Web browser.

■ Designing for Mobile Devices

↓
THE BOTTOM LINE

Designing a mobile application begins with planning. You can reduce the time needed for development and create a more efficient app by outlining and/or sketching the flow of the application.

There are many factors to consider when designing a mobile application. The UI should be simple and intuitive, yet appealing. The functionality of the app must be error-free, responsive to user input (meaning that it runs with minimal or delay), and useful. If you plan to distribute your app to an international audience, you'll need to localize and globalize the app. What about storage—will your application require access to a database?

For very basic and simple apps, you can jump right into an IDE and begin creating an app. For most apps though, Microsoft recommends that you plan your application using paper and pencil, first creating an outline of how the application works, and then sketching the layout of screens in the flow from one function to another. This step makes development a

CERTIFICATION READY
What tasks should be performed when planning a moderate to complex mobile application?
3.1

much easier and more efficient task, just as writing a technical book is easier when the author follows a detailed outline.

Proper planning also includes knowing about Windows Phone Marketplace requirements (covered in Lessons 1 and 8) so that, in the end, you provide the best possible application. Thoroughly testing your application during development and again before submission to the Marketplace are best practices every developer should follow.

Before you get to the first stage of development, however, you need to understand some fundamental design concepts.

Describing and Defining Mobile Design Concepts

Windows Phone apps use the Metro style as the foundation for UIs to achieve a consistent look and feel. When designing apps, be sure to make buttons and other controls large enough to be used easily on a touch screen. You should also ensure consistent and adequate spacing, or padding, between controls and between text and controls.

The *user experience*—what the user sees, clicks, touches, and interacts with—in Windows Phone apps is based on the Metro style, a visual interface design originally developed for Windows Phone 7. It's now the foundation for Windows Phone OS, Xbox, and Windows 8 interfaces.

Metro style is clean and simple, features relatively large buttons for ease of use, and may include Live Tiles that provide links to other applications and functions. Metro style uses the Segoe WP font family, and usually incorporates flat colors (versus gradients) for Tiles and other elements. The goal for creating a Metro style UI is an uncluttered, minimalistic presentation with intuitive functionality.

CERTIFICATION READY
What factors should be considered for laying out buttons and controls in a mobile app UI?
3.1

Button and control size is an important feature of Metro style apps. In any mobile application, you should consider touch screens of all sizes when sizing UI controls. They must be big enough to accommodate larger fingers and should be separated with adequate padding. In fact, the entire UI should present a balance of text (for identification or instruction), images (if any), controls (for functionality), and spacing or padding between all elements.

Figure 2-7 shows an example of the Weather Forecast sample application available from Microsoft. The user taps or selects an entry to display the forecast for that location.

Figure 2-7

An example of proper sizing and spacing

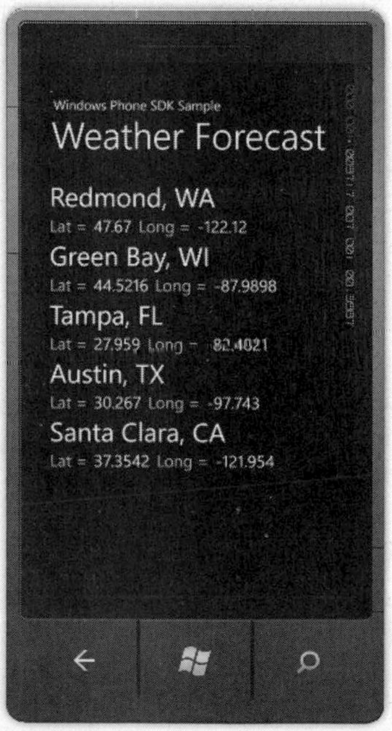

Windows Phone SDK Sample
Weather Forecast

Redmond, WA
Lat = 47.67 Long = -122.12

Green Bay, WI
Lat = 44.5216 Long = -87.9898

Tampa, FL
Lat = 27.959 Long = -82.4821

Austin, TX
Lat = 30.267 Long = -97.743

Santa Clara, CA
Lat = 37.3542 Long = -121.954

The UI control for each entry covers the area shown in Figure 2-7, which is adequately large for different types of fingers and input devices. In addition, the use of large and small font sizes, text color, and spacing around text gives the UI a clean look and feel, even though a lot of information is displayed. Potential improvements to this UI would be to eliminate the latitude and longitude lines, and create boxes for the city/state entries.

Buttons and related UI elements that are common to many apps are as follows:

- **Start:** The initial screen presented to users after powering on a device. The ***Start screen*** may display one or more Live Tiles to enable users to access app features or other apps. Start is always presented in portrait view.
- **Application Bar:** A row of buttons and an ellipsis displayed along the bottom of the phone's screen (see Figure 2-8). The ***Application Bar*** is designed for accessing the most common functionality in an application. The buttons are usually icons but may contain text labels.

Figure 2-8

An example of an Application Bar

TAKE NOTE *

Users press the Start hardware button to return to the Start screen, regardless of which application is running.

- **Status Bar:** An indicator bar for displaying system-level status information. May include information on signal strength, battery power level, Bluetooth status, and more.
- **Hardware buttons:** These include Power, Start, Volume, Back, and Search. (A sampling of buttons is shown in Figure 2-9.) Many devices also have a Camera button. The location of hardware buttons is device dependent, so they don't always appear in the same place from device to device.

Figure 2-9

Default hardware buttons

CREATE A UI FOR AN APP

GET READY. This exercise helps you create a simple Web browser application. To create the UI for the app, perform the following steps:

1. Open the Visual Studio IDE.

2. Open the MyFirstApp project by selecting **File > Open Project**, navigating to the **MyFirstApp** folder, if necessary, and double-clicking **MyFirstApp.sln**.

3. Ensure the Toolbox, Solution Explorer, and Properties window are displayed, along with the Code Editor and design surface. The IDE window should look like Figure 2-10.

Figure 2-10

MyFirstApp in the Visual Studio IDE

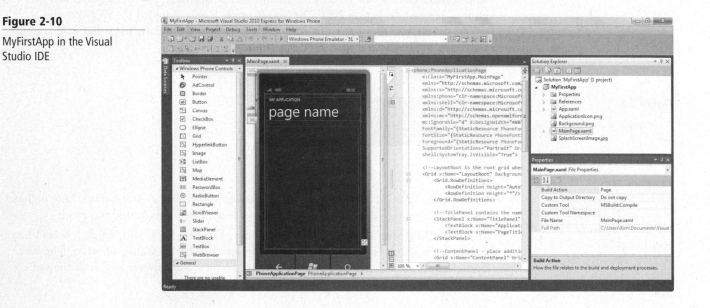

4. To change the default page name placeholder, click **page name** in the design surface. In the Properties window, change the Text property from page name to **My Browser**, as shown in Figure 2-11. Press **Enter**.

Figure 2-11

Changing the name of a control

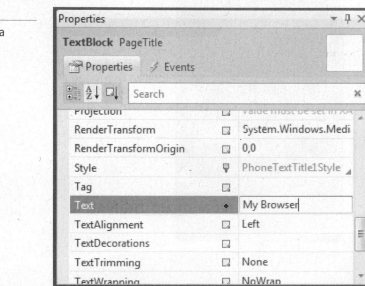

5. Modify the code in MainPage.xaml so the app can be used in portrait or landscape mode. Click the first line of the XAML code (**<phone:PhoneApplicationPage**) to display the PhoneApplicationPage properties in the Properties window. Using the drop-down list in the SupportedOrientation property, change the value to **PortraitOrLandscape**.

6. To add a text box to the app, in which users will enter Web addresses, drag the **TextBox** control from the Toolbox and drop it in the design surface just below the My Browser text. Use your mouse to resize the length of the box, dragging the right side toward the left, to make room for a Go button (which you'll add shortly).

7. Make the text box flexible so it displays properly with the Go button in either portrait or landscape orientation. With the TextBox control still selected, set the Height and Width properties in the Properties window to **Auto**. Set the HorizontalAlignment property to **Stretch** and the VerticalAlignment property to **Top**. Change the Text property to a Web address of your choice.

8. Change the background color for the box, if you want.

9. To create the Go button, drag the **Button** control from the Toolbox and drop it to the right of the text box. Move the control in place so it aligns with the text box, as shown in Figure 2-12. You might need to resize the Button control so the height matches the text box and the width leaves ample spacing between the button and the text box.

Figure 2-12

Adjusting the Button control

10. For the Go button, set the Content property to **Go**, the Height and Width properties to **Auto**, the HorizontalAlignment property to **Right**, and the VerticalAlignment property to **Top**.

11. To add the window that displays the Web site being visited, drag the **WebBrowser** control from the toolbox to the design surface. Drop the control below the text box and button you just added.

12. Resize the WebBrowser control so it fills most of the remaining space, similar to Figure 2-13.

Figure 2-13

Adjusting the size of the
WebBrowser control

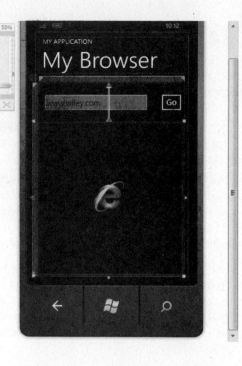

Figure 2-13

Adjusting the size of the
WebBrowser control

13. Set the Height and Width properties of the WebBrowser control to **Auto**, and the HorizontalAlignment and VerticalAlignment properties to **Stretch**.

14. Click **File > Save** to save the project.

15. Click the **Start Debugging** button to the left of the emulator drop-down list on the Visual Studio toolbar, or press **F5**, to view the app in the Windows Phone Emulator. The app should look similar to Figure 2-14.

Figure 2-14

The Web browser app UI

16. Leave the file and Visual Studio IDE open if you plan to complete the next exercise during this session.

➕ **MORE INFORMATION**

The "User Experience Design Guidelines for Windows Phone" Web page at http://bit.ly/jVjxwc and "General Design Principles" at http://bit.ly/xS0T4l should be your first two stops when using the Web to learn about creating the UI for Metro style applications. The "First Look at Windows Phone" Web page at http://bit.ly/JzKeoy describes common UI elements, from the Start menu to various buttons to the status bar.

Describing and Defining Globalization and Localization

> Localization and globalization ensure that people from other countries or who use a language other than the default language of your app enjoy the same user experience.

To make your app accessible to a wider audience, and potentially reach a broader sales market, you should develop your app for more than one language. Localization and globalization help you target your app to an international audience.

Localization is the process of translating text strings into other languages. A UI in a localized application displays in a user's local language. That means a developer also localizes the Application Bar if it contains text, and possibly the application title. (Some developers choose not to localize the app title to maintain branding.) Aside from English, the target languages based on highest smartphone sales per country in 2011 are Chinese, Japanese, German, French, Italian, Russian, Portuguese, and Hindi.

To achieve localization, you need to store resources like text strings, images, and videos in resource-only files, separating the resources from the application's code. See Figure 2-15. (You'll learn about the difference between resource and content files in Lesson 3.)

CERTIFICATION READY
What is the definition of localization?
3.1

Figure 2-15

A list of resource-only files in the Visual Studio IDE

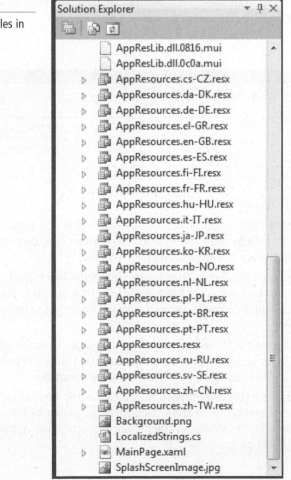

Localization and globalization are tightly related. *Globalization* is the process of making an application language-neutral. A globalized app presents data, such as currency and dates, in a format specific to a user's locale or culture. For example, if your application displays dollar amounts, your globalized app might display Euros for French users. You use the `CultureInfo` class in your code to provide information about a specific culture.

TAKE NOTE * Neither localization (in a language other than the native language of the app) nor globalization is necessary for Marketplace submission. However, if you decide to localize and globalize your app, it's easier to do so early on in development.

→ **LOCALIZE AN APPLICATION**

GET READY. As a simple example of localization, you'll localize just the title in the MyFirstApp application. To localize the title, perform the following steps:

1. In the Visual Studio IDE, open the **MyFirstApp** project file if it's not already open.

2. To add a resource file to the app, in Solution Explorer, right-click **MyFirstApp** and then select **Add > New Item** from the shortcut menu. In the Add New Item dialog box, select **Resources File**, enter **AppResources.resx** in the **Name** text box at the bottom of the dialog box, and click **Add**.

3. Enter **Title** in the first blank Name field. If you decide to localize other text strings, you must use a unique keyword for each string.

4. Enter **My Browser** in the Value field. This is the string that is displayed to the user in the application. You can add a comment in the Comment field or leave it blank. Your screen should look like Figure 2-16.

Figure 2-16

Adding a string to the localization table

Name	Value	Comment
Title	My Browser	Localizing the title that appears at the top of the application.

AppResources.resx* × MainPage.xaml

Strings ▾ | Add Resource ▾ | Remove Resource | Access Modifier: Internal

TAKE NOTE *

The "Culture and Language Support for Windows Phone" Web page at http://msdn. microsoft.com/en-us/ library/hh202918 lists regional data you may need to create resource files for other languages.

5. Create a resource file for each additional language that you want your app to support. In this example, let's localize the title for the German language, so create another resource file but name it **AppResources-de-DE.resx**.

6. In the new resource file, enter **Title** in the first blank Name field. Translate "My Browser" into German and enter the translated string, which is **Mein Browser**, into the Value field. Add a comment to the Comment field. Close the window and save it when prompted.

7. Edit the project file to define the additional language (German) your application will support. To do so, right-click the project file and select **Properties**. In the Application pane that appears, click **Assembly Information**.

8. Ensure that **English (United States)** is selected in the Neutral Language list at the bottom of the Assembly Information dialog box, as shown in Figure 2-17. This identifies the language of the strings in the default resources file, AppResources.resx. Click **OK** to close the dialog box.

Figure 2-17

Verifying the neutral language

9. Close the project and exit the Visual Studio IDE.

10. Open Notepad, select **File > Open**, open the drop-down list just above the Open button in the lower-right corner and then select **All Files (*.*).** files. Navigate to **My Documents\Visual Studio 2010\Projects\MyFirstApp\MyFirstApp** (or the location of your MyFirstApp folder) and open the **MyFirstApp.csproj** file, as shown in Figure 2-18.

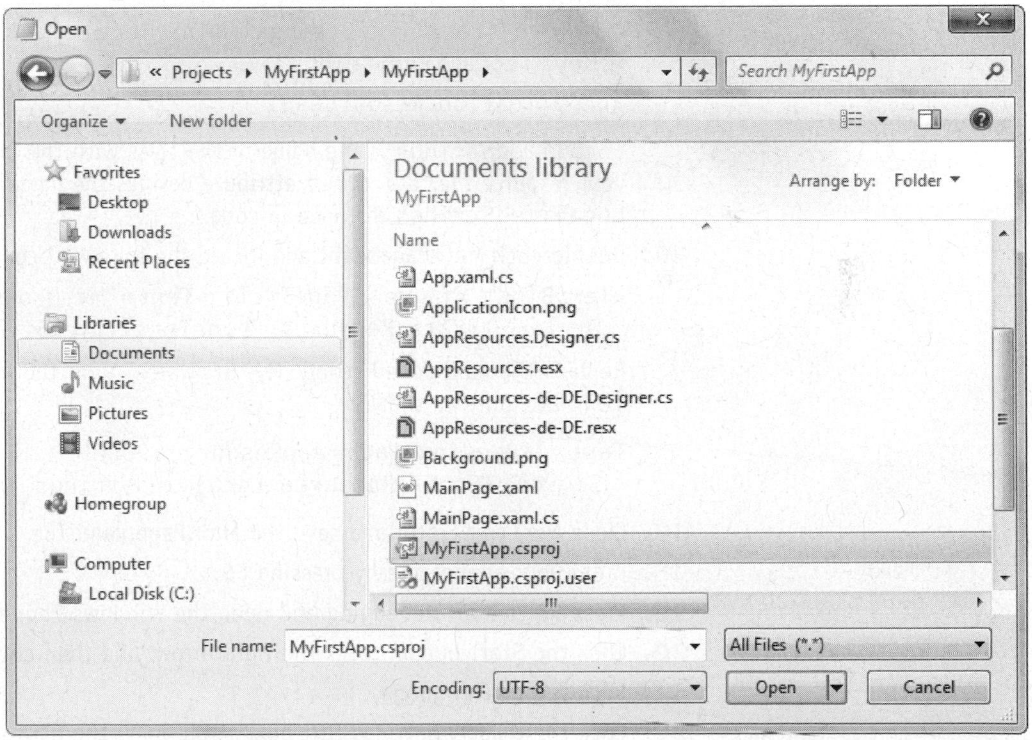

Figure 2-18

Opening MyFirstApp.csproj in Notepad

11. Locate the **<SupportedCultures>** tag and add the name of the additional culture (language) your app needs to support. For example, to add German to the tag, modify the tag so it looks like the following:

```
<SupportedCultures>de-DE;</SupportedCultures>
```

12. Save the file and close Notepad. Reopen the Visual Studio IDE and open the **MyFirstApp** project file.

13. To replace the hard-coded title string with the string in the resource files, double-click **AppResources.resx** in Solution Explorer. In the string editor pane, select **Public** from the AccessModifier drop-down list at the top of the pane. Close the string editor pane. Repeat this step for **AppResources-de-DE.resx**.

14. Define a class in MainPage.xaml.cs with a property that points to the resources. The following example, in C#, uses a LocalizedStrings class. This class contains a property that points to the AppResources resource file in the MyFirstAppnamespace:

```
public class LocalizedStrings
{
    public LocalizedStrings()
    {
    }

  private static AppResources localizedResources = new
AppResources();

  public AppResources AppResources { get { return
localizedResources; } }
}
```

15. Double-click the **App.xaml** file in Solution Explorer and add the local:LocalizedStrings XAML code to the <Application.Resources> section, as follows:

```
<Application.Resources>
    <local:LocalizedStrings xmlns:local="clr-namespace:MyFirstApp"
x:Key="LocalizedStrings" />
</Application.Resources>
```

LocalizedStrings is the name of the class with the property that returns your resource file. The x:Key attribute defines the name by which you refer to a LocalizedStrings instance in code.

16. Double-click **MainPage.xaml** and locate the following code:

```
<TextBlock x:Name="PageTitle" Text="My Browser" Margin="9,-7,0,0"
  Style="{StaticResource PhoneTextTitle1Style}"/>
```

Replace the hard-coded string "My Browser" with the following code, retaining the Text attribute as shown:

```
Text="{Binding Path=AppResources.Title,
  Source={StaticResource LocalizedStrings}}"
```

17. Close the Code Editor and save the **MainPage.xaml** file.

18. Build your application by pressing **F6**.

19. Press **F5** to start debugging and open the Windows Phone Emulator.

20. Click the **Start** button, click the right arrow, and then click **Settings**.

21. Click **region+language**.

22. Click the Display Settings text box, scroll down the list, and then click **German**. Restart the emulator.

23. Verify that your application title is in German.

24. Change the display setting in the emulator back to **English (United States)**.

25. Close the emulator and the Visual Studio IDE.

+ MORE INFORMATION

Visit the "Globalization and Localization for Windows Phone" Web page at http://bit.ly/dslsSb for details on globalization and localization.

Optimizing Mobile Applications

> The two most important factors in the user experience are startup time and responsiveness. You can *optimize* a mobile application by breaking the application into smaller assemblies, using the correct image format and size, using content rather than resource files, and much more.

Given the limited memory on most mobile devices, application optimization is an important part of proper app development. The two most important factors in application performance are startup time and responsiveness to the user.

The following tips help you develop optimized mobile apps:

- **Application startup:** If you need to display information on the splash screen, create a duplicate splash screen from the default splash screen, insert a custom image or content, and incorporate a method that displays the new splash screen for a short period of time. Another way to minimize startup time is to break your application into smaller assemblies that load only if needed.

- **Images:** Windows Phone supports JPG and PNG image files. Use the JPG format for images that are opaque, and use PNG for transparent images. In addition, limit the maximum size of images to 2000 × 2000 pixels. The maximum pixel size does not apply to icons, just photos, screen shots, and the like.

- **Content and resource files:** Lesson 3 discusses the difference between content and resource files. Content files offer better application performance than resource files because they are not compiled into an assembly when the application package file (.xap) is generated. Check the Build Action in the Properties window to ensure that any read-only files, such as images, are set to Content.

- **Progress bar:** Users like progress bars to know roughly when a task will complete. Because the `ProgressBar` control can actually reduce performance when it runs, use the `PerformanceProgressBar` control instead.

- **Storage space:** If your application creates temporary data in isolated storage, clear the data when it's no longer being used. This type of data is typically cached files. Also, give users the option to delete user-created data like photos or music files to free up storage space.

CERTIFICATION READY
What is the recommended maximum size (in pixels) for photos and screen shots in an application?
3.1

A very useful tool for analyzing and improving the performance of an application is Windows Phone Performance Analysis. You launch this tool from within the Visual Studio IDE (in the Debug menu) after building an application. The tool collects a sample of either execution or memory performance data and then displays performance metrics and a chart that you analyze.

You can find many more detailed tips and links to analysis tools on the "Performance Considerations in Applications for Windows Phone" Web page at http://bit.ly/JnudmT.

➔ EVALUATE AN APPLICATION FOR OPTIMIZATION

GET READY. To evaluate an application for optimization, perform the following steps:

1. In the Visual Studio IDE, open the **MyFirstApp** project file.
2. Check the Build Action on each of the image files. Are all image files set to Content? If not, change the Build Action value.

3. Save the project file.

4. To prepare for running the Windows Phone Performance Analysis tool, let's add a few lines of code that enable the application to search the Web. In Solution Explorer, click **MainPage.xaml** and then double-click **MainPage.xaml.cs**. In the Code Editor, add the two code statements that begin with `string site` and `webBrowser1`, as follows:

```
    private void button1_Click(object sender,
RoutedEventArgs e)
    {
        string site = textBox1.Text;
        webBrowser1.Navigate(new Uri(site, UriKind.Absolute));
    }
  }
}
```

5. Save the project file.

6. To run the Windows Phone Performance Analysis tool, you must first build the application by pressing **F6**.

7. When the build is complete, select **Debug > Start Windows Phone Performance Analysis**. Leave **Execution** selected in the window that appears, as shown in Figure 2-19. Click the **Launch Application** link. The tool connects to the Windows Phone Emulator.

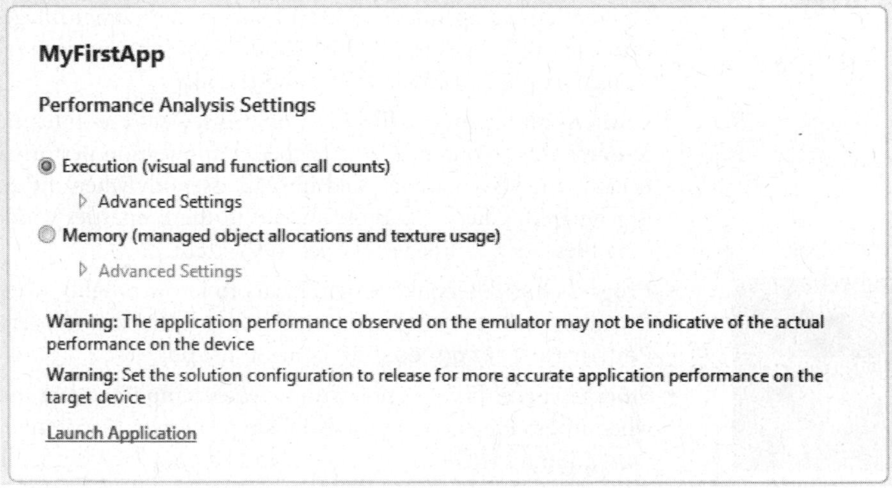

Figure 2-19

Selecting to profile execution performance data in the application

MyFirstApp

Performance Analysis Settings

⦿ Execution (visual and function call counts)

▷ Advanced Settings

○ Memory (managed object allocations and texture usage)

▷ Advanced Settings

Warning: The application performance observed on the emulator may not be indicative of the actual performance on the device

Warning: Set the solution configuration to release for more accurate application performance on the target device

Launch Application

8. Use the application in the emulator to try to connect to a few different Web sites.

9. Click the **Back** button in the emulator to stop the profiling. The performance data appears in chart form, as shown in Figure 2-20.

10. To get more information about a portion of the data, click and drag your mouse pointer over the timeline that corresponds to spikes or other unusual data points. The information appears below the chart, as shown in Figure 2-21.

11. Read through the issues and observation summaries to determine if you need to modify the application to improve performance. Remember, when running the tool in the emulator, problems revealed by the performance analyzer don't necessarily point to issues with the application—the computer may be the bottleneck.

12. Close the emulator, the MyFirstApp file, and the Visual Studio IDE.

Figure 2-20

The results of the profiling

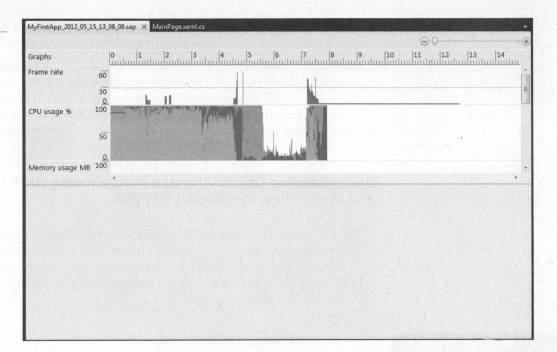

Figure 2-21

More information about profiled performance data

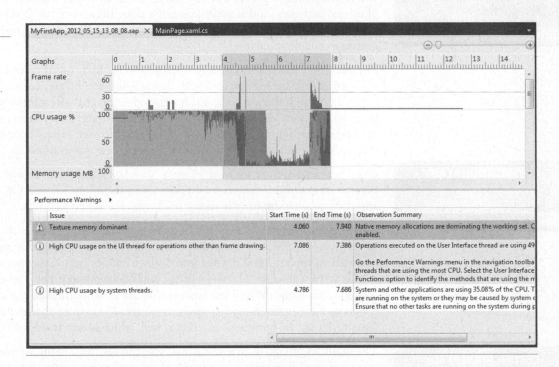

Understanding Asynchronous Programming/Threading

Asynchronous programming or threading enables an application to share a thread of execution to complete two or more activities in much less time than executing each activity sequentially and continuously.

In VB and C#, methods are executed continuously, which means once a method begins executing, it continues to do so until the method execution ends. A thread of control executes a given method. When a method is handled by a single thread and the method is waiting to complete a task, such as a file download, the user will experience a delay.

Asynchronous programming is a technique that enables multiple tasks to be processed at the same time by sharing threads. This creates discontinuous execution, where sequential activities are split into multiple methods. Discontinuity gives your application the ability to execute a thread that performs an activity while waiting for another activity to complete, like a file download. Asynchronous programming greatly improves the performance of an application.

Understanding Object-Oriented Programming (OOP) and Model View ViewModel (MVVM)

Object-oriented programming has been around for decades. It groups everything as objects, and uses encapsulation, polymorphism, and inheritance to enhance code re-use. The Model View ViewModel (MVVM) separates the front-end, or user interface, of an application from the back-end engine and data. MVVM also increases code re-use, and makes testing a much easier task.

CERTIFICATION READY
What is object-oriented programming (OOP)?
3.1

Object-oriented programming is a philosophy or an approach to software development in which everything is grouped as objects. In OOP, an object is something that can perform a set of related activities, and is an instance of a class. Because of its object-oriented nature, OOP takes advantage of encapsulation, polymorphism, and inheritance to increase code re-use and decrease code maintenance.

Encapsulation refers to grouping properties and methods together. In OOP, encapsulation is achieved mainly by creating classes. A class acts like a template, defining the properties of an object along with the methods, attributes, and events that affect those properties. Polymorphism is the ability to substitute one class for another. (Two different classes can contain the same method names, but each method can still return different results because of the code behind each method.) Inheritance is the ability to create new classes based on existing classes.

CERTIFICATION READY
What is an example of separation of concern?
3.1

OOP has been around for over 30 years, so it has a long track record of use and acceptance. Several programming languages support OOP, including VB and C#. However, another approach to programming is taking hold, which is called MVVM.

Model View ViewModel (MVVM) is a design pattern that separates the UI from a database or the layer in a program that accesses data. MVVM is an example of *separation of concerns*, in which an application is divided into distinct features (software concerns) that have minimal overlap in functionality. The way HTML and CSS work together is an example of separation of concerns. Similarly, the business logic of software is a concern, and the interface through which a person uses the business logic is another concern. If you must change the interface, you shouldn't have to change the business logic code as well, which is exactly what MVVM is all about.

CERTIFICATION READY
What is the advantage of the Model View ViewModel pattern?
3.1

The main advantage of MVVM is that you can test your application's back-end (engine) separate from the UI, potentially reducing development time. MVVM also enables you to re-use code more efficiently.

The Model describes your application domain, which is a set of classes that represents your data, data entities, business objects, services, and more. The data can be from almost any source, such as in local storage on the device, in a database locally or remotely, or accessed via a Web service.

The View is your application UI, which are the Silverlight screens that you build in the Visual Studio IDE.

The ViewModel is a middleman between the Model and the View. Here you can gather and customize the data you want to present to the user, which will be bound to a View. Using a ViewModel, the View doesn't know the source of data and doesn't have to retrieve it.

The ViewModel typically accomplishes data capture and transfer using services, or service agents. For example, you can create a service agent class that calls remote services from Silverlight. The service agent initiates the service call, captures the data that's returned, and forwards the data to the ViewModel. You can re-use the service agent across multiple ViewModel classes.

Figure 2-22 illustrates the MVVM pattern and where services can be integrated.

Figure 2-22

The MVVM model with integrated services

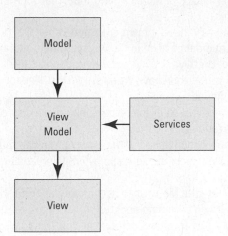

The ViewModel may consist of the following:

- **Properties:** These are strings or objects. Notifies binding clients using the INotifyPropertyChanged interface whenever a bound element changes.
- **Collections:** This is usually ObservableCollection, a dynamic data collection that provides notifications when any bound element changes.
- **Commands:** Implements the ICommand, which binds an action as a property, maintaining separation between the ViewModel and the View. For example, the ICommand might retrieve data from a Web service and then display the data when the user pushes a button.

The important thing to remember is that binding properties of a View to a ViewModel eliminates the need to write code in a ViewModel that directly updates a View. When creating a complex application, this separation enables one person or group to develop the back-end while another person or group designs and creates the UI.

⊙ EXPLORE MVVM

GET READY. To explore the concepts of MVVM, perform the following steps:

1. In a Web browser, browse to the following two Web pages and read both articles:

   - The Basics of MVVM (Paul Sheriff): http://bit.ly/jw9OG6
   - MVVM QuickStart (Microsoft): http://bit.ly/gQY00r

2. Compare MVVM to the "Localize an Application" exercise earlier in this lesson. Is app localization a form of separation of concerns?

3. Write a summary report (no longer than one page) that presents the similarities between MVVM and the procedure for localizing a mobile application.

✚ MORE INFORMATION

To learn more about OOP, visit the "Object-Oriented Programming (C# and Visual Basic)" Web page at http://msdn.microsoft.com/en-us/library/dd460654.aspx. MSDN Magazine provides a highly informative article on MVVM at http://msdn.microsoft.com/en-us/magazine/dd419663.aspx.

SKILL SUMMARY

IN THIS LESSON YOU LEARNED:

- You can develop mobile applications using platform-specific tools or multiplatform tools. A multiplatform tool enables you to create mobile apps for a variety of platforms. PhoneGap and Rhodes are two examples of multiplatform tools that support Windows Phone 7, among other platforms.
- The Visual Studio integrated development environment, or IDE, provides several tools that enable you to create and debug code in C#, VB, and other programming languages. To create applications specifically for Windows Phone, you can use the Windows Phone Add-in for Visual Studio if you already have Visual Studio installed, or use Visual Studio 2010 Express for Windows Phone.
- The .NET Framework provides all of the technologies needed to create, test, and run Windows-based applications.
- Designing a mobile application begins with planning. You can reduce the time needed for development and create a more efficient app by outlining and/or sketching the flow of the application.
- Windows Phone apps use the Metro style as the foundation for UIs to achieve a consistent look and feel. When designing apps, be sure to make buttons and other controls large enough to be used easily on a touch screen. You should also ensure consistent and adequate spacing, or padding, between controls and between text and controls.
- Localization and globalization ensure that people from other countries or who use a language other than the default language of your app get the same user experience.
- The two most important factors in the user experience are startup time and responsiveness. You can optimize a mobile application by breaking the application into smaller assemblies, using the correct image format and size, using content rather than resource files, and much more.
- Asynchronous programming or threading enables an application to share a thread of execution to complete two or more activities in much less time than executing each activity sequentially and continuously.
- Object-oriented programming has been around for decades. It groups everything as objects, and uses encapsulation, polymorphism, and inheritance to enhance code re-use.
- The Model View ViewModel (MVVM) separates the front-end, or user interface, of an application from the back-end engine and data. The MVVM enhances application testing and code re-use.
- MVVM is an example of separation of concerns, in which an application is divided into distinct features (software concerns) that have minimal overlap in functionality.

■ Knowledge Assessment

Fill in the Blank

Complete the following sentences by writing the correct word or words in the blanks provided.

1. _____ is an integrated development environment (IDE) used by programmers and developers to create all kinds of applications and user interfaces (UIs). The IDE includes a code editor and debugger, and natively supports the C++, VB.NET, C#, and F# programming languages.

2. _____ is a Visual Studio IDE available as a stand-alone software package or as an add-in for Visual Studio Professional or higher.

3. In Visual Studio 2010 Express for Windows Phone, a file's code appears in the _____, where you can modify the code.

4. _____ errors prevent code from being compiled in an IDE.

5. In a Windows Phone app, _____ may display one or more Live Tiles to enable users to access app features or other apps.

6. _____ is the process of translating text strings into other languages.

7. _____ is the process of making an application language-neutral.

8. _____ programming is a technique that enables multiple tasks to be processed at the same time by sharing threads.

9. _____ programming is a philosophy or an approach to software development in which everything is grouped as objects.

10. _____ is a design pattern that separates the UI from a database or the layer in a program that accesses data.

Multiple Choice

Circle the letter that corresponds to the best answer.

1. In Visual Studio 2010 Express for Windows Phone, which term best describes the IDE element that displays a generic device called a phone skin, which you can use to design an application UI?
   a. Windows Phone Emulator
   b. Design surface
   c. Design Editor
   d. Toolbox

2. In Visual Studio 2010 Express for Windows Phone, which of the following is pressed to create a release build of an application?
   a. F1
   b. F5
   c. F6
   d. F10

3. Which of the following is responsible for presenting data, such as currency and dates, in a format specific to a user's locale or culture?
   a. Localization
   b. Binding
   c. Globalization
   d. Metro style

4. Which .NET Framework technology enables you to create rich user interfaces that may include 2D graphics, 3D graphics, multimedia, and documents?
   a. ADO.NET
   b. Windows Workflow Foundation (WF)
   c. Windows Communication Foundation (WCF)
   d. Windows Presentation Foundation (WPF)

5. Which of the following are ways to optimize a mobile application? (Choose all that apply.)
   a. Break the application into smaller assemblies.
   b. Use the correct image format and size.
   c. Use resource rather than content files.
   d. Run the Windows Phone Emulator.

6. Which of the following is *not* a common feature of a Metro style UI?
   a. Live Tiles
   b. Color gradients
   c. Relatively large buttons
   d. The Segoe WP font family

7. Which of the following is an aspect of asynchronous programming?
   a. Discontinuous execution
   b. Continuous execution
   c. Bottlenecks
   d. Lack of thread sharing

8. Which of the following are important concepts in object-oriented programming? (Choose all that apply.)
   a. Globalization
   b. Inheritance
   c. Encapsulation
   d. Polymorphism

9. What are the three main components of MVVM?
   a. ViewModel
   b. Model
   c. Microsoft .NET
   d. View

10. What is the main purpose of the Windows Phone Performance Analysis tool?
    a. Testing and improving how well an application runs
    b. Debugging an application
    c. Creating a release build of an application
    d. Packaging an application for distribution

True/False

Circle T if the statement is true or F if the statement is false.

T   F   1. The two most important factors in the mobile app user experience are the appeal of the UI and responsiveness.

T   F   2. In MVVM, the `ViewModel` describes the application domain, which is a set of classes that represent data, data entities, business objects, services, and more.

T   F   3. Runtime errors are unexpected or incorrect behaviors that occur while an application runs.

T   F   4. In a Windows Phone app, Start may be presented in portrait or landscape view.

T   F   5. The way HTML and CSS work together, and MVVM, are examples of separation of concerns.

■ Competency Assessment

Scenario 2-1: Select an IDE to Create Windows Phone Apps

Marty wants to make some money in his spare time and has decided to create and sell some Windows Phone applications. He's not sure which tools to use and asks for your advice. What do you tell him?

Scenario 2-2: Design an Application

Marty decided to use Visual Studio 2010 Express for Windows Phone to create applications. He starting to create his first app but stopped because it contained too many screens and became too complex to work with. He's disillusioned with app development because the process seems too hard. What do you suggest to Marty to help him begin another app development project?

■ Proficiency Assessment

Scenario 2-3: Create an App for an International Audience

Naveen wants to make his photo-sharing application highly usable by English speakers in the United States, as well as people in China, Germany, and France. His application includes icons and photos but no text other than the title, and the app includes dates. He doesn't want to translate the title, but does want the dates associated with photos to appear in the order commonly used by people in the four countries. However, the dates differ depending on the locale. What can Naveen do to ensure the dates appear properly depending on the user's locale?

Scenario 2-4: Optimize an App

Christiane works for a marketing firm and is close to finishing a mobile application for a client that owns a chain of theaters. The application lists movies that are currently playing in the theaters and includes images of movie posters. The problem is that the app starts up and runs much more slowly than it did earlier in development. What tips do you share with Christiane to decrease the startup time and increase the responsiveness of the app?

Exploring Networked Data and Data Stores

3 LESSON

EXAM OBJECTIVE MATRIX

SKILLS/CONCEPTS	MTA EXAM OBJECTIVE	MTA EXAM OBJECTIVE NUMBER
Using Data Stores	Using data stores.	2.2
Working with Networked Data	Working with networked data.	2.1

KEY TERMS

ADO.NET

Choosers

content files

data binding

data store

database

database schema

event

event handler

isolated storage

key/value pair

Language-Integrated Query (LINQ)

Launchers

LINQ to SQL

merge replication

occasionally connected application (OCA)

remote storage

resource files

SQL Server replication

Sync Framework

Web service

Windows Azure

Windows Communication Foundation (WCF)

You've been working with the application developer team at BoxTwelve Mobile on a mobile app for Glide, a winter sports equipment and apparel reseller. To continue your training with the developers at BoxTwelve Mobile, you've been asked to help determine the proper type of data store and/or Web service to use for a custom-ordering app for a client. You also need to learn about data linking and binding.

■ Using Data Stores

↓
THE BOTTOM LINE

A data store is a data repository or container that stores data. The repository can be a database or a type of structured flat file.

Mobile applications use all kinds of data, such as dates and events in a calendar app, support ticket information in a help desk app, and task items in a to-do list. The same applies to apps that use pictures, music, and video. How does a small device with limited storage space handle so many different types of data? The big-picture answer is data stores, which may be located on the device or remotely over the Internet.

CERTIFICATION READY
What is a data store?
2.2

A *data store* is simply a data repository—a container that stores data. The repository can be a database, or it can be a flat file, like a spreadsheet, that contains data structured into rows and columns. Even a text file can be a data repository as long as the data is structured consistently, so that it resembles rows and columns (see Figure 3-1). Items in a data store are called objects, which are integrated within the data store and may come from multiple sources.

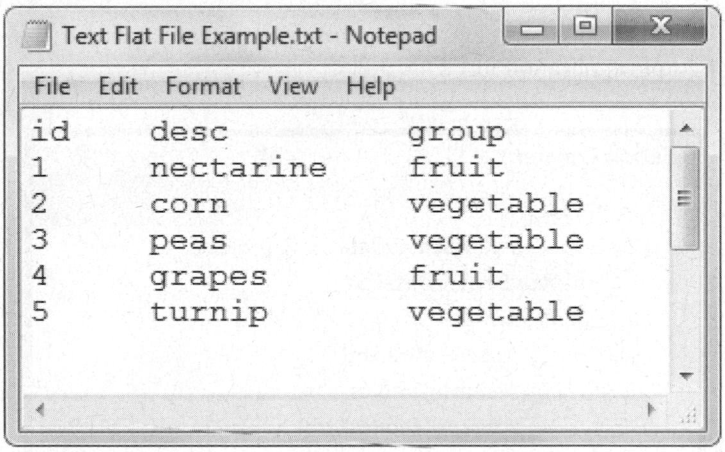

Figure 3-1

An example of a text file as a flat-file repository

Text Flat File Example.txt - Notepad

File Edit Format View Help

id	desc	group
1	nectarine	fruit
2	corn	vegetable
3	peas	vegetable
4	grapes	fruit
5	turnip	vegetable

This lesson examines types of data used by mobile apps, how they're stored, and how an app accesses and uses that data.

Using Different Types of Storage

Files and databases are the predominant forms of storage for mobile devices. To optimize an app's performance, you should apply a Content build action to read-only files when creating an app. A Resource build action is applied to files that are compiled into assemblies, which can affect an app's startup time.

To understand how an app accesses and uses data, you first have to understand mobile app data storage. "Storage" in this sense refers to files and databases—the containers in which data resides.

Files

A typical application created in the Visual Studio IDE includes some files you should know about:

- **C# or Visual Basic (VB):** Code file that contains either C# or VB code. C# files have a .cs file extension and VB files have a .vb file extension. This code is the programming language instruction used to define the application.

CERTIFICATION READY
How are Windows Phone applications integrated with XML?
2.2

- **XAML:** Extensible Application Markup Language (XAML) was developed by Microsoft and is used to create the user interface for mobile apps. XAML files are XML-based and have an .xaml file extension.

- **XAP:** This is the compressed output file for applications created in the Visual Studio IDE. It contains all of the files, XAML, and .NET code needed to run the app. It's like a .zip file but with an .xap extension. You usually don't work with the XAP file until the later testing phases of mobile app development and when you're ready to submit your app to the Windows Phone Marketplace.

- **Images:** Not every mobile app has images. For those that do, Joint Photographic Experts Group (JPEG) and Portable Network Graphics (PNG) are the image file format of choice. They are both generally small in file size and support millions of colors. Windows Phone supports both .jpg and .jpeg file extensions for JPEG files. PNG files are lossless, unlike JPEG files. PNG files have a .png file extension.

TAKE NOTE*

A lossless image uses compression that enables you to enlarge the image, within reason, without losing quality. On the other hand, a lossy image shows degradation and pixelated distortion when the image is enlarged.

You can see the C#, XAML, and image files in an expanded view of Solution Explorer for a sample application in Figure 3-2.

Figure 3-2

Files for a sample app written in C#

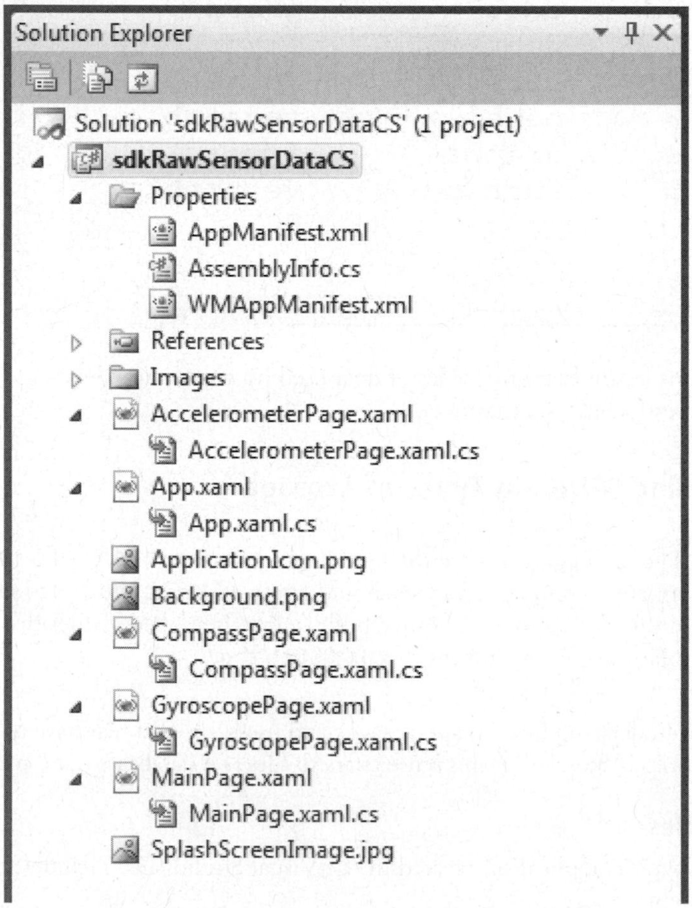

Two important file types in applications built in the Visual Studio IDE are content files and resource files. These files are read-only local files, which are generally image files. (You'll learn about local versus remote files after the next exercise.)

TAKE NOTE *

In Windows Phone applications, an assembly is a data link library (DLL) file. You can use the same assembly in different application packages.

Content files offer better application performance than resource files because they are not compiled into an assembly when the application package file (.xap) is generated. Instead, the assemblies contain pointers to content files, and many assemblies can share content files in a package. By not including content files in the assemblies, an application starts faster.

Resource files are embedded in the project assembly, so they're always available whether you deploy the assemblies inside or outside of the application package. Because resource files are compiled in the assemblies, resource files can affect the length of time an application needs to start. With few resource files in an app, the user won't notice the difference. As the number of resource files grows, the startup lag will be noticeable. Developers typically use resource files when they know they won't need to modify the files once the assembly is compiled, and when the size of any files called during startup are small enough so they don't affect the app's startup time.

You choose whether a file is content or resource using the Build Action feature in the Visual Studio IDE. Figure 3-3 shows the Properties window for an image file in a sample application. The build action is currently set to Content, but clicking the down arrow to the right of the field opens a menu where you can select another type of build action, including Resource.

Figure 3-3

Specifying the Content or Resource build action for a file

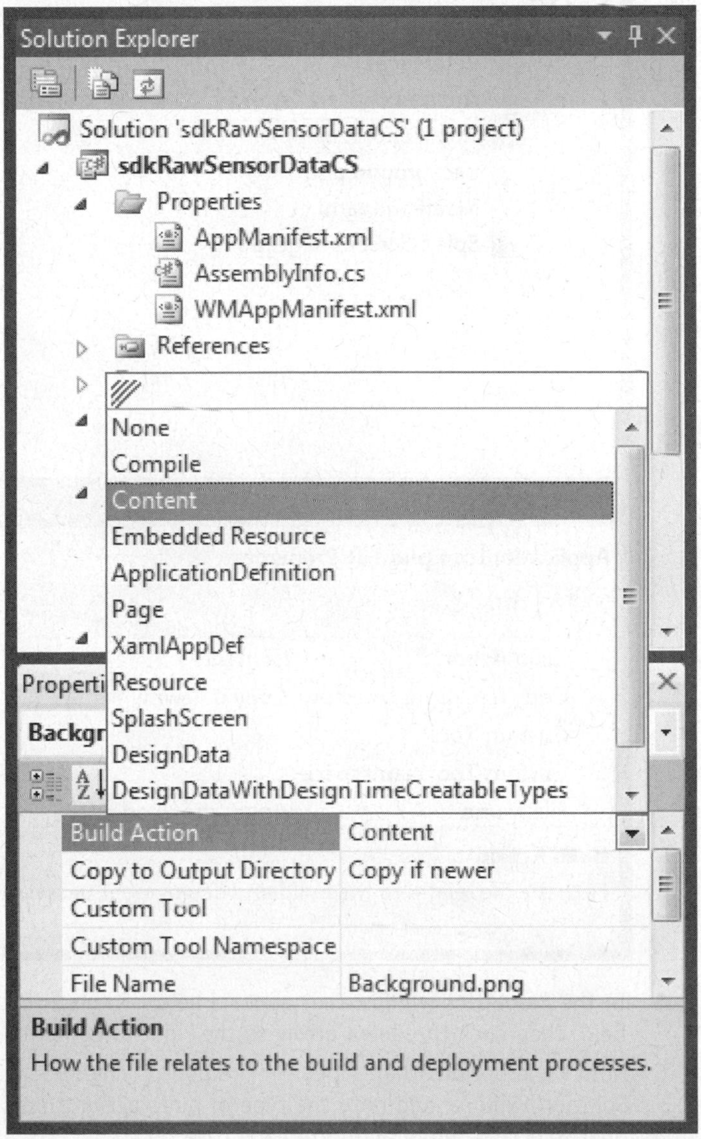

TAKE NOTE *

When you begin building your own apps, remember that the build action in Visual Studio is set to Resource by default. You need to change it to Content for each image to improve app performance.

CHECK THE BUILD ACTION OF SPECIFIC FILES

GET READY. To check the build action of specific files, perform the following steps:

1. In the Visual Studio IDE, open the Network and Device Information (sdkNetworkAndDeviceInfo) sample project that you downloaded in Lesson 1.

2. Open Solution Explorer.

3. Click **ApplicationIcon.png** to select it, and then click the **Properties** button on the toolbar in Solution Explorer, as shown in Figure 3-4.

Figure 3-4

The Properties window in Solution Explorer

Properties button

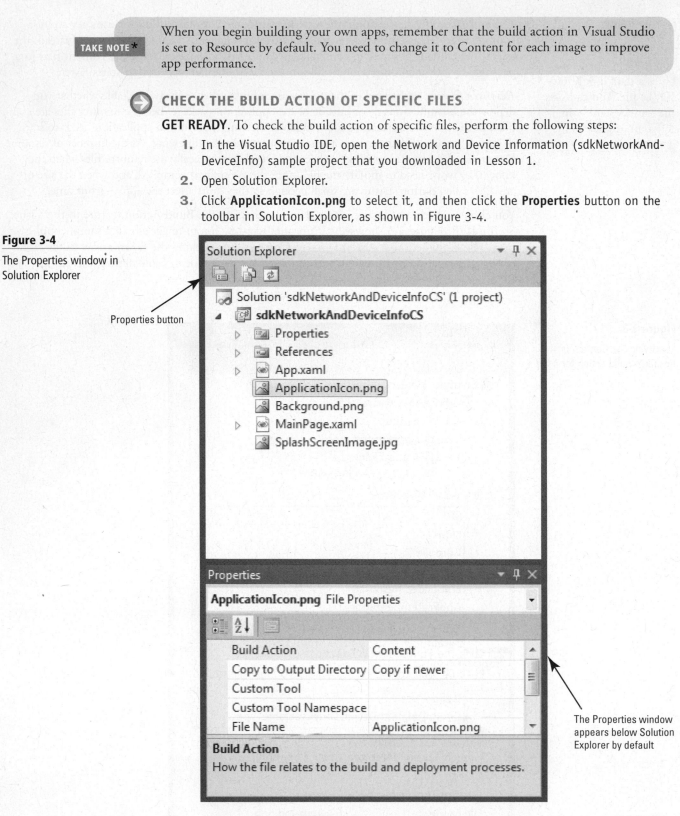

The Properties window appears below Solution Explorer by default

4. In the Properties window that appears below Solution Explorer, click the **Build Action** field, then click the **down arrow** to the right of Content.

5. Notice the options that appear in the pop-up menu. Select each PNG file listed in Solution Explorer and note the type of build action that's selected. Why did the developer select the build action in each case?

6. Close the code sample file and leave the Visual Studio IDE open if you continue to the next exercise during this session.

TAKE NOTE * You can access resource files using the `Application.GetResourceStream` method, and access content files using the `XElement.Load` method.

Databases

A *database* is a collection of information organized in a structure that's designed for convenient access. You can easily make changes to data in a database, reorganize the fields, and search the database for specific types of information.

CERTIFICATION READY
What are the two primary types of data storage?
2.2

Many databases are "relational," which means two or more tables within a database are linked to one another (related). When you perform a search, the search engine can check all of the linked tables instead of just one. A well designed relational database helps to eliminate duplicate data storage requirements, thus making it easier to maintain accurate data. Because the data is stored once and related to other tables, any update only needs to be done in one location.

For example, a simple healthcare relational database might contain a physician table (with physician names, addresses, phone numbers, and specialties), a patient table (with patient information, health record number, date of birth, prescriptions, etc.), and an appointments table (with physician identifier, patient identifier, and appointment date). One doctor can see many different patients, and patients can make one or more appointments, so linking the three tables is much more efficient than trying to organize all of the information in a single table.

Another important concept is a *database schema*, which is the structure of a database defined in a formal language. The schema defines the tables in a relational database, the fields in each table, and the relationships between fields and tables.

Microsoft SQL Server is an example of a widely used, relational database program. Data that a mobile device user generates can be kept in a database on the device or accessed on a remote server that runs SQL Server.

⊙ EXPLORE AN APPLICATION THAT USES A DATABASE

GET READY. To explore an application that uses a database, perform the following steps:

1. On the Start page in the Visual Studio IDE, access the Code Samples for Windows Phone Web page.
2. Click the **Fundamental Concepts** category.
3. Click **C#** next to the Local Database Sample entry and download it to your Visual Studio 2010\Projects folder. (You can download a similar code sample if the Local Database sample is no longer available.)

TAKE NOTE * You can download the VB code if you prefer, but the following steps and figures are based on C#. You would need to modify the steps slightly to accommodate VB.

4. Extract the Zip file in Windows Explorer, and then open the project in the Visual Studio IDE.
5. Open Solution Explorer, click the **App.xaml** entry to expand it, and then double-click **App.xaml.cs**.
6. Browse the code, a portion of which is shown in Figure 3-5. Which section of code looks for an existing database and creates one if a database doesn't exist?

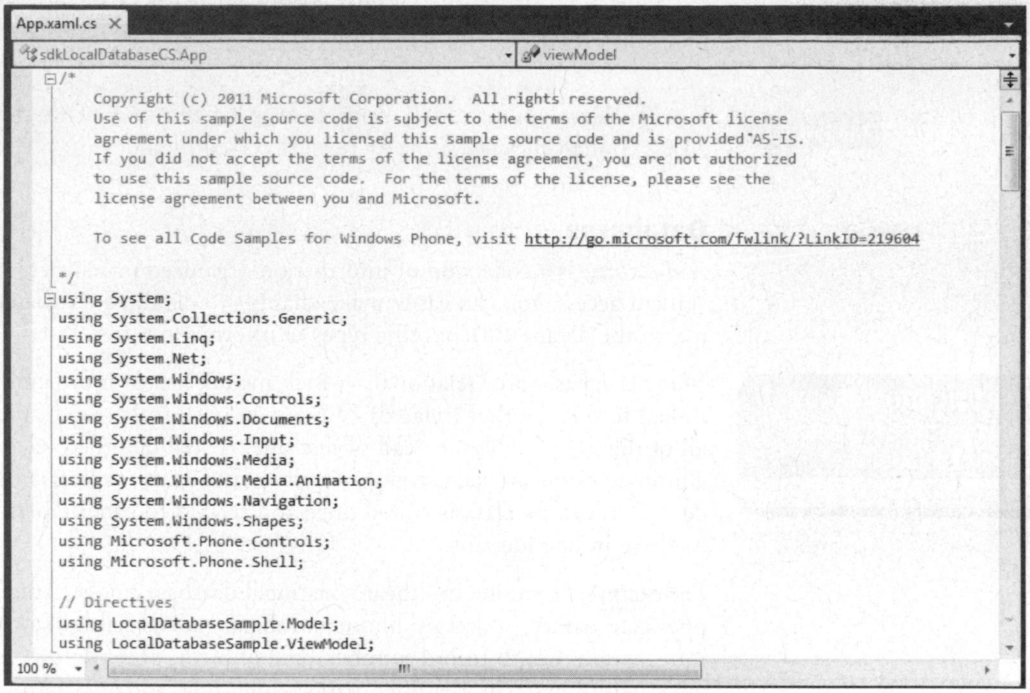

Figure 3-5

A portion of code from App.xaml.cs in the Local Database sample

```
App.xaml.cs ×
sdkLocalDatabaseCS.App                                    viewModel
/*
    Copyright (c) 2011 Microsoft Corporation.  All rights reserved.
    Use of this sample source code is subject to the terms of the Microsoft license
    agreement under which you licensed this sample source code and is provided "AS-IS.
    If you did not accept the terms of the license agreement, you are not authorized
    to use this sample source code.  For the terms of the license, please see the
    license agreement between you and Microsoft.

    To see all Code Samples for Windows Phone, visit http://go.microsoft.com/fwlink/?LinkID=219604

*/
using System;
using System.Collections.Generic;
using System.Linq;
using System.Net;
using System.Windows;
using System.Windows.Controls;
using System.Windows.Documents;
using System.Windows.Input;
using System.Windows.Media;
using System.Windows.Media.Animation;
using System.Windows.Navigation;
using System.Windows.Shapes;
using Microsoft.Phone.Controls;
using Microsoft.Phone.Shell;

// Directives
using LocalDatabaseSample.Model;
using LocalDatabaseSample.ViewModel;

100 %
```

7. Close the code sample file and leave the Visual Studio IDE open if you continue to the next exercise during this session.

Describing and Defining the Benefits of Different Storage Locations

> Windows Phone OS 7.1 can use local storage on a device, and a special area of local storage called isolated storage to hold user-specific data. Data can also be accessed remotely—across an internal network or the Internet.

Windows Phone OS 7.1 enables you to store data locally or remotely. Local, read-only data is stored within the application itself. Data that's specific to the user, such as preferences, e-mail addresses, and game scores, can be stored in special local containers called *isolated storage*. Users can also access data remotely, from a server located on the Internet, using Web services. An illustration of the various types of storage are shown in Figure 3-6.

Figure 3-6

Local, isolated, and remote storage in Windows Phone OS 7.1

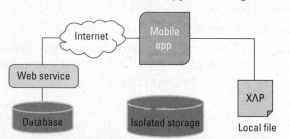

Local Storage and Isolated Storage

Local files may be XML, text, APIs, or other types of files, and are located on the device. As mentioned in the last section, you can compile local files as content files or resource files. Some local files are static, which means they don't change, and can be read-only.

Other local files are dynamic, like a database file, and are located in isolated storage. This keeps them separated so no other applications can access that data. User-specific data is generally dynamic data that's kept in isolated storage.

There are three ways to use isolated storage. You can save data:

- As key/value pairs by using the `IsolatedStorageSettings` class; the syntax is similar to the following:

```
public void SaveStringObject()
{
    var settings = IsolatedStorageSettings.ApplicationSettings;
    settings.Add("key", value");
}
```

- In files and folders using the `IsolatedStorageFile` class; the syntax is similar to the following:

```
IsolatedStorageFile myIsolatedStorage =
IsolatedStorageFile.GetUserStoreForApplication();

myIsolatedStorage.CreateDirectory("NewFolder");
```

- In a database

A **key/value pair** is a set of data items. The key is unique. It can be a keyword or ID, for example. The value is a data item or a pointer to where that data item is stored. This method of file storage is useful for application settings and query strings when searching a database. The following are examples of key/value pairs:

client=Internet Explorer 9

q=bing.com

If two applications must access the same data, the data can't be local to either application. In this case you need to use remote storage through a Web service, which generally means the data resides in storage on the Internet (also referred to as "in the cloud"). Many applications can share data that's in the cloud, and some apps allow users to keep a local copy in isolated storage as well.

Remote Storage

Remote storage, as mentioned, is data located on a server across the Internet that requires Web services for a client to access. An application can use one of several Web protocols to access Web services. The protocols include HTTP, XML, and Simple Object Access Protocol (SOAP), among others.

A **Web service** acts like a proxy between a client (the mobile app) and remote storage (database server). The proxy acts as an intermediary, passing along requests from the client seeking resources, such as data, from the server. The proxy also passes data from the server to the client.

Now let's take a look at Web services commonly used by mobile apps. The following are Web service technologies that enable you to work with remote data:

- **Windows Communication Foundation (WCF) services:** This is a framework for building and accessing Web services. You use WCF to make a class accessible as a service and then exchange objects between your app and that service.
- **WCF Data Services (OData services):** This is a widely used framework for accessing data. WCF data services can turn .NET code into an Open Data Protocol (OData) Web service. This means apps can use HTTP to run queries against a remote database, and to create, modify, and delete data in the database.
- **Windows Azure Services:** **Windows Azure** provides cloud storage that can be used by Windows Phone applications. Because cloud storage is scalable, this service works well if you need to store large amounts of data. You access Windows Azure in much the same way you use a Web service.

CERTIFICATION READY
What are the differences between local, isolated, and remote storage?
2.2

TAKE NOTE*

Developers use the term "expose" when referring to making a class accessible as a service.

TAKE NOTE*

You'll learn more about WCF later in this lesson.

To access any Web service from a Silverlight-based app, use the HTTP classes `HttpWebRequest` and `HttpWebResponse` or `WebClient` classes in the System.Net namespace. These classes work with HTTP to provide the "link" between an app and a Web service.

 EXPLORE AN APPLICATION THAT USES A WEB SERVICE

GET READY. To explore an application that uses a Web service, perform the following steps:

1. On the Start page in the Visual Studio IDE, access the Code Samples for Windows Phone Web page.

2. Click the **Fundamental Concepts** category.

3. Click **C#** next to the Weather Forecast Sample entry and download it to your Visual Studio 2010\Projects folder. (You can download a similar code sample if the Weather Forecast sample is no longer available.)

TAKE NOTE * You can download the VB code if you prefer, but the following steps and figures are based on C#. You would need to modify the steps slightly to accommodate VB.

4. Extract the ZIP file in Windows Explorer, and then open the project in the Visual Studio IDE.

5. Open Solution Explorer, click the **ForecastPage.xaml** entry to expand it, double-click **ForecastPage.xaml.cs**, and then close Solution Explorer.

6. Browse the code, a portion of which is shown in Figure 3-7. Where does the remote data exist? Which HTTP class(es) does this code sample use—`HttpWebRequest`/`HttpWebResponse` or `WebClient`?

Figure 3-7

A portion of code from ForecastPage.xaml.cs in the Weather Forecast sample

```
ForecastPage.xaml.cs  ×

sdkWeatherForecastCS.ForecastPage                         forecast

/*
    Copyright (c) 2011 Microsoft Corporation.  All rights reserved.
    Use of this sample source code is subject to the terms of the Microsoft license
    agreement under which you licensed this sample source code and is provided AS-IS.
    If you did not accept the terms of the license agreement, you are not authorized
    to use this sample source code.  For the terms of the license, please see the
    license agreement between you and Microsoft.

    To see all Code Samples for Windows Phone, visit http://go.microsoft.com/fwlink/?LinkID=219604

*/
using System.Windows.Controls;
using Microsoft.Phone.Controls;
using System.Windows.Navigation;


namespace sdkWeatherForecastCS
{
    public partial class ForecastPage : PhoneApplicationPage
    {
        Forecast forecast;

        public ForecastPage()
        {
            InitializeComponent();
        }

        /// <summary>
        /// Event handler to handle when this page is navigated to

100 %
```

7. Close the code sample file and leave the Visual Studio IDE open if you continue to the next exercise during this session.

MORE INFORMATION

To learn more about how to get data into your Windows Phone application, go to http://bit.ly/eWJZx1. The "Generic local data storage for Windows Phone 7.1 (Mango) apps" blog entry at http://bit.ly/HchFYV can help you more easily understand local storage. These Web sites provide information on local and isolated storage: "Local Data Storage for Windows Phone" at http://bit.ly/HJSAXm and "Isolated Storage Overview for Windows Phone" at http://bit.ly/wNFtZK.

Accessing Native Data and Functionalities

Launchers and Choosers are APIs that are called from within an original application, temporarily use built-in applications on a device, and then return the user to the original application. A Chooser API can return data to the original application but a Launcher API cannot.

CERTIFICATION READY
How do you access built-in data and functionalities on a mobile device?
2.2

Launchers and *Choosers* are APIs that provide access to built-in Windows Phone features, such as placing a phone call, getting contact information, or taking a picture. The APIs work from within an app you develop by temporarily opening a new application, letting the user perform tasks in the new application, and then closing the new application and returning the user to the original app. A Chooser API can return data to the original application but a Launcher API cannot.

For example, the Phone Number Chooser launches the Contacts application, enabling the user to search for a specific contact. If the contact information is found, an event is raised, the event handler receives a phone number, and the phone number is returned to the user.

TAKE NOTE*

In programming, an *event* is the result of something occurring in an object. An example of a user-generated event is tapping a button on a device. The object in which the event occurs is called the "event generator." In this example, the button is the event generator, and when the user taps the button an event occurs. The object performing the task when the event occurs is the *event handler*. An event handler is usually a software routine that responds to actions, such as tapping. One or more event handlers may be needed for a single event.

 EXPLORE A CHOOSER

GET READY. To see how a Chooser works, perform the following steps:

1. On the Start page in the Visual Studio IDE, access the Code Samples for Windows Phone Web page.
2. Click the **Cameras and Photos** category.
3. Click **C#** next to Photos Sample and download it to your Visual Studio 2010\Projects folder. The Photos sample code enables you to capture a photo using the built-in Camera application, crop the photo, and save it.

TAKE NOTE*

You can download the VB code if you prefer, but the following steps and figures are based on C#. You must modify the steps slightly to accommodate VB.

4. Extract the ZIP file in Windows Explorer, and then open the project in the Visual Studio IDE.
5. In the Visual Studio IDE, close the Code Samples for Windows Phone window by clicking the **X** in the tab.

6. Click **Open project** on the Start page, or select **File > Open Project**.

7. Double-click the code sample's folder in the Projects folder, select the **.sln** file, and click **Open**.

8. Click the **Find in Files** button on toolbar, type **CameraCaptureTask** in the Find and Replace dialog box, and then click **Find All**. (See Figure 3-8.)

Figure 3-8

Searching for CameraCaptureTask in the code sample

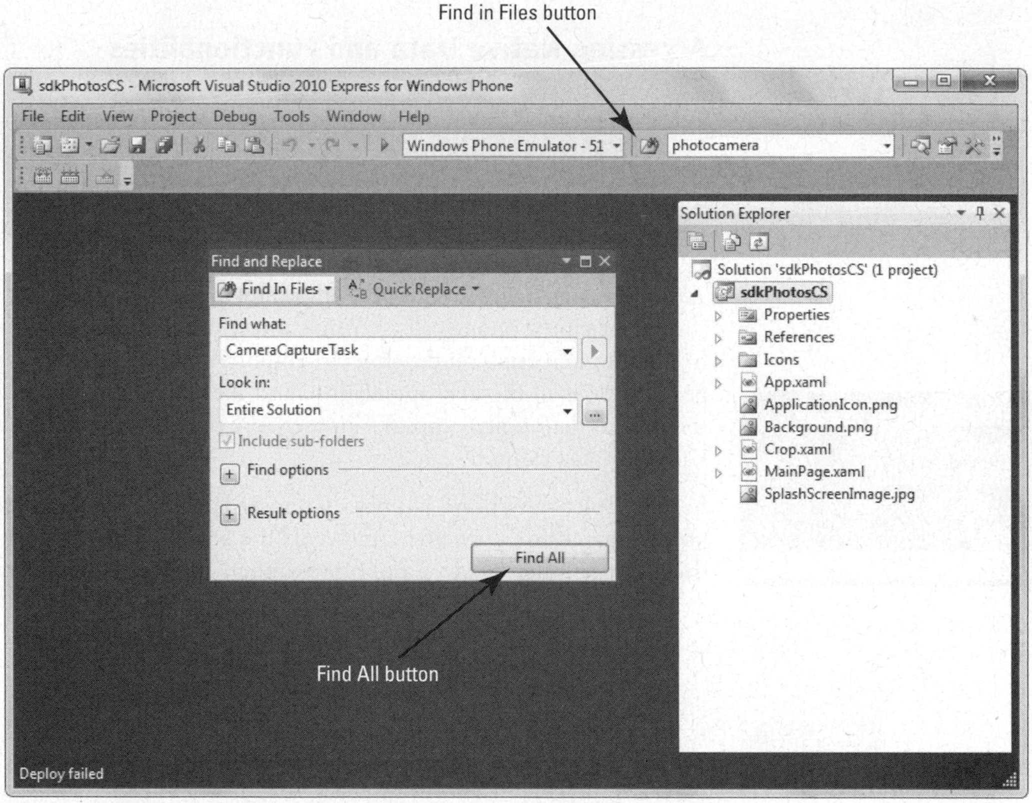

9. The names of files containing CameraCaptureTask appear in the Find Results window, shown in Figure 3-9. Notice that the two listings indicate the MainPage.xaml.cs file.

Figure 3-9

The Find Results window

```
ind Results 1, "Entire Solution"
\Projects\sdkPhotosCS\sdkPhotosCS\MainPage.xaml.cs(45):          CameraCaptureTask ctask;
\Projects\sdkPhotosCS\sdkPhotosCS\MainPage.xaml.cs(84):             ctask = new CameraCaptureTask();
 Total files searched: 9
```

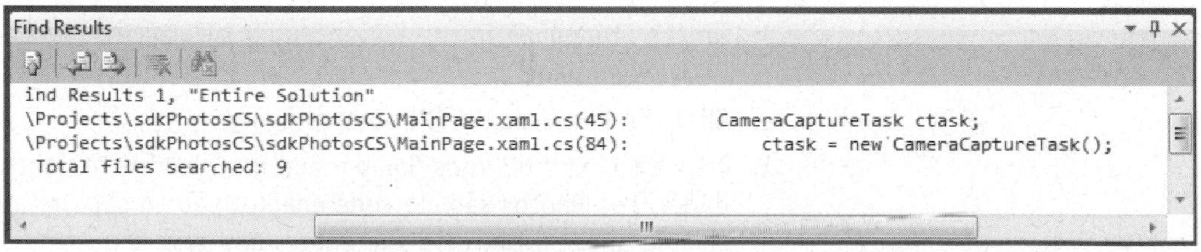

10. Open Solution Explorer, locate the **MainPage.xaml** entry, click to expand the entry, and then double-click the **MainPage.xaml.cs** file name.

11. Close Solution Explorer and the Find Results window to free up window space. Browse the code, a portion of which is shown in Figure 3-10. To locate the instances of CameraCaptureTask, press **Ctrl+F**, type **CameraCaptureTask** in the Find what text box, and then click **Find Next**.

12. Click **Find Next** again to find the next instance of CameraCaptureTask. Examine the associated event handlers. Can you determine which part of the code returns data to the user?

Figure 3-10

Camera capture code in a sample file

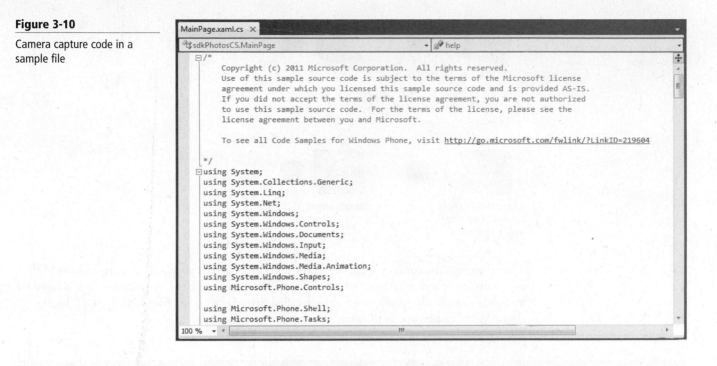

13. Close the code sample file and leave the Visual Studio IDE open if you continue to the next exercise during this session.

➕ MORE INFORMATION

To learn more about Launchers and Choosers, visit the "Launchers and Choosers Overview for Windows Phone" Web page at http://msdn.microsoft.com/en-us/library/ff769542(v=VS.92).aspx.

Handling Offline Situations

> An occasionally connected application (OCA) synchronizes data on a client device with a remote server, so that the user can work with server-based information while offline.

A mobile app that requires a user to access data from a remote source fails when the device doesn't have network connectivity. This is a common problem even for PC users who sometimes can't access online email accounts when their Wi-Fi connection is down. A workaround for mobile app developers is to make the application run in offline mode by using an **occasionally connected application (OCA)**. An OCA is an application that synchronizes a local (client) database with a remote (server) database when a connection is active, and then allows the user to work with the data offline. An advantage of OCA is that local data access is faster than remote data access, so the user isn't limited by the speed of the device's network connection.

Here's how it works: An OCA retrieves data from the remote server and stores it locally on the user's device. The user can use the app and data locally. When a network connection is available, the OCA synchronizes the data between the client and server so a current copy resides in both data stores. See Figure 3-11 for an illustration of the process.

CERTIFICATION READY
How do you allow a mobile app to access data available on a remote server while the mobile device is offline?
2.2

Figure 3-11

Data synchronization and
offline mode

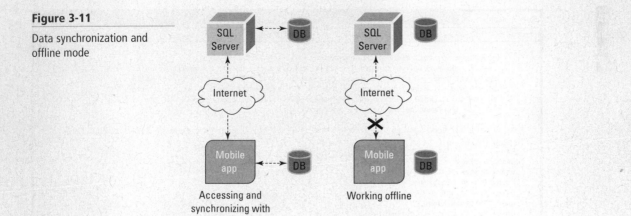

The server may be running SQL Server, or you can program your app to sync with an SQL data store on Windows Azure. In a Windows Phone environment, synchronization is handled by Sync Framework, which was formerly called Sync Services for ADO.NET. You'll learn about Sync Framework in the next section.

■ Working with Networked Data

THE BOTTOM LINE

Networked data is located on an internal company server or across the Internet. To create apps that use networked data, developers must determine which type of database engine to use, where data will be located, how to access the data, how to synchronize data between a client and server, and how to optimize app performance and bandwidth.

As you learned previously, a mobile application that must store data can use a database for data storage. If the database is remote and must be accessed over a network or the Internet ("networked data"), the app should build in a process for synchronizing the data between the mobile device and the remote database.

CERTIFICATION READY
What is networked data?
2.1

The following sections explain how to integrate your apps with databases, which technologies to use to access data locally and remotely, and how to bind data. You'll also learn how to optimize the performance of your apps that use databases so they transfer as little data as possible.

➕ **MORE INFORMATION**

Visit the MSDN "Networking in Silverlight for Windows Phone" Web page at http://bit.ly/Jh7tlV for additional details on working with networked data.

Integrating with Databases

Windows Phone 7.1 can access a remote Microsoft SQL Server server; the engine that runs locally on a mobile device is Microsoft SQL Server Compact Edition (SQL CE). You can also use SQLite on a mobile device, which is an embedded relational database system.

Windows Phone 7.1 can work with a backend database such as Microsoft SQL Server or SQLite. Because a mobile device has limited local storage space, Microsoft SQL Server

CERTIFICATION READY
Which database engines
can a Windows Phone
mobile app use?
2.1

Compact Edition (SQL CE) and SQLite are used to support local databases. The full version of SQL Server runs on a server and is accessed over an internal network or the Internet.

The Microsoft Windows Phone 7.1 SDK includes support for LINQ to SQL, which enables you to access SQL Server Compact databases on the mobile device. Sync Services for ADO. NET (ActiveX Data Objects for .NET) enables you to synchronize remote data with a local database on a mobile device.

TAKE NOTE * SQLite is not simply a "lite" version of SQL Server. SQLite is an embedded relational database system that doesn't require a server, and its source code is in the public domain.

Using LINQ to SQL

LINQ to SQL makes the connection between an application, the data it needs to access, and the database engine.

Language-Integrated Query (LINQ) is a set of .NET extension methods that enable developers to run queries on data from different sources. Windows Phone apps use *LINQ to SQL* to perform all local SQL-related database tasks, such as defining the schema, querying and selecting data, inserting and updating data, deleting data, and saving changes to the database.

With LINQ, you can write queries in C# or VB using Query syntax, which is a shorthand way for expressing queries. A LINQ to SQL query expression usually begins with a `From` clause and ends with a `Select` clause. You indicate the data you want to query using the `From` clause, and indicate the type of data you want returned in the `Select` clause. The `Where` clause filters the data.

The following is an example of LINQ query syntax:

```
var db = new BoxtwelveEntities();

var query = from c in db.Customers
where c.Country == "USA"
select c.CompanyName;
```

LINQ to SQL filters and orders data within the database layer, which improves performance. To do this, LINQ queries written in C# or VB are converted to simpler SQL queries, and then sent to the database to execute. The translated SQL query is:

```
SELECT
[Extent1].[CompanyName] AS [CompanyName]
FROM [dbo].[Customers] AS [Extent1]
WHERE N'USA' = [Extent1].[Country]
```

To enable basic LINQ functionality in an application created in the Visual Studio IDE, you first add a reference to System.Core.dll, which you select through the Project > Add Reference menu. Then you add a directive or Imports statement for System.Linq to your source code.

VIEW LINQ TO SQL CODE

GET READY. To view LINQ to SQL code in a sample application, perform the following steps:
1. In the Visual Studio IDE, open the Network and Device Information (sdkNetworkAnd-DeviceInfo) sample project.
2. Open Solution Explorer, click the **MainPage.xaml** entry to expand it, and then double-click **MainPage.xaml.cs**.
3. Browse the code, a portion of which is shown in Figure 3-12. Where is the directive for LINQ?
4. Close the code sample file and the Visual Studio IDE.

CERTIFICATION READY
What is the purpose of
LINQ?
2.1

Figure 3-12

A portion of code from
MainPage.xaml.cs in
the Network and Device
Information sample

```
MainPage.xaml.cs  ×
sdkNetworkAndDeviceInfoCS.MainPage                              MainPage()

/*
    Copyright (c) 2011 Microsoft Corporation.  All rights reserved.
    Use of this sample source code is subject to the terms of the Microsoft license
    agreement under which you licensed this sample source code and is provided AS-IS.
    If you did not accept the terms of the license agreement, you are not authorized
    to use this sample source code.  For the terms of the license, please see the
    license agreement between you and Microsoft.

    To see all Code Samples for Windows Phone, visit http://go.microsoft.com/fwlink/?LinkID=219604

*/
using System;
using System.Linq;
using System.Net;
using System.Windows;
using Microsoft.Phone.Controls;

// Namespaces added for the sample
using Microsoft.Phone.Net.NetworkInformation;
using System.Text;
using System.Net.Sockets;


namespace sdkNetworkAndDeviceInfoCS
{
    public partial class MainPage : PhoneApplicationPage
100 %
```

LEARN MORE ABOUT SQLITE

GET READY. To learn more about SQLite, perform the following steps:

1. Using a Web browser, go to the SQLite Web site at **http://www.sqlite.org/**.
2. Click the **Documentation** link on the menu bar.
3. Click the **About SQLite** link and read the resulting Web page.
4. Click the **Back** button, click the **Appropriate Uses for SQLite** link, and then browse the page to understand situations that lend themselves to using SQLite versus those that do not.
5. Close the Web browser.

➕ **MORE INFORMATION**

Visit the MSDN "LINQ to SQL" Web page at http://msdn.microsoft.com/en-us/library/bb386976.aspx for additional details on working with networked data.

Synchronizing and Replicating Data

Synchronizing data between a local database on a mobile device and a server keeps the information in both sources up to date. You can use Sync Framework or SQL Server replication to accomplish synchronization.

Sync Framework, formerly Sync Services for ADO.NET, is a part of the Microsoft Sync Framework (MSF). Sync Framework enables you to add synchronization to your applications, so that the data on a client (such as a mobile device) matches data in a store at a remote location.

Sync Framework works with ADO.NET-enabled databases. ***ADO.NET*** is a set of classes that provide access to data services such as SQL Server and XML. You can code an application to use ADO.NET to connect to a data source, and then work with the data as usual.

Any database that uses Sync Framework can exchange data with other data sources that are supported by MSF, whether the data source is a Web service or a data store.

Synchronization can also be achieved with ***SQL Server replication***. Replication copies data and objects between multiple databases, and then maintains an exact copy of the data through synchronization.

Although transactional replication is generally used to synchronize data between servers, ***merge replication*** is geared toward mobile applications to enable data exchange between a device and a server.

A developer must first create an SQL mobile database and provision the database, and then set up and configure SQL Server for merge replication.

+ MORE INFORMATION

Visit the SQL Server Replication Web page at http://msdn.microsoft.com/en-us/library/ms151198.aspx for general replication information.

Implementing Data Binding

> Data binding sets up the relationship between a data source and a control (called a target). Silverlight app data can be bound using XAML or with C# or VB code.

Most Windows Phone apps display data, which can come from a database. The data might also be the color to use in a control in the app. A control can be a list box, a text box, a combo box, or something similar. For example, an app might display stock quotes, enabling the user to click a quote and display more detailed information in a text box. Or the color of a text box might change depending on the type of data being displayed.

Data binding is a process that sets up the relationship between a data source and a control (called a target). Silverlight app data can be bound using XAML or with C# or VB code. Data binding provides a simple way to connect the user interface to the data that it displays, and enables the user to modify and save changes to the data using the interface.

You create the binding in XAML using the {Binding} syntax and set the source using the `DataContext` property in the C# code.

The following code snippets show both the XAML and C# code for binding the foreground color (target) of a text box to a `SolidColorBrush` object (source) so that the color of the text changes when the data changes. The code is modified from the example on the Microsoft MSDN "Data Binding" Web page at http://bit.ly/LaVObx.

An example of the XAML code is as follows:

```
<TextBox x:Name = "MyTextBox" Text = "Text"
Foreground = "{Binding myBrush, Mode = OneWay}"/>
```

The C# might look like the following:

```
// Create an instance of the MyColors class
// that implements INotifyPropertyChanged.
MyColors textcolor = new MyColors();
```

```
// myBrush set to SolidColorBrush with Blue color.
textcolor.myBrush = new SolidColorBrush(Colors.Blue);

// Set the DataContext of the TextBox MyTextBox.
MyTextBox.DataContext = textcolor;

// Create a class that implements
//INotifyPropertyChanged.
public class MyColors : INotifyPropertyChanged
{
    private SolidColorBrush_myBrush;

    // Declare the PropertyChanged event.
    public event PropertyChangedEventHandler PropertyChanged;

    // Create the property to act as the
    // binding source.
    public SolidColorBrush myBrush
    {
      get { return_myBrush; }
      set
      {
        _myBrush = value;
        // Call NotifyPropertyChanged when
        // the source property changes.
        NotifyPropertyChanged("myBrush");
      }
    }

    // NotifyPropertyChanged raises the
    // PropertyChanged event, passing the
    // source property that is being updated.
    public void NotifyPropertyChanged(string propertyName)
    {
      if (PropertyChanged != null)
      {
          PropertyChanged(this,
            new
PropertyChangedEventArgs(propertyName));
      }
    }
}
```

VIEW A DATA BINDING EXAMPLE IN C#

GET READY. To view a data binding example in C#, perform the following steps:

1. On the Start page in the Visual Studio IDE, access the Code Samples for Windows Phone Web page.

2. Click the **Application Features** category.

> **TAKE NOTE** *
>
> You can download the VB code if you prefer, but the following steps and figures are based on C#. You would need to modify the steps slightly to accommodate VB.

3. Click **C#** next to the Contacts and Calendar Sample entry and download it to your Visual Studio 2010\Projects folder.

4. Extract the Zip file in Windows Explorer, and then open the project in the Visual Studio IDE.

5. Open Solution Explorer, click the **MainPage.xaml** entry to expand it, and then double-click **MainPage.xaml.cs**.

6. Browse the code, a portion of which is shown in Figure 3-13. Can you locate the section of code that binds data? What is the specific code used for data binding in this sample?

Figure 3-13

A portion of code from MainPage.xaml.cs in the Contacts and Calendar sample app

```
/*
    Copyright (c) 2011 Microsoft Corporation. All rights reserved.
    Use of this sample source code is subject to the terms of the Microsoft license
    agreement under which you licensed this sample source code and is provided AS-IS.
    If you did not accept the terms of the license agreement, you are not authorized
    to use this sample source code. For the terms of the license, please see the
    license agreement between you and Microsoft.

    To see all Code Samples for Windows Phone, visit http://go.microsoft.com/fwlink/?Link
*/
using System;
using System.Windows;
using System.Windows.Controls;
using System.Windows.Input;
using Microsoft.Phone.Controls;
using Microsoft.Phone.UserData;

namespace sdkContactsCS
{
    public partial class MainPage : PhoneApplicationPage
    {
        FilterKind contactFilterKind = FilterKind.None;

        // Constructor
```

7. Close the code sample file and leave the Visual Studio IDE open if you continue to the next exercise during this session.

➕ MORE INFORMATION

AppHub has links to resources that explain data binding in more detail. Visit http://bit.ly/eWJZx1. You can also visit the MSDN "Data Binding" Web page at http://bit.ly/7A7jro.

Minimizing Data Traffic for Performance and Cost

It's important to create apps that minimize the transfer of data between a device and a remote location to improve application performance and minimize costs to the end user.

One goal of every mobile app developer is to create apps that transfer as little data as possible. The reasons include app and device performance, and cost.

When a user runs an app that must connect to networked data, connectivity speeds vary depending on the user's location and whether the connection is cellular or Wi-Fi. A slow, unreliable connection can be frustrating to a user, and can be a business liability for company employees that must get information quickly. Apps that are written to run from a remote source (not just get data from remote storage) are even more at risk of performing poorly due to connectivity issues. This type of app requires all data to be downloaded at every request because it doesn't reside on the device.

CERTIFICATION READY
How is data traffic minimized for a mobile application?
2.1

TAKE NOTE* Although 4G cellular network connections are available for mobile devices today, the slower 3G service is still widely used, which also consumes more bandwidth.

Regarding costs, if the user has a relatively small amount of data time through a cellular plan, slow app response time can, over time, consume the user's allotted data transfer quota and result in overage charges.

With these considerations in mind, when planning and developing mobile apps, be sure to contain the entire app on the mobile device whenever possible, especially for consumer applications.

Many enterprise apps are developed using a three-tier approach. A three-tier architecture uses a server to check user credentials for security purposes and to control bandwidth, which reduces the size of the part of the app that resides on the device. The middle tier is usually some type of middleware or service, such as WCF. An alternative is to create a mobile-enabled Web application that runs from a Web browser on the device.

Using Windows Communication Foundation (WCF) Web Services and Representational State Transfer Protocol (REST)

Windows Communication Foundation (WCF) services work with Representational State Transfer Protocol (REST) to expose resources on the Web that clients can access and use.

CERTIFICATION READY
How do WCF services and REST work together?
2.1

Windows Communication Foundation (WCF) was briefly described earlier in this lesson. It is a framework for building applications and implementing Web services, and it provides an interface from which other applications can retrieve data over the Web.

WCF services provide a unified way for different applications to communicate using "endpoints," and uses XML as the bridge between them. This is an important concept because many apps, especially Web applications, may use many other applications to provide the entire user experience. For example, when you log in to a social networking site that provides games, the games aren't programmed into the social network site software. The games are separate and called from the social network site software. When you interact with the social network site, the site's software interacts with other applications.

With WCF services, you don't have to program voluminous amounts of code. Instead, it uses a set of standards called REST, or Representational State Transfer Protocol, to "expose" resources on the Web that clients can access and use. The Bing search engine is an example of a Web site that provides service via REST.

WCF services expose data as an Open Data Protocol (OData) feed. OData is a Web protocol for querying and updating data and uses the Get, Put, Post, and Delete HTTP instructions.

You can use WCF in many different ways, from weather reports to instant messaging to delivering news feeds. A few advantages of WCF include speed, safety/security, and support for multiple bindings including HTTP.

+ MORE INFORMATION
To learn more about WCF services and OData, go to http://bit.ly/BJpZj.

SKILL SUMMARY

IN THIS LESSON YOU LEARNED:

- A data store is a data repository or container that stores data. The repository can be a database or a type of structured flat file.
- Files and databases are the predominant forms of storage for mobile devices. To optimize an app's performance, you should apply a Content build action to read-only files when creating an app. A Resource build action is applied to files that are compiled into assemblies, which can affect an app's startup time.
- Windows Phone OS 7.1 can use local storage on a device, and a special area of local storage called isolated storage to hold user-specific data. Data can also be accessed remotely—across an internal network or the Internet.
- Launchers and Choosers are APIs that are called from within an original application, temporarily use built-in applications on a device, and then return the user to the original application. A Chooser API can return data to the original application but a Launcher API cannot.
- An occasionally connected application (OCA) synchronizes data on a client device with a remote server, so that the user can work with server-based information while offline.
- Networked data is located on an internal company server or across the Internet. To create apps that use networked data, developers must determine which type of database engine to use, where data will be located, how to access the data, how to synchronize data between a client and server, and how to optimize app performance and bandwidth.
- Windows Phone 7.1 can access a remote Microsoft SQL Server server; the engine that runs locally on a mobile device is Microsoft SQL Server Compact Edition (SQL CE). You can also use SQLite on a mobile device, which is an embedded relational database system.
- LINQ to SQL makes the connection between an application, the data it needs to access, and the database engine.
- Synchronizing data between a local database on a mobile device and a server keeps the information in both sources up to date. You can use Sync Framework or SQL Server replication to accomplish synchronization.
- Data binding sets up the relationship between a data source and a control (called a target). Silverlight app data can be bound using XAML or with C# or VB code.
- It's important to create apps that minimize the transfer of data between a device and a remote location to improve application performance and minimize costs to the end user.

■ Knowledge Assessment

Fill in the Blank

Complete the following sentences by writing the correct word or words in the blanks provided.

1. A database _____ defines the tables in a relational database, the fields in each table, and the relationships between fields and tables.

2. A _____ acts like a proxy between a client (the mobile app) and remote storage (database server), passing along requests from the client seeking resources, such as data, from the server.

3. You can use _____ to make a class accessible as a Web service and then exchange objects between your app and that service.

4. _____ storage is data located on a server on an internal network or across the Internet.

5. _____ storage is a special area of local storage.

6. _____ replication is geared toward mobile applications to enable data exchange between a device and a server.

7. _____ provides cloud storage that can be used by Windows Phone applications.

8. _____ and _____ are APIs that provide access to built-in Windows Phone features.

9. _____, formerly Sync Services for ADO.NET, is a part of the Microsoft Sync Framework (MSF).

10. _____ is a set of classes that provide access to data services such as SQL Server and XML

Multiple Choice

Circle the letter that corresponds to the best answer.

1. Which of the following was developed by Microsoft and is used to create the user interface for mobile apps?
   a. C#
   b. VB
   c. XAML
   d. XAP

2. Which of the following is the compressed output file for applications created in the Visual Studio IDE?
   a. C#
   b. VB
   c. XAML
   d. XAP

3. You want to embed read-only data in the assemblies of your application. Which build action should you choose in Visual Studio?
   a. Content
   b. Resource
   c. Page
   d. None

4. You don't want to embed read-only data in the assemblies of your application. Which build action should you choose in Visual Studio?
   a. Content
   b. Resource
   c. Page
   d. None

5. Which of the following is a framework that can turn .NET code into an Open Data Protocol (OData) Web service?
   a. WCF Data Services
   b. SQL Server
   c. LINQ to SQL
   d. OCA

6. Which of the following is a type of application that synchronizes a local database with a remote database when a connection is active, and then allows the user to work with the data offline?
   a. Launcher
   b. Chooser

    c. LINQ to SQL

    d. OCA

7. Which of the following are valid ways to save data to isolated storage? (Choose all that apply.)

    a. As key/value pairs using the IsolatedStorageSettings class

    b. In files and folders using the IsolatedStorageFile class

    c. In a database

    d. In files and folders in a database

8. The construct client=Internet Explorer 9 is an example of:

    a. a class

    b. a key/value pair

    c. a declaration

    d. none of the above

9. To access any Web service from a Silverlight-based app, which of the following can you use?

    a. HttpWebRequest class

    b. HttpWebResponse class

    c. Both a and b

    d. Neither a nor b

10. To use a LINQ to SQL filter, which language can you use to write LINQ queries for conversion? (Choose all that apply.)

    a. SQL

    b. C#

    c. VB

    d. WCF

True/False

Circle T if the statement is true or F if the statement is false.

T   F   1. A data store can be an XML file or a database.

T   F   2. Language-Integrated Query (LINQ) is part of the .NET Framework.

T   F   3. Local files on a mobile device are always read-only.

T   F   4. To improve performance, you should contain the entire app on the mobile device whenever possible.

T   F   5. WCF uses a set of standards called REST to synchronize local data with data in SQL Server.

■ Competency Assessment

Scenario 3-1: Speed Up the Start Time of an Application

Giovani, a co-worker, wants to improve the startup time of an application he created. He says the app has a lot of PNG files, but they're small in size. He wants to know what he can do to make his application start faster. How do you answer him?

Scenario 3-2: Use a Built-in Application

Shivani is developing an application that enables the user to enter contact information. She wants the text box for the email field to change color when a complete and syntactically correct email address is entered. How do you advise her?

■ Proficiency Assessment

Scenario 3-3: Use the Same Data Store for Two Applications

Robert wants to create two applications that use the same data store. He's not sure where to locate the data, such as locally, in isolated storage, or remotely. How do you respond?

Scenario 3-4: Understand Databases Accessible by Mobile Apps

Shivani works in the IT department and is the administrator of the Web and database servers. She has been asked by a few developers about which database engines a mobile app can use but she's not sure. How do you answer?

Exploring Mobile Device Networking

EXAM OBJECTIVE MATRIX

SKILLS/CONCEPTS	EXAM OBJECTIVE DESCRIPTION	EXAM OBJECTIVE NUMBER
Understanding Networking for Mobile Devices	Network for mobile devices.	3.2

KEY TERMS

HttpWebRequest class

HttpWebResponse class

multicast

NetworkAvailabilityChanged event

push notifications

raw notification

Tile notification

toast notification

WCF RIA Services

WebClient class

Windows Phone Notifications (WPNs)

The BoxTwelve Mobile application developer team needs to add networking functionality to the latest mobile apps for Glide, its biggest client. One app will access inventory and sales databases via a Web service, and the other will send push notifications to salespersons to notify them when new products go live in the online catalog. You've been asked to help with the development of both apps.

■ Understanding Networking for Mobile Devices

↓ **THE BOTTOM LINE**   Windows Phone networking functionality runs the gamut from detecting network changes automatically in relation to a single device, to receiving push notifications, to using Web services across the Internet.

Networking is an important part of the Windows Phone user experience. Networking enables you to send and receive email and text messages, use a chat application, browse the Web, receive notifications, and retrieve data from a company server or across the Internet.

This lesson addresses several network-related concepts associated with Windows Phone. The first section shows you how to use the NetworkAvailabilityChanged event to enable an application to detect network changes. After that, you'll also dive into Web services and how to use HttpWebRequest or WebClient to retrieve data for your applications, as well as explore multicast communications, push notifications, and Windows Communication Foundation (WCF) Rich Internet Application (RIA) Services.

> **➕ MORE INFORMATION**
>
> To learn more about general network functionality for Windows Phone devices, visit the "Networking and Web Services Overview for Windows Phone" Web page at http://msdn.microsoft.com/en-us/library/ff637518(v=vs.92).aspx.

Creating Robust Server/Cloud Communications

> Robust communications on a Windows Phone device include the ability to switch between cellular and wireless connectivity and close connectivity when it best suits the apps running on the device. The NetworkAvailabilityChanged event enables this kind of functionality.

In Lesson 1, you learned that Windows Phone devices provide both cellular and Wi-Fi (802.11) connectivity. Windows Phone apps use the DeviceNetworkInformation class to provide networking information such as the cellular mobile operator, whether the cellular network allows roaming, and whether a Wi-Fi network is available, among other information. The properties for the DeviceNetworkInformation class are:

- CellularMobileOperator
- IsNetworkAvailable
- IsCellularDataEnabled
- IsCellularDataRoamingEnabled
- IsWiFiEnabled

The properties are static, so you can access them directly in code rather than creating an instance of the class first.

For many Windows Phone apps with network functionality, you want the phone to be able to switch from its current network to a different network, such as from cellular to Wi-Fi when a high-speed Wi-Fi network is available or vice versa when the device moves out of range of the Wi-Fi network. The Microsoft.Phone.Net.NetworkInformation namespace provides several classes that enable applications to interact with network interfaces. One class is NetworkNotificationEventArgs, which provides data to the NetworkAvailabilityChanged event. The *NetworkAvailabilityChanged event* listens for network availability changes.

The following code enables the NetworkAvailabilityChanged event to detect changes to network availability:

```
{
    InitializeComponent();

    // Subscribe to the NetworkAvailabilityChanged
    // event
DeviceNetworkInformation.NetworkAvailabilityChanged += new
EventHandler<NetworkNotificationEventArgs>(OnNetwork
AvailabilityChanged);
}

void OnNetworkAvailabilityChanged(object sender,
NetworkNotificationEventArgs e)
{
    //Insert your code here
}
```

The NetworkAvailabilityChanged event fires whenever the network changes, such as a connection, disconnection, or configuration change.

⊕ EXPLORE THE NETWORKAVAILABILITYCHANGED EVENT

GET READY. To explore use of the NetworkAvailabilityChanged event, perform the following steps:

1. This exercise dissects C# code for detecting network changes for a Windows Phone. To implement and test the code, you need a Windows Phone device with access to cellular and Wi-Fi connections. For purposes of this exercise, we'll simply step through the code to understand how it works.

   The following code lists directives that you add to the top of the page code-behind file for your main application:

   ```
   using Microsoft.Phone.Net.NetworkInformation;
   using System.Windows;
   using Microsoft.Phone.Tasks;
   ```

2. The following variable declarations must be added to the MainPage class. The first declaration lists changes detected while the application is running. The second declaration keeps track of the currently available network interfaces.

   ```
   public ObservableCollection<string> Changes { get; set; }
   public ObservableCollection<string> NetworkInterfaces { get;
   set; }
   ```

3. The next set of code subscribes the device to the NetworkAvailabilityChanged event and determines what changes were made. Notice the use of the NotificationType and NetworkInterface properties of NetworkNotificationEventArgs. These properties show the type of notification that was received and display the name of the associated network interface.

   ```
   // Constructor
   public MainPage()
   {

       InitializeComponent();

       // Subscribe to the NetworkAvailabilityChanged
       // event

   DeviceNetworkInformation.NetworkAvailabilityChanged += new
   EventHandler<NetworkNotificationEventArgs> (NetworkAvailability
   Changed);
   }
   void NetworkAvailabilityChanged(object sender,
   NetworkNotificationEventArgs e)
   {
       string change = string.Empty;
       switch (e.NotificationType)
       {
         case
   NetworkNotificationType.InterfaceConnected:
           change = "Connected to ";
           break;
         case
   ```

```
NetworkNotificationType.InterfaceDisconnected:
        change = "Disconnected from ";
        break;
    case
NetworkNotificationType.CharacteristicUpdate:
        change = "Characteristics changed for ";
        break;
    default:
        change = "Unknown change with ";
        break;
  }
  string changeInformation = String.Format(" {0} {1} {2} ({3})",
      DateTime.Now.ToString(), change,
  e.NetworkInterface.InterfaceName,

    e.NetworkInterface.InterfaceType.ToString());
  . . . }
```

4. For additional learning, if you have a Windows Phone device with access to cellular and Wi-Fi access for testing, perform the steps described on the "How To: Detect Network Changes for Windows Phone" Web page at http://bit.ly/yxIlll. You will work in the MainPage.xaml and MainPage.xaml.cs (code-behind) files in the project you create.

Accessing Web Services

Web services provide a relatively easy way to enable many different kinds of interactive, network-connected applications such as Really Simple Syndication (RSS) feeds, maps, and so on.

Lesson 3 introduced Web services, which act like proxies between clients (mobile apps) and remote storage (database servers). The proxy acts as an intermediary, passing along requests from the client seeking resources, such as data, from the server. The proxy also passes data from the server to the client. You can host Web services on your own server, but it's common to interact with a hosted service such as Windows Azure or another third party.

CERTIFICATION READY
What kinds of activities can an end user perform with Web services running in the background?
3.2

Windows Phone applications often need to connect to and consume Web services, which enable users to receive RSS feeds, use maps, interact with social media, and more. The services may be Simple Object Access Protocol (SOAP), HTTP, or Representational State Transfer (REST). Extensible Markup Language (XML) is used to tag data and deliver it to the client for parsing and display.

Understanding the HttpWebRequest/HttpWebResponse and WebClient Classes

To access Web services from a Silverlight-based application and to retrieve data, you can use the HTTP classes `HttpWebRequest` and `HttpWebResponse` or the `WebClient` class in the System.Net namespace. These classes work with HTTP to provide the "link" between an app and a Web service.

The classes retrieve data from a Uniform Resource Identifier (URI), which is a pointer to data or resources on a server or the Internet (like a URL). Whether you use WebClient or

CERTIFICATION READY
Which classes are used to access Web services from Silverlight-based applications?
3.2

HttpWebRequest/HttpWebResponse, the communications are asynchronous rather than synchronous. Asynchronous communications do not occur in real time and can result in a noticeable delay from the user's perspective.

The HttpWebRequest and HttpWebResponse classes work together. The *HttpWebRequest class* contains a request for the data or resource you want to access. The *HttpWebResponse class* provides a container for the incoming data from the server. An alternative is to use the *WebClient class*, which sends data to and from a URI. WebClient is useful for quick-and-easy (usually one-time) data retrieval from a Web service, whereas the HttpWebRequest/HttpWebResponse combination enables you to have more control over a Web service request.

When you access Web services using the HttpWebRequest and HttpWebResponse classes, referred to as making an HTTP call, the following steps are involved for applications that request and receive data from a service:

- Create an instance of the HttpWebRequest, which contains a request for data.
- Get the response stream from the Web service.
- Create an instance of HttpWebResponse, which provides a container for the incoming response.
- Read, parse, and display the returned data, which is often in XML format.
- Close the call.

The HttpWebRequest represents the first part of the call, which is made from the client to the server. After the server receives the request, it returns the requested data to the client in the form of an HttpWebResponse. The client can access that response with GetResponse or BeginGetResponse/EndGetResponse.

The WebClient class is actually built on top of HttpWebRequest and simplifies many common tasks, resulting in less code. Using WebClient, you don't have to deal with the details of Web requests and responses.

CREATE AN RSS FEED APP USING WEBCLIENT

GET READY. RSS is a family of data format used for providing users with frequently updated content. To create an RSS feed using the WebClient class, perform the following steps:

1. In your Visual Studio IDE, create a new project by selecting **File > New Project**.
2. In the New Project dialog box, select **C# Silverlight for Windows Phone** in the Installed Templates pane on the left and **Windows Phone Application** in the middle pane. In the Name field near the bottom of the dialog box, name the project **RSSFeedWebClient**, as shown in Figure 4-1. Click **OK**.
3. In the New Windows Phone Application dialog box, leave Windows Phone OS 7.1 selected and click **OK**.
4. To create the UI, double-click **MainPage.xaml** in Solution Explorer if it's not already open.
5. Edit the page title, which currently displays "page name," by selecting the page name UI element in the design surface. Scroll through the Code Editor to see the associated code highlighted. Replace "page name" with **RSS Feed**, as shown in Figure 4-2.
6. To add a button to the interface that will download the RSS feed, and a text block that will display the feed data, open the Toolbox and drag the **Button** control to the design surface, in the area just under the RSS Feed page title. Drag the **TextBlock** control from the Toolbox to the design surface and drop it under the Button control.

Figure 4-1

Creating the RSS feed project

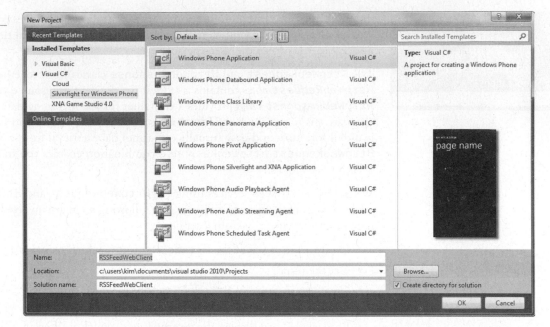

Figure 4-2

Modifying the page title

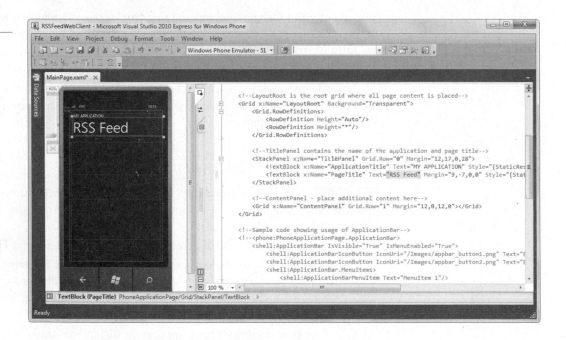

7. To configure the button and text block, locate the Content Panel section in Code Editor. Change the `Button` and `TextBlock` code to the following:

```
<Button Content="Download" Height="72" HorizontalAlignment="Left"
    Margin="6,6,0,0" Name="btnDownload" VerticalAlignment="Top"
    Width="444" Click="btnDownload_Click" />

<TextBlock Height="30" HorizontalAlignment="Left"
    Margin="21,84,0,0" Name="txtStatus" Text=""
    VerticalAlignment="Top" Width="328" />
```

Figure 4-3

The interface with a button and text block

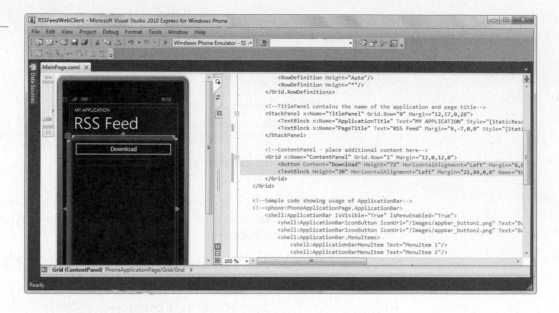

8. The layout should look similar to Figure 4-3. Close the Toolbox and save the file.

9. Now you need to add some code to the application to make it work. In Solution Explorer, expand **MainPage.xaml** and then double-click the **MainPage.xaml.cs** file. This is the code-behind file.

10. Create an instance of the WebClient class by inserting the following code in the MainPage class, as shown in Figure 4-4.

```
WebClient client = new WebClient();
```

Figure 4-4

Creating an instance of the WebClient class

```
namespace RSSFeedWebClient
{
    public partial class MainPage : PhoneApplicationPage
    {
        WebClient client = new WebClient();

        // Constructor
        public MainPage()
        {
            InitializeComponent();
        }
    }
}
```

11. In the Constructor section, add the event handlers for the two events associated with the WebClient object. The events are DownloadProgressChanged and DownloadStringCompleted. See Figure 4-5.

```
client.DownloadProgressChanged += new
    DownloadProgressChangedEventHandler
    (client_DownloadProgressChanged);
```

```
client.DownloadStringCompleted += new
    DownloadStringCompletedEventHandler
    (client_DownloadStringCompleted);
```

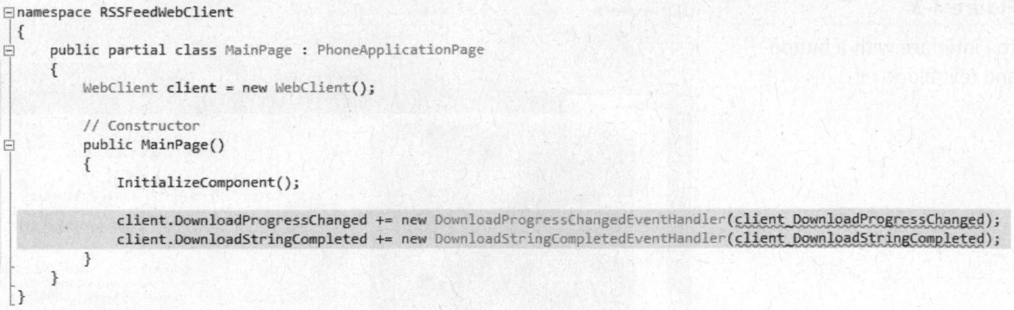

Figure 4-5

Creating event handlers

```
namespace RSSFeedWebClient
{
    public partial class MainPage : PhoneApplicationPage
    {
        WebClient client = new WebClient();

        // Constructor
        public MainPage()
        {
            InitializeComponent();

            client.DownloadProgressChanged += new DownloadProgressChangedEventHandler(client_DownloadProgressChanged);
            client.DownloadStringCompleted += new DownloadStringCompletedEventHandler(client_DownloadStringCompleted);
        }
    }
}
```

12. Sometimes feeds take a while to download, so it's a good idea to display the progress of the RSS feed download. Code the `DownloadProgressChanged` event handler as follows (see Figure 4-6):

```
void client_DownloadProgressChanged(object sender,
    DownloadProgressChangedEventArgs e)
{
    if (e.UserState as string == "MSDN")
    {
        txtStatus.Text = e.BytesReceived.ToString()
            + " bytes received.";
    }
}
```

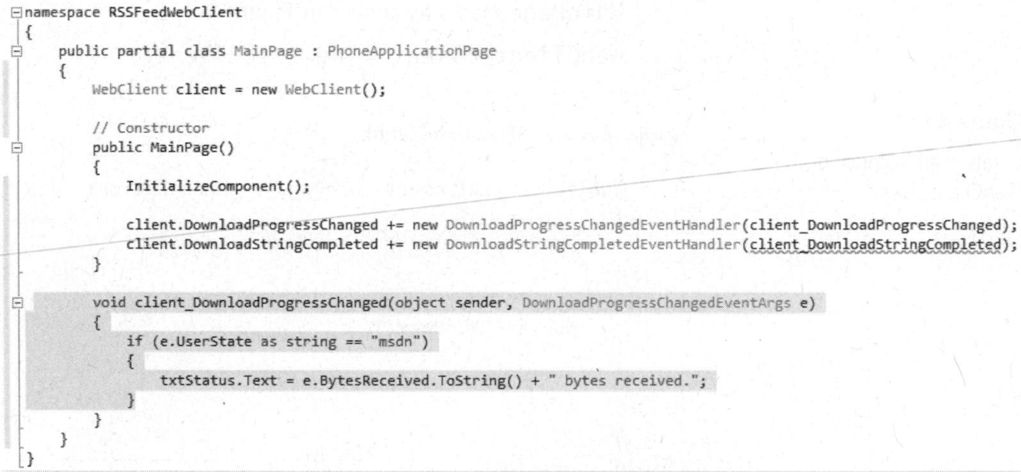

Figure 4-6

Adding a progress indicator

```
namespace RSSFeedWebClient
{
    public partial class MainPage : PhoneApplicationPage
    {
        WebClient client = new WebClient();

        // Constructor
        public MainPage()
        {
            InitializeComponent();

            client.DownloadProgressChanged += new DownloadProgressChangedEventHandler(client_DownloadProgressChanged);
            client.DownloadStringCompleted += new DownloadStringCompletedEventHandler(client_DownloadStringCompleted);
        }

        void client_DownloadProgressChanged(object sender, DownloadProgressChangedEventArgs e)
        {
            if (e.UserState as string == "msdn")
            {
                txtStatus.Text = e.BytesReceived.ToString() + " bytes received.";
            }
        }
    }
}
```

The `UserState` property identifies the origin of the RSS feed; in this case, the feed is coming from the Microsoft Developer Network (MSDN). The `BytesReceived` property displays the number of bytes downloaded.

13. The `DownloadStringCompleted` event fires when the download of the RSS feed finishes. Add the following code to store the content using the `Result` property (see Figure 4-7):

```
void client_DownloadStringCompleted(object sender,
    DownloadStringCompletedEventArgs e)
{
    if (e.Error == null && !e.Cancelled)
        MessageBox.Show(e.Result);
}
```

Figure 4-7

Coding for the
`DownloadString-`
`Completed` event

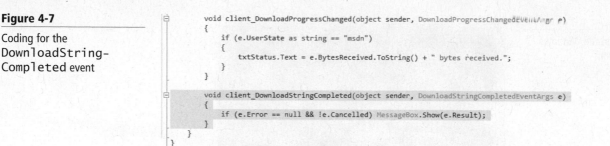

```
void client_DownloadProgressChanged(object sender, DownloadProgressChangedEventArgs e)
{
    if (e.UserState as string == "msdn")
    {
        txtStatus.Text = e.BytesReceived.ToString() + " bytes received.";
    }
}

void client_DownloadStringCompleted(object sender, DownloadStringCompletedEventArgs e)
{
    if (e.Error == null && !e.Cancelled) MessageBox.Show(e.Result);
}
```

14. Save the file.

15. Click the **MainPage.xaml** file tab if the file is still open, or double-click the file in Solution Explorer.

16. Double-click the **Download** button in the design surface.

17. Add the following code to the button-click event handler all on one line, as shown in Figure 4-8. This code includes the URI for the RSS feed.

```
client.DownloadStringAsync(new Uri("http://msdn.microsoft.com/
    en-us/magazine/rss/default.aspx?z=z&iss=1"), "MSDN");
```

Figure 4-8

Coding the Download button

```
void client_DownloadStringCompleted(object sender, DownloadStringCompletedEventArgs e)
{
    if (e.Error == null && !e.Cancelled) MessageBox.Show(e.Result);
}

private void btnDownload_Click(object sender, RoutedEventArgs e)
{
    client.DownloadStringAsync(new Uri("http://msdn.microsoft.com/en-us/magazine/rss/default.aspx?z=z&iss=1"), "msdn");
}
```

18. Save the file, and then click the **Start Debugging** button on the toolbar (or press **F5**) to view the file in the Windows Phone Emulator.

19. In the emulator, after the application fully loads, click the **Download** button. The RSS feed should appear, as shown in Figure 4-9.

20. Close the emulator and click **OK** in the dialog box that appears in the Visual Studio IDE.

21. Close the project file and the Visual Studio IDE.

➕ **MORE INFORMATION**

For details about Windows Phone and Web services, browse the "Networking and Web Services Overview for Windows Phone" Web page at http://msdn.microsoft.com/en-us/library/ff637518(v=vs.92).aspx.

Understanding Windows Azure

Lesson 1 introduced you to Windows Azure, a cloud computing and services platform that can be used by Windows Phone applications. You can use Windows Azure for file storage, or use Azure services to build new applications or to extend existing apps. Azure enables you to offer Web service login with authentication, send push notifications to client devices, access data tables and queues stored on Windows Azure, and manage user permissions, among other activities.

Windows Azure supports industry-standard Web protocols such as SOAP and REST so you don't have to modify code to work with proprietary protocols.

Figure 4-9

The RSS feed in the Windows
Phone Emulator

To more easily create mobile apps that use the Windows Azure services, you can use the
Windows Azure Toolkit for Windows Phone. The toolkit includes several Windows Phone
project templates for Visual Studio, class libraries optimized for Windows Phone, and sample
applications.

SIGN UP FOR A WINDOWS AZURE SUBSCRIPTION

GET READY. To sign up for a free 90-day trial subscription on Windows Azure, perform the
following steps:

1. Using a Web browser, go to the Windows Azure free trial Web page at
   http://www.windowsazure.com/en-us/pricing/free-trial/.

2. Click the **try it free** button. On the resulting screen, sign in to your Windows Live
   account. (If you don't have a Windows Live account, click the **Sign up** link and follow
   the prompts.)

3. The Windows Azure sign up process begins automatically. Follow the prompts to sign
   up for a subscription.

The first screen indicates you need a mobile phone and credit card (see Figure 4-10). Microsoft states that the credit card is for identification purposes only, and that you can continue a paid subscription to Windows Azure after your trial period ends by modifying the spending limit in your account.

4. Continue through all screens until you click **Finish** to complete the sign-up process.

Figure 4-10

The first Windows Azure free trial subscription sign-up screen

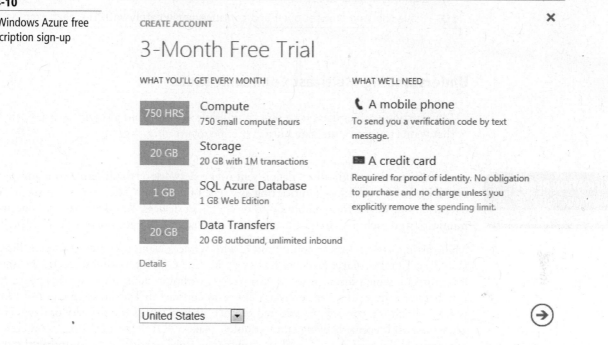

5. You're directed to the Windows Azure subscriptions profile Web page, as shown in Figure 4-11.

Figure 4-11

Windows Azure subscriptions profile Web page

6. Sign out of your account.

7. Go to windowsazure.com, click the **SIGN IN** button, sign in using your Windows Live account, and then click **MANAGE**. The portal page for your Windows Azure account appears. Notice that you can create your own hosted service, a storage account, a database, or a virtual network.

8. Click the appropriate link to read about how to set up a hosted service.

9. Sign out of your account.

10. Leave the Web browser open and continue immediately with the next exercise.

Understanding Multicast Communications

Multicasting enables data to be sent to multiple devices from a single device. Each device that wants to receive the data must subscribe to a multicast group.

CERTIFICATION READY
What is multicasting?
3.2

In a *multicast* communication, data is sent over a network or the Internet to many devices at one time. You can think of multicasting as a type of broadcast, like a television signal: You send data from one device for distribution to several other devices. You don't have to send the communication to each device individually—devices that want to get the broadcast subscribe to it.

Multicasting uses sockets to communicate with services using the User Datagram Protocol (UDP), a Transport layer protocol that's part of the TCP/IP protocol suite. It's a connectionless protocol, which means it sends data packets without establishing or managing a connection between the sender and receiver. (This is in contrast to Transmission Control Protocol (TCP), which is a connection-oriented protocol that manages the delivery of data between the sender and receiver.) Being connectionless makes UDP a fast protocol, but there's no guarantee of delivery. A UDP socket receives data from a service by monitoring the port associated with the service. When data arrives, UDP processes the data.

A multicast group has an Internet Protocol (IP) address called a multicast group address. IP version 4 (IPv4) addresses are in the format of four octets, similar to XXX.XXX.XXX.XXX. An octet can have one to three numbers. For example, 192.168.0.1 is a commonly used IPv4 address. A multicast group address must be in the range from 224.0.0.0 to 239.255.255.255, which is reserved for multicast communications. A multicast communication also uses a port number.

Each device subscribes to the multicast group address. When a subscribed device sends packets to the multicast group, all other subscribed device receive the packets.

Windows Phone OS 7.1 uses the UdpAnySourceMulticastClient class in the System.Net. Sockets namespace to enable devices to join a multicast group.

EXPLORE MULTICASTING

GET READY. To explore multicasting, perform the following steps:

1. In your Visual Studio IDE, go to the Start page, and click **Code Samples for Windows Phone** in the Learning Resources section.

2. Download and install the **Multicast Sockets Sample** to your Projects folder. (If you're not sure how to access this code sample, refer to the Download a Code Sample exercise in Lesson 1.) This code sample is for a Rock Paper Scissors game that demonstrates multicast group communication in which players join a multicast group to discover each other.

3. Open the project in your Visual Studio IDE, and then double-click the **UdpAnySourceMulticastChannel.cs** file in Solution Explorer. The file appears in the Code Editor, as shown in Figure 4-12.

Figure 4-12

The contents of the
`UdpAnySource`
`MulticastChannel`
file

4. What is the specific code that creates new instances of the
   UdpAnySourceMulticastChannel class? There may be more than one instance.

5. In Solution Explorer, double-click **GamePlay.cs** to open the file in Code Editor.

6. What is the multicast group IP address being used?

7. What is the port number being used?

8. Close the project file but leave the Visual Studio IDE open if you plan to complete
   the next exercise during this session.

➕ **MORE INFORMATION**

For a detailed walkthrough of multicasting, visit the "How to: Send and Receive Data in a Multicast Group for
Windows Phone" Web page at http://msdn.microsoft.com/en-us/library/hh286407(v=vs.92).aspx.

Exploring Push Notifications

> Push notifications, or Windows Phone Notifications (WPNs), are data or messages sent
> from a Web service to a client device. Windows Phone uses three types of push notifica-
> tions: toast, Tile, and raw.

Multitasking, in relation to mobile devices, means having several applications or tasks running at the same time. For example, a mobile device user might have a Twitter application
open to receive updates while using a chat application to connect with a co-worker. Because
the energy resources of a mobile device are limited, multitasking can quickly drain a battery.
Push notifications provide an alternative approach to multitasking.

Push notifications, also referred to as *Windows Phone Notifications (WPNs)*, allow a Web
service to send data to a Windows Phone device. Many notifications allow a user to receive
messages without running the associated application continuously. Windows Phone 7 provides three types of push notifications:

- *Toast notifications:* Appear at the top of the screen, often in text format similar to a
  short text message.

- *Tile notifications:* Can update Tiles on the device's Start screen. Tiles are part of the
  Metro style and usually contain an icon and two strings. A Tile notification alerts the

CERTIFICATION READY
What is a push
notification?
3.2

user to some type of event, like an impending storm in the area or receipt of an email, by changing the icon, strings, and/or the tile's background.

- *Raw notifications:* Occur only when the associated app is running. Raw notifications enable you to push custom data to an application, such as updated stock quotes, without notifying the user.

Toast notifications and Tile notifications occur when the associated app is not running. A user receives a notification message and can then run the app only when needed, extending battery life.

For push notifications to work, you establish a communications channel between a Windows Phone device and an application that provides notification data. A client subscribes to a channel, so when new information is available, the service pushes that information to the client.

The Windows Phone namespace for push notifications is Microsoft.Phone.Notification. You must create a new channel or find an existing channel through which to send notifications using the HttpNotificationChannel class. The ChannelName property identifies the channel name, and the ChannelURI property identifies the source of the current active channel.

A few of the commonly used methods in the HttpNotificationChannel class are BindToShellToast and BindToShellTile. These methods associate a HttpNotificationChannel channel instance to toast and Tile notifications. The UnbindToShellToast and UnbindToShellTile methods disassociate toast and tiles subscriptions from a channel. To close the channel and remove all subscriptions, use the Close method of the HttpNotificationChannel class.

EXPLORE A TOAST NOTIFICATION APP

GET READY. To explore a toast notification application, perform the following steps:

1. In your Visual Studio IDE, go to the Start page, and click **Code Samples for Windows Phone** in the Learning Resources section.

2. Download and install the **Toast Notification Sample** to your Projects folder. The sample contains two projects: one that enables a Windows Phone device to receive notifications and another that sends notifications.

3. Open the project named sdkToastNotification in your Visual Studio IDE, (see Figure 4-13) and then open the **MainPage.xaml.cs** file from Solution Explorer.

Figure 4-13

The contents of the MainPage.xaml code-behind file

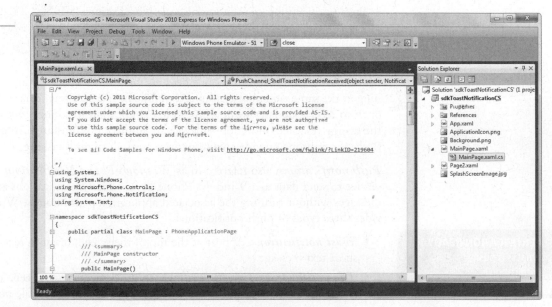

4. Locate the **HttpNotificationChannel** class. You might have to expand statements in the code to see all of the code.

5. Does the code include the **BindtoShellToast** method? What is the statement that includes the method?

6. Start the Windows Phone Emulator by clicking the **Start Debugging** button on the toolbar or by pressing **F5**. What is the URI for this application?

7. Close the project file but leave the Visual Studio IDE open if you plan to complete the next exercise during this session.

➕ **MORE INFORMATION**

To learn more about push notifications in Windows Phone, visit the "Push Notifications Overview for Windows Phone" Web page at http://msdn.microsoft.com/en-us/library/ff402558.

Understanding the Application Model in Relation to Windows Communication Foundation (WCF) Rich Internet Application (RIA) Services

WCF RIA Services enable a developer to create n-tier applications that include server-side code that is automatically pushed to a client. The client is updated on the fly whenever the code is modified and recompiled.

Windows Communication Foundation (WCF) is a framework for building and accessing Web services. WCF enables you to make a class accessible as a service and then exchange objects between your app and that service. Rich Internet Applications (RIAs) are Web-based applications that look and feel like desktop applications, and offer user interfaces (UI) that may include interactivity, audio, video, and more. With RIAs, the UI is usually located on the client, whereas the application's logic and functionality originates from the server but is used by the client.

CERTIFICATION READY
What are WCF RIA Services?
3.2

Introduced in .NET Framework 4 and Silverlight 4, *WCF RIA Services* is a server-side technology that automatically generates client-side objects that handle communication between the client and server. WCF RIA Services makes it much easier for you to develop n-tier RIAs. N-tier architecture splits an application into tiers, or layers, so that the layers are reusable and can be modified without having to change the entire application. Figure 4-14 shows a simplified version of an n-tier application.

Figure 4-14

An n-tier application using a WCF RIA Services architecture

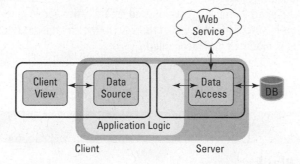

WCF RIA Services enables you to write server code and make parts of that code available on the client without writing client-side code to access it. The server code includes services, domain entities, and supporting logic. This code generates corresponding classes for the client, from which you call services. The client is aware of and can use the application logic that actually resides on the server. Whenever a developer modifies and recompiles the application on the server, the client is automatically updated with latest application logic.

➡ EXPLORE WCF RIA SERVICES

GET READY. To explore WCF RIA Services, perform the following steps:

1. Use a Web browser to perform research for this exercise. Take notes while performing research.

2. Research how to open a WCF RIA Services application to Windows Phone 7 clients using SOAP. Write an outline of the major steps or create a flowchart.

3. How does WCF RIA expose data in the OData format?

4. Which Microsoft .NET Framework tools are required to create a WCF RIA Services application?

5. Write a one- to two-page summary report of your findings.

6. Close all open windows.

➕ MORE INFORMATION

For more information about WCF RIA Services, visit the MSDN "WCF RIA Services" Web page at http://bit.ly/1euj3T.

SKILL SUMMARY

IN THIS LESSON YOU LEARNED:

- Windows Phone networking functionality runs the gamut from detecting network changes automatically in relation to a single device, to receiving push notifications, to using Web services across the Internet.

- Robust communications on a Windows Phone device include the ability to switch between cellular and wireless connectivity, and close connectivity, when it best suits the apps running on the device. The `NetworkAvailabilityChanged` event enables this kind of functionality.

- Web services provide a relatively easy way to enable many different kinds of interactive, network-connected applications such as Really Simple Syndication (RSS) feeds, maps, and so on.

- Multicasting enables data to be sent to multiple devices from a single device. Each device that wants to receive the data must subscribe to a multicast group.

- Push notifications, or Windows Phone Notifications (WPNs), are data or messages sent from a Web service to a client device. Windows Phone uses three types of push notifications: toast, Tile, and raw.

- WCF RIA Services enable a developer to create n-tier applications that include server-side code that is automatically pushed to a client. The client is updated on the fly whenever the code is modified and recompiled.

■ Knowledge Assessment

Fill in the Blank

Complete the following sentences by writing the correct word or words in the blanks provided.

1. The _____ class contains a request for the data or resource you want to access from a Web service. This class works with an associated Web response class.

2. The _____ class provides a container for the incoming data from a Web service.

3. In a _____ communication, data is sent over a network or the Internet to many devices at one time.

4. The `NetworkNotificationEventArgs` class in the Microsoft.Phone.Net. NetworkInformation namespace provides data to the _____ event.

5. Introduced in .NET Framework 4 and Silverlight 4, _____ is a server-side technology that automatically generates client-side objects that handle communication between the client and server.

6. An alternative to `HttpWebRequest/HttpWebResponse` is the _____ class, which is useful for one-time data retrieval from a Web service.

7. _____ allow a Web service to send data and alerts to a Windows Phone device.

8. Windows Phone OS 7.1 uses the _____ class in the System.Net.Sockets namespace to enable devices to join a multicast group.

9. _____ is a connectionless Transport layer protocol that's part of the TCP/IP protocol suite.

10. _____ is a cloud computing and services platform that can be used by Windows Phone applications for file storage or to build new applications or to extend existing apps.

Multiple Choice

Circle the letter that corresponds to the best answer.

1. Which of the following is an event that enables a mobile device switch from cellular to Wi-Fi when a high-speed Wi-Fi network is available?
   a. `IsNetworkAvailable`
   b. `IsCellularDataEnabled`
   c. `IsWiFiEnabled`
   d. `NetworkAvailabilityChanged`

2. Which of the following is used to tag data in a Web services communication and deliver it to the client for parsing and display?
   a. SOAP
   b. HTTP
   c. XML
   d. REST

3. The construct `using Microsoft.Phone.Net.NetworkInformation;` is listed at the top of a MainPage.xaml file. What is this construct called?
   a. Variable
   b. Declaration
   c. Namespace
   d. Class

4. Which method associates an `HttpNotificationChannel` instance to toast notifications?
   a. `BindToToast`
   b. `BindToShellToast`
   c. `UnbindToToast`
   d. `UnbindToShellToast`

5. Which of the following commonly uses the `UdpAnySourceMulticastChannel` class?
   a. A multicasting application
   b. A network availability application
   c. A Voice over IP application
   d. Windows Azure

6. Which of the following occur only when an application is running?
   a. Toast notifications
   b. Tile notifications
   c. Raw notifications
   d. All push notifications

7. Which of the following is not an example of an activity associated with consumption of a Web service?
   a. Place a phone call
   b. Get RSS feeds
   c. Use maps
   d. Interact with social media

8. Which type of architecture splits an application into reusable layers so that they can be modified without having to change the entire application?
   a. N-layer
   b. X-layer
   c. N-tier
   d. None of the above

9. WCF is a framework for building and accessing Web services. What is an RIA?
   a. A Web-based application
   b. A type of database
   c. A protocol for accessing Web services
   d. A type of Web service

10. A customer receives an alert at the top of her Windows Phone device screen when her prescription is ready to be picked up at the pharmacy. What is this type of notification?
    a. Toast
    b. Tile
    c. Raw
    d. None of the above

True/False

Circle T if the statement is true or F if the statement is false.

T   F   1. A multicast group has an IP address called a multicast group address.

T   F   2. UDP is a connection-oriented protocol that guarantees delivery of data packets.

T   F   3. In a Visual Studio IDE, MainPage.xaml is a code-behind file.

T   F   4. Push notifications require a communications channel between a Windows Phone device and an application that provides notification data.

T   F   5. A URI is a pointer to data or resources on a server or the Internet.

■ Competency Assessment

Scenario 4-1: Understand WCF RIA Services

Juan is a new intern at BoxTwelve Mobile and wants to learn about WCF RIA Services. He understands the essentials of WCF but doesn't understand what WCF RIA Services can accomplish. What do you tell him?

Scenario 4-2: Use HttpWebRequest and HttpWebResponse

Leeann is taking a Silverlight course and was just introduced to Web services and the various ways to use them. She asked you to send her an email that provides a quick overview of the steps involved in using HttpWebRequest and HttpWebResponse. What do you send to her in the email?

■ Proficiency Assessment

Scenario 4-3: Create a Push Notification App

Santy is a busy construction project manager who's often in the field working with contractors, vendors, and clients. He wants a to-do list application for his Windows Phone device that notifies him when a list item is due. He's searched the Windows Phone Marketplace but can't find exactly what he wants, and needs to hire a contract programmer to build the application. He asked you for advice as to how to word the project description properly.

Scenario 4-4: Determine Whether to Use HttpWebRequest or WebClient

Leeann is beginning to develop a simple test application that retrieves quotes for two different stocks from a source on the Web, and then displays them in text blocks in her application. She is including a Refresh button, for now, that will update the data. She wants to know whether she should use HttpWebRequest and WebClient. How do you advise her?

Understanding Silverlight and Mobile Code

EXAM OBJECTIVE MATRIX

SKILLS/CONCEPTS	MTA EXAM OBJECTIVE	MTA EXAM OBJECTIVE NUMBER
Understanding Silverlight	Understanding Silverlight.	3.3
Understanding Code for Mobile Applications	Code for Mobile Applications.	3.5

KEY TERMS

audio element

canvas element

Cascading Style Sheets (CSS)

controls

Extensible Application Markup Language (XAML)

geolocation

HTML5

JavaScript

managed code

media query

Microsoft Silverlight

Panorama control

Pivot control

Silverlight for Windows Phone

vendor prefixes

video element

Visual Basic .NET (VB.NET)

Visual C#

XNA framework

Glide, a client of BoxTwelve Mobile, has requested that the BoxTwelve application developer team create a custom game app that involves simulated winter sports, to be distributed to Glide customers and prospects as a marketing tool. Glide wants BoxTwelve to write a proposal that provides details about the application's functionality, such as whether it will exist as a standalone app or a mobile Web application, the framework and language to be used to develop the app, and the development process in general. You've been asked to participate in this project by shadowing the client-facing BoxTwelve project manager and the development team lead. You will learn about Silverlight.

■ Understanding Silverlight

↓
THE BOTTOM LINE

Silverlight for Windows Phone is a version of the Microsoft Silverlight framework. Silverlight uses XAML to create user interfaces, and it uses code created in C# or VB to make applications run.

Microsoft Silverlight is a Web application framework that enables you to create Rich Internet Applications (RIAs). Using a Silverlight plug-in, a Web browser can deliver media similar to an Adobe Flash experience. *Silverlight for Windows Phone* is a specific version of Silverlight geared toward applications that run on Windows Phone devices.

CERTIFICATION READY
Silverlight is tightly coupled with which declarative language?
3.3

As you learned in Lesson 1, Silverlight uses the declarative language *Extensible Application Markup Language (XAML)*, pronounced "zamel," to create the user interface (UI). Silverlight is similar to Windows Presentation Foundation (WPF) and relies on XAML to implement a user interface. XAML is "tightly coupled" with the Silverlight framework—its purpose is to create instances of the classes that the framework contains. Silverlight generally uses C# or VB as the code behind the UI (see Figure 5-1), which makes the application run. This is referred to as *managed code* because they rely on the Common Language Runtime for execution. Code-behind files mainly handle events from application controls, like the `Button`, `TextBox`, and `TextBlock` controls used in exercises in previous lessons. You'll learn more about controls later in this lesson.

TAKE NOTE*

Managed code is a Microsoft term that refers to source code written in any of 20+ languages available for use in the .NET Framework, which include C# and VB. Within the framework, these languages share a set of class libraries and rely on the Common Language Runtime (CLR) for execution, and therefore is managed by CLR for such things as memory allocation and cleanup.

Figure 5-1

An XAML file and an associated code-behind file in the Visual Studio IDE

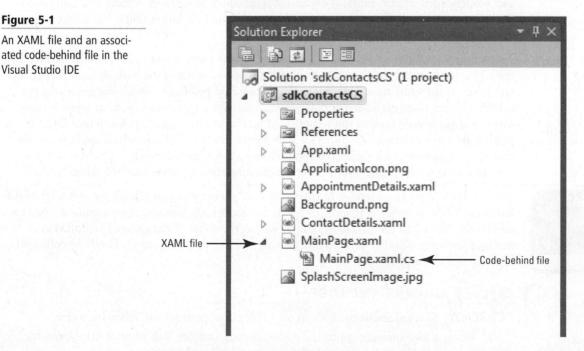

Although Silverlight for Windows Phone supports most of the features of Silverlight, it excludes some features that aren't appropriate for the phone. One Silverlight feature that's not supported in Silverlight for Windows Phone is something called an HTML DOM bridge, which accesses

the HTML Document Object Model (DOM) from managed code and can call managed code from JavaScript. Silverlight for Windows Phone includes other features that are specific to touch input, such as gesture-aware controls and manipulation events like tap, double-tap, and hold.

The next section takes a detailed look at the differences between Silverlight and the XNA framework, which is used to create mobile games. It also introduces HTML5, the latest Web markup language that may eventually become the primary mobile app development language.

> **➕ MORE INFORMATION**
>
> For additional details, visit the "Features Differences Between Silverlight and Silverlight for Windows Phone" Web page at http://bit.ly/d7ynTU and the "Class Library Support for Windows Phone" Web page at http://bit.ly/LkErkA.

Exploring the Differences between Silverlight, XNA, and HTML5

> Silverlight applications use an event-driven model, whereas XNA applications use a game loop and polling. With Silverlight, you can integrate video and other multimedia elements into applications, but XNA can render 3D video games. HTML5 is a platform-independent markup language used to create HTML documents and Web applications. HTML5 is also regarded as a family of technologies that include HTML, CSS3, and JavaScript.

Silverlight for Windows Phone is the platform that developers use most often when creating data- and event-driven mobile applications. The ability to create an RIA user interface means you can mimic the look and feel of desktop applications, while including interactivity, audio, video, and more. In addition, Silverlight enables you to render many different types of shapes, from straight lines and rectangles to ellipses and paths (similar to freehand drawings).

The *XNA framework*, which is a set of Visual Studio libraries, is designed primarily for multi-screen 2D and 3D game development. XNA tools enable you to use and manage assets like models, sprites (2D graphical objects), backgrounds or textures, effects, and animations. For 2D games, you define sprites and backgrounds based on bitmap files. Modeling and animations figure heavily in 3D games.

The action of an XNA game, in which graphical objects move around the screen, is affected by the XNA game loop. You can think of the game loop as a series of methods or steps that occur repeatedly as the game runs. User interaction is based on polling, in which the game asks the system whether some event-driven task has occurred, like a tap, mouse click, or joystick movement. The game continues to run regardless of user input, but does respond to user input when polling indicates a change in input. This is in contrast to Silverlight, in which applications are mainly event-driven. That means the application waits for the user to click a button or tap a control on the screen, which fires an event instructing the app to perform the related action.

The exercises in previous lessons of this book have shown you that Silverlight uses a lot of different methods to perform actions. In XNA, the game loop uses only two methods: Update and Draw. The Draw method draws things within the scene of the game. The Update method performs all other actions, like moving objects, updating scores, handling collisions between objects, and so on.

> **CERTIFICATION READY**
> Which framework is ideal for 3D game development?
> 3.3

➡ EXPLORE AN XNA GAME LOOP

GET READY. To learn about the code in an XNA game, perform the following steps:

1. Using a Web browser, go to the App Hub code samples Web page at http://create.msdn.com/en-US/education/catalog/article/wp7_code_samples.

2. Download **Hello XNA Framework Sample** to your Projects folder and expand the archive file. This sample is for a basic XNA Framework application that moves two graphics boxes around the screen and plays a sound when the boxes collide.

3. Open the project in your Visual Studio IDE. To see how the game works, click the **Start Debugging** button on the toolbar or press **F5** to open the application in the Windows Phone Emulator. The game displays in the emulator, as shown in Figure 5-2, and runs automatically.

Figure 5-2

The Hello XNA Framework Sample game running in the emulator

4. Allow the game to run for about 30 seconds or until the first collision occurs. Close the emulator.

5. In the Visual Studio IDE, click **OK** to close the dialog box that indicates that you lost the connection to the emulator. Double-click the **Game1.cs** file in Solution Explorer. The code displays in the Code Editor, as shown in Figure 5-3.

Figure 5-3

The Game1.cs file in the Hello XNA Framework sample

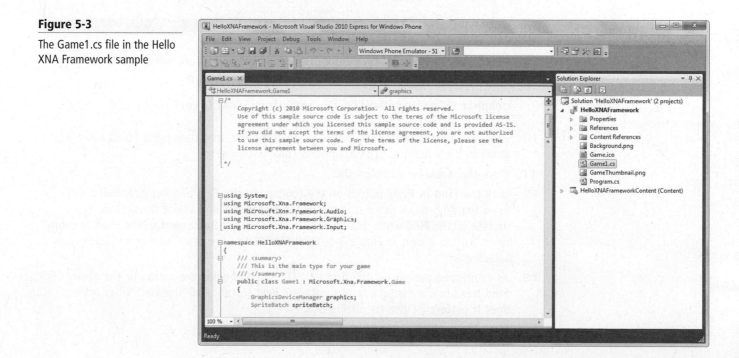

6. At the beginning of the code, after the initial comment section, notice the XNA. Framework directives. This clearly indicates use of the XNA framework.

7. Scroll down, if necessary, to the namespace. The Game1 class first defines two fields—graphics and spriteBatch—and then defines sprites, textures, and a sound effect. The Game1 constructor initializes the graphics field, setting the Content property, and setting a time for the game loop. The associated code is as follows:

```
graphics = new GraphicsDeviceManager(this);
    Content.RootDirectory = "Content";

// Frame rate is 30 fps by default for Windows Phone.
    TargetElapsedTime = TimeSpan.FromTicks(333333);
```

8. Scroll down to see the code that initializes the game and then loads content. After that, the action of the game begins with the first Update method, shown in Figure 5-4.

Figure 5-4

The action of the game begins here

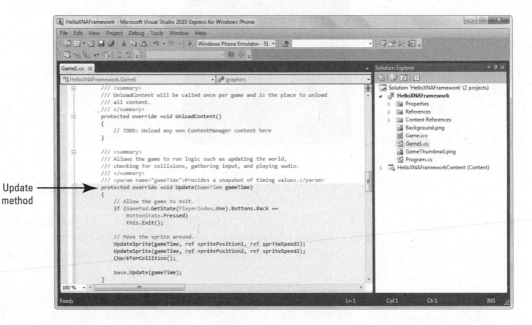

9. Scroll through the code to the end. Locate the Draw method, which draws the background using the following code:

```
graphics.GraphicsDevice.Clear(Color.CornflowerBlue);
```

10. Change CornflowerBlue to **LimeGreen**, save the file, and then press **F5** to run the game in the emulator. The background color is changed.

11. Close the emulator and click **OK**.

12. Click the **Find in Files** button on the toolbar. In the Find and Replace dialog box, open the drop-down list at the top of the dialog box and select **QuickFind**. Type **update** in the Find what text box and select **Current Document** in the Look in drop-down list, as shown in Figure 5-5. Click **Find Next**. The first instance of "update" is selected.

13. As mentioned previously, the first Update method begins the action of the game. Click **Find Next** in the dialog box to locate the next instance of "update." What action does it perform? Close the dialog box.

14. Close the project file and exit the Visual Studio IDE.

Figure 5-5

The Find and Replace dialog box

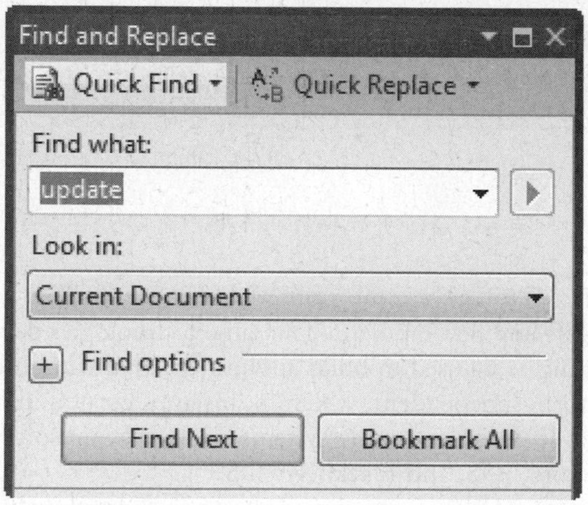

Although XNA is geared primarily toward game development and Silverlight for UI-based applications, many developers also create games using Silverlight. Starting with Windows Phone 7.5, you can combine features of Silverlight for Windows Phone and the XNA framework in a Windows Phone app.

➕ **MORE INFORMATION**

The "Silverlight and XNA Frameworks for Windows Phone" Web page at http://bit.ly/NoaEcC provides many links to specific information for both platforms, including application development and class libraries.

Introducing HTML5 and Its Relationship to Mobile Applications and Silverlight

Windows Phone is capable of running HTML5 Web applications. **HTML5** (logo shown in Figure 5-6) is the latest draft specification of Hypertext Markup Language (HTML), the language of the Web. An important point to understand about HTML5 is that it is both a standard and a family of new HTML markup tags, CSS, JavaScript, and other related technologies. **Cascading Style Sheets (CSS)** defines styles for HTML, usually in a separate file so you can easily change fonts, font sizes, and other attributes within the CSS file and the changes are reflected across all HTML files that reference the CSS file. The latest version of CSS is CSS3. **JavaScript** is a scripting language that adds interactivity to Web pages. (A scripting language is a programming language that uses scripts and requires no compiler.)

Figure 5-6

The HTML5 logo

This work is attributed to the W3C.

TAKE NOTE *

W3C® is a trademark (registered in numerous countries) of the World Wide Web Consortium; marks of W3C are registered and held by its host institutions MIT, ERCIM, and Keio.

The World Wide Web Consortium (W3C) is the main standards body developing specifications for HTML5, which is targeted for finalization in 2014 but could occur much later. Many parts of the specification are considered stable and are already in use across many Web sites.

Although the HTML5 family is most often used to create Web pages, you can also use HTML5 in mobile app development. The same technologies developers use to build Web pages are beginning to be used to build applications that run on different mobile devices. HTML5 is platform-independent, which means apps created in HTML5 can run on different desktop and mobile device operating systems, such as Microsoft Windows, Windows Phone, Mac OS X, Android, iOS, and Blackberry OS.

CERTIFICATION READY
What types of platforms support HTML5?
3.3

Some of the HTML5 features that are important to mobile applications include the following:

- **Audio and video tags:** With the use of relatively little markup, the *audio elements* and *video elements* embed audio and video multimedia in an application, complete with playback controls. Media that uses HTML5 audio and video plays back more efficiently and smoothly than media played through Silverlight or Flash plug-ins, and helps to conserve a device's battery charge.

- **Canvas:** The *canvas element* creates a container for graphics and uses JavaScript to draw 2D shapes and bitmap graphics as needed. Graphics are rendered by the browser on the fly, rather than created and stored within the application and then simply displayed. This is similar to creating and rendering graphics in Silverlight, and many of the properties are the same.

- **Fluid grids and layouts:** HTML5 includes the ability to create flexible and fluid grids and layouts, where "flexboxes" and grids resize themselves automatically to adjust to different screen sizes. These elements replace traditional HTML tables and other hard-coded layout structures, and are especially handy when a mobile device changes orientation from portrait to landscape.

- **Geolocation:** Most mobile devices have built-in GPS hardware, and HTML5 uses JavaScript to detect the geographic positioning of a client device. *Geolocation* is the identification of a device's geographic position, and it works with a device's Accelerometer, Compass, and Gyroscope features.

- **Media queries:** A *media query* is a CSS3 feature that detects a user's type of screen and sizes the output accordingly. Companies have struggled for years to create Web sites that accommodate both PCs and mobile devices. Many maintain separate pages—two different versions of the same page, where one is optimized for PC screens and the other for mobile device screens. Media queries enable you to maintain a single Web page that checks for the presence of certain media features, such as height, width, orientation, and screen resolution, and then loads a CSS file or parts of a CSS file particular to that type of client device.

Unlike Silverlight, HTML5 apps do not require users to download a plug-in or use devices that have plug-in support. Instead, you can use any Web browser that supports HTML5, whether on your PC or mobile device, and run apps with audio, video, and other multimedia elements. That statement comes with a few disclaimers. Because HTML5 is still in draft format, not all major browsers today support all HTML5 features. Some features, such as grid layouts, render properly only in Microsoft Internet Explorer 10 (as of this writing). Other features require developers to include vendor prefixes in the CSS code. *Vendor prefixes* are code workarounds that simply add a keyword surrounded by dashes to the front of a CSS3 property name. The most common vendor prefixes are described as follows:

- Mozilla Firefox supports the -moz- prefix.
- Microsoft Internet Explorer uses the -ms- prefix.
- Opera uses the -o- prefix.
- Google Chrome and Apple Safari support the -webkit- prefix.

For example, the CSS3 display:flexbox element creates flexible layout boxes. To apply the flex style to elements so they render properly in the Firefox browser, you need to use the display:-moz-flexbox property.

TAKE NOTE * The lack of browser support will improve over time as the HTML5 specification matures. Major browsers continue to adopt HTML5 features and provide native support in each new release.

An important difference between Silverlight and HTML5 is that Silverlight is defined within XAML, which is then parsed to create the UI. As mentioned previously, Silverlight and XAML are tightly coupled—Silverlight relies on XAML to create the UI. In comparison, HTML and JavaScript are only loosely coupled. HTML uses tags to describe the structure of a document, and a browser parses the document to create a DOM. The browser uses JavaScript to expose an application programming interface (API) for manipulating the DOM. HTML can exist without JavaScript and vice versa, but Silverlight cannot exist without XAML.

⊙ CREATE A WEB PAGE USING HTML5

GET READY. To learn how easy it is to use HTML5, let's create a simple Web page that includes the audio element, which creates playback controls automatically. Perform the following steps:

1. Locate an MP3 audio clip on your computer or download a public domain clip from the Internet.

2. Open Notepad or another text editor on your computer. Create a file with the following markup, substituting the name of your MP3 file for sample.mp3. The MP3 file should be in the same folder as the HTML file you're creating.

```
<!doctype html>
<html>
  <head>
    <meta charset="UTF-8">
    <title>Audio Example</title>
  </head>
<body>
  <audio src="sample.mp3" controls="controls">
  </audio>
</body>
</html>
```

3. Save your file as **audio.html**.

4. Open a Web browser such as Internet Explorer. Select **File** > **Open**, click **Browse** and navigate to the location of the audio.html file, select the file, and click **OK**. You should see something similar to Figure 5-7.

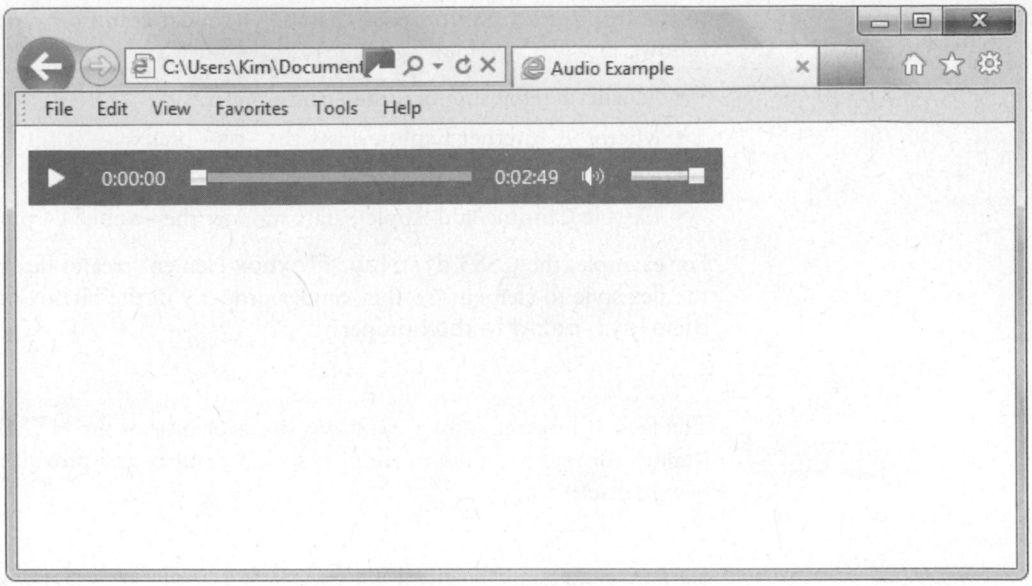

Figure 5-7

HTML5 default audio controls
in a Web browser

5. Click the Play button to start the audio clip. Notice that the default controls include a mute button and a volume slider.

6. Close any open files, including Notepad and the Web browser.

➕ MORE INFORMATION

Brandon Satrom is an expert on Web technologies and HTML5 in particular, and is a former Web evangelist for Microsoft. Browse his *MSDN Magazine* article titled "Building Apps with HTML5: What You Need to Know" at http://msdn.microsoft.com/en-us/magazine/hh335062.aspx. Brandon also blogs at userinexperience.com. The MSDN *Magazine* article "Practical Cross-Browser HTML5 Audio and Video" by John Dyer at http://msdn.microsoft.com/en-us/magazine/hh781023.aspx provides a terrific explanation of the HTML5 audio and video elements.

Which Technology Should You Use to Create Windows Phone Apps?

You can use Silverlight for event-driven applications, especially business-type applications, and games that display a lot of text, use the software keyboard, and that access Windows Phone controls. XNA framework is designed for multi-screen 2D and 3D games. HTML5 is still emerging but is used to provide some features, such as audio, video, and canvas graphics, in browser-based applications.

Knowing how to use Silverlight, XNA, and HTML5 is one thing, but knowing when to use them is another.

When it comes to gaming, both Silverlight and XNA framework work well for games with modest graphics and animations. However, Silverlight excels at games that display a lot of text, such as high-score statistics. For high-performance gaming, especially for multi-screen 2D and 3D games, use the XNA framework.

Silverlight is, and will continue to be in the near future, the choice of developers who want to create event-driven applications with RIA user interfaces. Silverlight also makes development easier for applications that will use the built-in UI controls on a Windows Phone; XNA framework developers must create controls that match the look and feel of a Windows Phone UI. The same applies to applications that use the software keyboard that displays automatically on a Windows Phone device for input—Silverlight can access that control by default, but XNA framework developers must create their own software keyboard control.

As you learned earlier in the lesson, you can combine Silverlight and XNA in a single application. Certain scenarios make this combination a good choice, such as an XAML-based, event-driven application that incorporates a high-performance game. You can also combine platforms to create a multi-screen 3D arcade-style game, for example, with an RIA user interface.

You can reliably use some HTML5 features (such as audio, video, geolocation, and canvas graphics) in the WebBrowser control provided in the Visual Studio IDE. The HTML5 specification is still under development, so browser compatibility is an issue and requires research and testing on the part of the developer to know which HTML5 features currently render properly in the Windows Phone Internet Explorer browser.

EXPLORE AN APPLICATION THAT COMBINES SILVERLIGHT AND XNA

GET READY. To see how Silverlight and XNA can be combined in a single application, perform the following steps:

1. In your Visual Studio IDE, go to the Start page, and click **Code Samples for Windows Phone** in the Learning Resources section.

2. Download the **My Little Teapot Sample** to your Projects folder and expand the archive file.

3. Open the project in your Visual Studio IDE. To see how the application works, click the **Start Debugging** button on the toolbar or press **F5** to open the application in the Windows Phone Emulator. The application displays in the emulator, as shown in Figure 5-8.

Figure 5-8

The My Little Teapot sample code running in the emulator

Slider controls →

4. Use the slider bar controls in the application to change the color of the teapot. For example, click and hold the white box on the green slider and then slide it to the right. Do the same for the red and blue slider bars. Click a colored box below the sliders, and then move each of the slider bars again. Close the emulator.

5. In the Visual Studio IDE, click **OK** to close the dialog box that indicates that you lost the connection to the emulator.

6. Open Solution Explorer if it's not already open. Do several files look familiar? For example, this application includes MainPage.xaml, which you've seen many times in previous lessons.

7. Expand the **MainPage.xaml** entry and double-click the code-behind file. This example uses the C# version of the application code, but you could use the VB version as well. The code displays in the Code Editor, as shown in Figure 5-9.

Figure 5-9

The My Little Teapot MainPage.xaml.cs file code

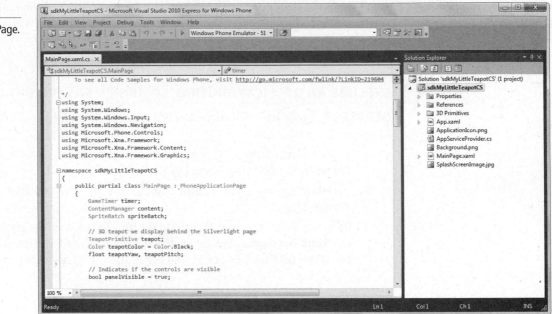

8. Press **Ctrl+F** and use the Find and Replace dialog box to find instances of "draw." Locate the code that draws the teapot, as follows:

```
private void OnDraw(object sender, GameTimerEventArgs e)
    {
        // Render the Silverlight controls using
        // the UIElementRenderer
        elementRenderer.Render();

        // Clear the screen to a solid color

SharedGraphicsDeviceManager.Current.GraphicsDevice.Clear(Color.
CornflowerBlue);
        // Draw the teapot
        DrawTeapot(e);

        spriteBatch.Begin();
        // Using the texture from the
        // UIElementRenderer,
        // draw the Silverlight controls to
        // the screen
        spriteBatch.Draw(elementRenderer.Texture, Vector2.Zero,
Color.White);
        spriteBatch.End();
    }
```

This code renders the Silverlight controls you used in the application. The UIElementRenderer class, in the Microsoft.Xna.Framework.Graphics namespace, renders a Silverlight UIElement into a texture.

9. Scroll further down the code to see the Manipulation events, which also control the 3D rendered teapot.

10. Close the project file but leave the Visual Studio IDE open if you plan to complete the next exercise during this session.

➕ MORE INFORMATION

If you need help deciding whether to use Silverlight or XNA, browse the "Silverlight and XNA Frameworks for Windows Phone" at http://bit.ly/NoaEcC. To see all the steps involved in creating a sample application that combines Silverlight and XNA, visit the "Developing a Windows Phone Application from Start to Finish" Web page at http://bit.ly/hs6gzQ.

Identifying Silverlight Controls

Silverlight for Windows Phone uses most of the same controls, which are visible elements that comprise the user interface, as are found in Silverlight. Some controls enable a user to interact with the application, whereas others display data or images, provide hyperlinks, or act as containers for other controls.

The visible elements that make up a user interface are called **controls**, and the Visual Studio IDE includes controls like `Button`, `MediaElement`, and `WebBrowser` among many others (see Figure 5-10).

Many Silverlight controls have been modified slightly from standard PC desktop controls to work well with Windows Phone touch displays. The Toolbox in Visual Studio 2010 Express for Windows Phone displays many of the available controls. The source

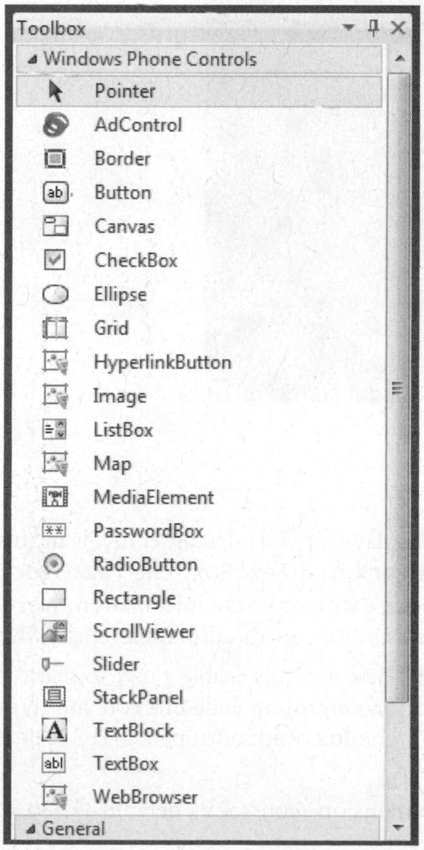

CERTIFICATION READY
What is the purpose of a control in Silverlight?
3.3

Figure 5-10

The default Windows Phone controls in the Toolbox

Toolbox
◢ Windows Phone Controls
▸ Pointer
AdControl
Border
Button
Canvas
CheckBox
Ellipse
Grid
HyperlinkButton
Image
ListBox
Map
MediaElement
PasswordBox
RadioButton
Rectangle
ScrollViewer
Slider
StackPanel
TextBlock
TextBox
WebBrowser
◢ General

of these controls is the System.Windows.Controls namespace in the .NET Framework Class Library for Silverlight or the Microsoft.Phone.Controls namespace in Windows Phone.

Controls fall into one of the following categories:

- **Navigation:** These controls enable a user to move from one page of content to another. The default navigation controls include PhoneApplicationFrame and PhoneApplicationPage. In a Windows Phone 7 app, PhoneApplicationPage defines the default UI content placeholder. PhoneApplicationFrame is the top-level container for the entire application, which contains PhoneApplicationPages. A PhoneApplicationFrame is created automatically when an application initializes.

- **Layout and grouping:** These controls help to create layouts and often serve as containers for other controls or visual objects. The default layout and grouping controls include Border, Canvas, ContentControl, Grid, Panorama, Pivot, StackPanel, VirtualizingStackPanel, and ScrollViewer. Figure 5-11 shows the Grid control.

Figure 5-11

An example of the Grid control

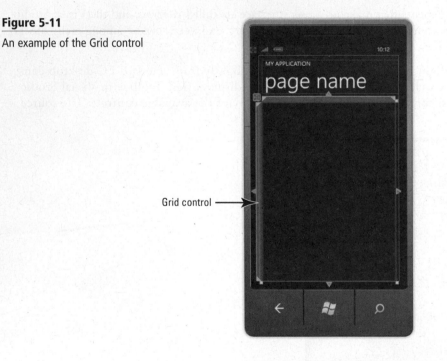

Grid control

- **Text:** These controls display text. The default controls in this category include PasswordBox, TextBlock, and TextBox. The TextBlock control displays text without allowing the user to edit the information, whereas TextBox allows user input. The PasswordBox control displays asterisks when a user inputs text.

- **Button and selection:** These controls enable a user to select items or navigate through an app. The default button controls include Button and HyperlinkButton, and the selection controls are CheckBox, RadioButton, and Slider. Figure 5-12 shows the CheckBox control.

- **List:** This category contains one control by default—ListBox—which displays list items.

Figure 5-12

An example of the
`CheckBox` control

Checkbox
control

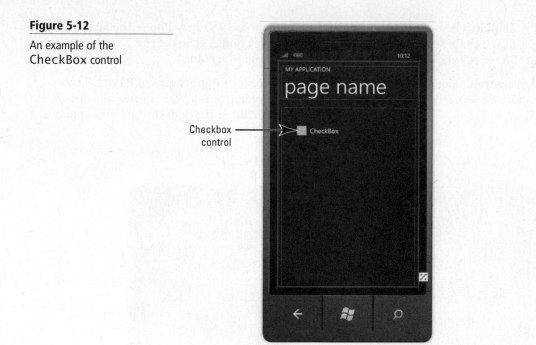

- **Image, map, and media:** These controls display JPG and PNG images and Bing maps, and playback controls for audio and video files. The default controls in this category include `Image`, `Map`, and `MediaElement`. Figure 5-13 shows the Map control.

Figure 5-13

An example of the `Map` control

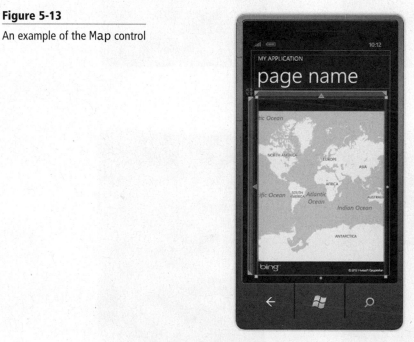

- **HTML:** The lone control in this category is `WebBrowser`, which displays a mini Internet Explorer Web browser that's fully functioning.
- **Progress and message:** These controls provide feedback to users. The `ProgressBar` control displays a visual status of a time-intensive operation, like a large file download. The `Popup` control displays a message, such as an alert or an error message, on top of content currently displayed.

- **Toolkit:** These controls are part of the Silverlight for Windows Phone Toolkit. The controls include AutoCompleteBox, ListPicker, LongListSelector, ContextMenu, DatePicker, TimePicker, ToggleSwitch, and WrapPanel.

Two controls unique to Silverlight for Windows Phone are Panorama and Pivot. The *Panorama control* displays content horizontally, extending beyond the edges of the display, as shown in Figure 5-14. This figure shows a panoramic list in the built-in Panorama application

Figure 5-14

An example of the Panorama control

Figure 5-15

An example of the Pivot control

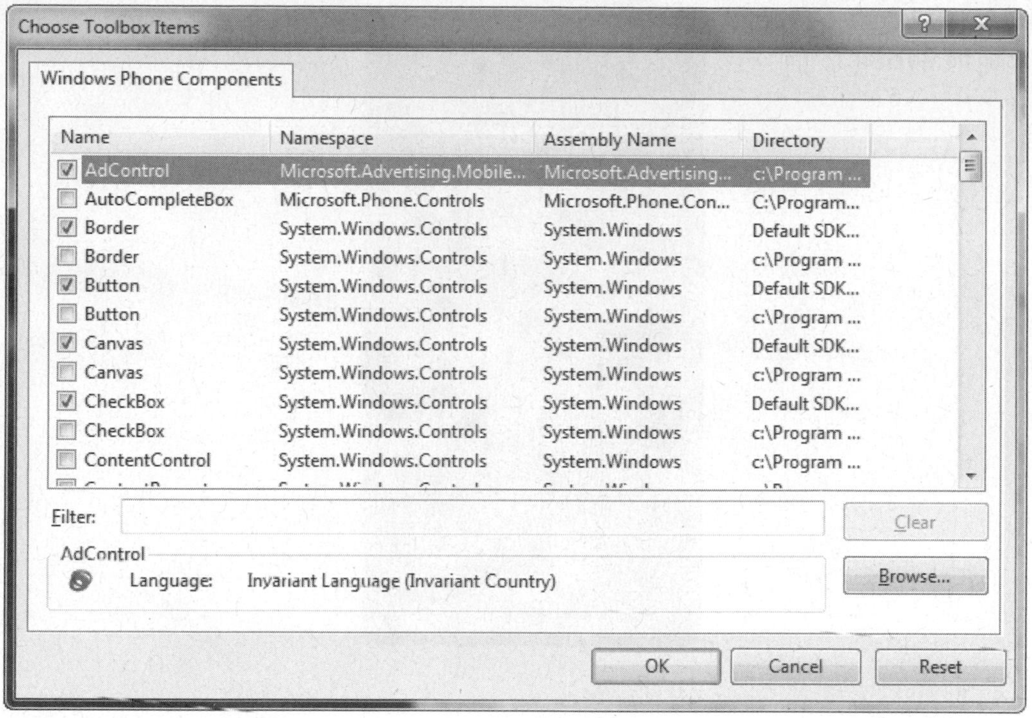

Figure 5-16

The Choose Toolbox Items
dialog box

CROSS REFERENCE *

Lesson 7 covers how to
use Windows Phone
controls within applica-
tions in detail.

in the Visual Studio IDE. The `Panorama` control is often used to display pictures as well.
The ***Pivot*** *control* switches between different views of an application or data, as shown in
Figure 5-15. This figure shows a pivot view of list data, using the built-in Pivot application
in the Visual Studio IDE. Windows Phone includes calendar and email applications that also
use the `Pivot` control.

The Visual Studio IDE Toolbox displays only a portion of the available controls. To see all
controls, right-click an empty area of the Toolbox and select Choose Items. In the Choose
Toolbox Items dialog box (see Figure 5-16), check the controls that you want to appear in the
Toolbox and then click OK.

A long list of controls supported in Silverlight for Windows Phone are listed and
described on the "Controls in Silverlight for Windows Phone" Web page at http://bit.ly/
KQAbdx. The page also lists controls that are not supported in Silverlight for Windows
Phone.

→ EXPERIMENT WITH CONTROLS

GET READY. You've already used the `Grid`, `TextBox`, `TextBlock`, and `WebBrowser` controls in the Visual Studio IDE in this and other lessons. To learn about a few other controls,
perform the following steps:

1. In the Visual Studio IDE, start a new project using the **Windows Phone Application**
   template. This example uses the Silverlight for Windows Phone C# version of the
   template.

2. Name the project **ControlsPractice**. The target OS is Windows Phone 7.1 OS.

3. Open the Toolbox, and then drag the **Border** control to the Grid element in the design
   surface, as shown in Figure 5-17.

Figure 5-17

Using the Border control

4. To create a colored border around some text, modify the MainPage.xaml code for the Border control as follows. You can modify the XAML directly in the Code Editor or make the changes to the properties by using the Properties window:

```
<Border Background="Coral" Width="300" Padding="10"
    CornerRadius="20">
        <TextBlock FontSize="30">Text and a Border</TextBlock>
</Border>
```

5. Resize the height of the border by dragging the upper or lower edge of the Border control in the design surface.

6. Drag the **Map** control from the Toolbox to the design surface, placing the Map control just under the Border control. Resize the Map control so you can easily see the map.

7. Drag the HyperlinkButton control from the Toolbox to the design surface, placing the HyperlinkButton control just under the Map control. Resize the HyperlinkButton control however you like.

8. With the HyperlinkButton control selected, open the Properties window. To make the control interactive, enter **http://www.wiley.com** or the URL of your choice in the NavigateURI property textbox.

9. In the TargetName property textbox, type **_blank**. (The HyperlinkButton control requires this property to indicate where to load the hyperlink response. _blank indicates that it will load in a new blank window.)

10. Save the file. The practice application design surface should look similar to Figure 5-18.

11. Press **F5** to debug the application and test the application in the Windows Phone Emulator. You'll revisit this application in Lesson 7 when you learn about controls in depth.

12. Close the Windows Phone Emulator, close the project file, and leave the Visual Studio IDE open if you plan to complete the next exercise during this session.

Figure 5-18

The Border, Map, and HyperlinkButton controls in the design surface

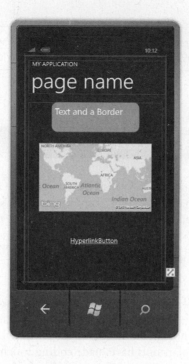

➕ **MORE INFORMATION**

The "Controls for Windows Phone" Web page at http://bit.ly/K25hMd provides links to information about Windows Phone controls. The App Hub "Types of Controls" Web page at http://bit.ly/M7FBC9 describes controls and control categories, and provides a Windows Phone Emulator image of a control in each category. The video at http://bit.ly/M04T2c walks you through the code for enabling the **PasswordBox**, **CheckBox**, **RadioButton**, **ListBox**, and **ScrollViewer** controls.

Using Silverlight and HTML5 Applications

HTML5 is used mainly for Web applications accessed from a mobile device using the WebBrowser control in the Visual Studio IDE, but the trend is for HTML5 to eventually replace Silverlight as a mobile application development solution.

For Web-related applications, both Silverlight and HTML5 are good choices. Only Silverlight can use the WebBrowser control that creates a mini Internet Explorer browser. You can use HTML5 code (markup tags for elements and their associated attributes and properties, and CSS properties for styling HTML content) within the control, which then gets bundled into the final application. Some developers believe that HTML5 should be used for audio and video delivery because of its higher performance and ease of use (no plug-in needed!). All major browsers support the HTML5 audio and video elements.

Much like any mobile application, HTML5 enables developers to package their apps and distribute them through an app store. However, because HTML5 is a relatively new technology, developers still use Silverlight as the primary tool for creating Windows Phone event-driven apps, and they are beginning to use HTML5 for many different types of applications accessed via a browser from a mobile device.

Although Microsoft will continue to support Silverlight for quite some time, the company encourages exploration and use of HTML5 rather than Silverlight. Microsoft calls HTML5 "the only true cross-platform solution for everything."

CERTIFICATION READY
Which language or framework offers better performance when playing back audio and video in a Web-based application?
3.3

+ MORE INFORMATION

Browse Brandon Satrom's MSDN Magazine article titled "Using HTML5 to Create Mobile Experiences" at http://msdn.microsoft.com/en-us/magazine/hh975346.aspx for an inside look at HTML5 for the mobile landscape.

■ Understanding Code for Mobile Applications

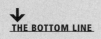 **THE BOTTOM LINE**

C#, VB, and XAML are at the heart of most Windows Phone applications today, and HTML5 is the newcomer that's beginning to gain traction. It's essential to know the high-level differences between these technologies, and to understand the customer's environment and needs, to be able to make good planning decisions and meet requirements.

CERTIFICATION READY
What is the importance of understanding code for mobile applications?
3.5

Learning how to develop mobile applications for your own personal interests and to share with friends can be a lot of fun. Developing applications in a business setting requires detailed knowledge of the technologies available to you. Improvements to each release of the Visual Studio IDE and similar tools have made coding much easier and less error-prone than in the past, but the graphical user interfaces (GUIs) also keep you just a step away from working with the actual code and understanding the subtle and major differences between languages.

Becoming a proficient developer often means immersing yourself in at least a few different languages and platforms. You should become familiar with the differences between languages that accomplish the same tasks, and whether those differences represent advantages or disadvantages to mobile applications. In addition, a proficient developer learns which questions to ask the customer throughout the application development life cycle in order to meet requirements, and to understand the customer's true needs and expectations.

Distinguishing Among Programming Languages and Programs

The programming languages most often associated with Windows Phone applications are XAML for the UI and C# and VB for defining an application. Microsoft supports only C# for XNA framework apps. C# and VB are both object-oriented programming languages and share similar feature sets and functionality. HTML5 is a markup language that requires JavaScript for user interactivity.

You can develop Windows Phone applications using the object-oriented programming languages *Visual Basic .NET (VB.NET)* or *Visual C#*. They are often referred to simply as VB and C# but differ slightly from the classic VB and C# programming languages. VB.NET is a subset of the classic VB (version 6.0 and earlier) and is the version implemented in the Visual Studio IDE. Visual C# is Microsoft's implementation of the C# specification; when you see "C#" in the Visual Studio IDE, it's actually Visual C#.

VB.NET or Visual C# code is the programming language instructions used to define an application. Because both languages support similar feature sets and functionality, the language you decide to use for developing applications is your preference.

Although the features sets are similar, the syntax that accomplishes the same tasks varies between the two languages. For example, take a look at `for` loop code snippets for each language. A sample `for` loop in VB might look like this:

```
For n = 1 To 10
    MsgBox("The number is " & n)
Next

For Each prop In obj
    prop = 38
Next prop
```

A sample `for` loop in C# might look like this:

```
for (int i = 1; i <= 10; i++)
 MessageBox.Show(string.Format(
   "The number is {0}", i);
foreach(int prop in obj)
{
 prop=38;
}
```

In addition, each language has some constructs not included in the other. For example, VB uses a `with` construct, which isn't found in C#.

VB generally has simpler event handling (syntactically). A method can declare that it handles an event, rather than the handler having to be set up in code.

It's easy to distinguish C# and VB files from each other because C# files have a .cs file extension and VB files have a .vb file extension.

| TAKE NOTE* | For a detailed list of similarities and differences, visit the Wikipedia "Comparison of C Sharp and Visual Basic .NET" Web page. |

CERTIFICATION READY
Which programming language does Microsoft support in the XNA framework?
3.5

XNA Framework uses C# to create games—Microsoft Xbox 360 games in particular. Although it's possible to use VB with XNA, Microsoft supports only C# with XNA and provides only C# templates in the Visual Studio IDE. However, the majority of console games around the world are written in C++, usually with a popular scripting language such as Lua or Python or a custom solution. Some developers use other languages, such as C, Objective C, and Java for game creation, but they're less popular than C++.

| TAKE NOTE* | Programmers well versed in C++ can make a relatively easy transition to C# because the syntax used in both languages is very similar. |

Silverlight uses XAML to define user interfaces. Microsoft developed XAML for the .NET Framework, particularly for Windows Presentation Foundation, Silverlight, and Windows Workflow Foundation (WF). Visual Studio 11 for Windows 8 Metro applications also use XAML. The Windows 8 nod is significant, considering the push toward HTML5 as the future mobile app and Web development platform.

XAML is similar to HTML and Extensible Markup Language (XML), and the "X" in XAML stands for Extensible. You can identify XAML files by their .xaml file extension.

HTML5 is a markup language that uses tags to define content. HTML documents have an .html or .htm file extension.

CERTIFICATION READY
Which file extensions
does HTML support?
3.5

HTML tags come in pairs, such as the following example for creating a first-level heading in an HTML document:

```
<h1>Green Bay Is TitleTown USA</h1>
```

HTML documents for the Web (aka a Web page) begin with a `doctype` declaration that indicates the language or rules to be used by the browser when rendering the page. The HTML5 `doctype` is very simple compared to previous HTML version, and it looks like this:

```
<!doctype html>
```

HTML documents generally include the `<html>`, `<head>`, `<title>`, and `<body>` tags, at a minimum. A tag pair is also called an element, which describes content, inserts graphics, or creates hyperlinks. Not all tags describe data on their own or at least not in enough detail for rendering, so some elements must include attributes, which are keywords that modify or extend HTML elements and provide additional information. For example, the `<a>` (or anchor) tag creates hyperlinks, but the opening and closing `<a> </a>` tags don't have much meaning by themselves. Including the `href` attribute with a specific Web address as the attribute's value makes much more sense:

```
<a href="http://www.wiley.com">Wiley Web site</a>
```

Figure 5-19 shows the markup for a simple HTML document. This document includes some inline CSS code for styling the content, and some JavaScript code that enables interactivity with the user. (Some of the JavaScript code is collapsed, or hidden from view, to reduce the height of the figure.) Most HTML documents separate the CSS code to a separate document, but it's acceptable to include inline code if you have a few simple, standalone Web pages.

Figure 5-19

A simple HTML document with HTML markup, CSS code, and JavaScript code

```
<!doctype html>

<html>
  <head>
    <title>Detect Touch Screen</title>
    <meta charset="utf-8" />

    <style type="text/css">
      #canvas{background-color: dodgerblue;}
    </style>

    <script type="text/javascript">

        document.addEventListener("DOMContentLoaded", init, false);

        function init()...

        function detect()...

    </script>

  </head>

  <body>
    <canvas id="canvas" width="100" height="100"></canvas>
    <br />
    <p>Click the box to start touch screen detection.</p>
  </body>
</html>
```

⊙ IDENTIFY DIFFERENCES BETWEEN C# AND VB

GET READY. To identify differences between C# and VB, perform the following steps:

1. Open the **Weather Forecast** sample application in the Visual Studio IDE.

2. If you don't have both versions of the application (C# and VB), go to the code samples for Windows Phone Web page at http://msdn.microsoft.com/en-us/library/ff431744(v=vs.92).aspx. Download the same code sample in the language other than the one you already have. For example, if you opened the C# version of the Weather Forecast sample, download the VB version and expand the archive file to make the files accessible.

3. Compare the MainPage code-behind files for the two versions of the application. Hint: Print the page for each, and then match up comments and review the code that follows each comment to see how the action of the application is handled.

4. Close the project file and exit the Visual Studio IDE.

➕ MORE INFORMATION

For more information on VB and C#, check out the "Getting Started with Visual Basic" Web page at http://msdn.microsoft.com/en-us/library/8hb2a397.aspx and the "Getting Started with Visual C#" Web page at http://msdn.microsoft.com/en-us/library/a72418yk.aspx. The "XAML Overview" Web page is located at http://msdn.microsoft.com/en-us/library/cc189036(VS.95).aspx. You can learn more about XNA by browsing the "Getting Started with XNA Game Studio Development" Web page located at http://msdn.microsoft.com/en-us/library/bb203894.aspx. A great resource for all kinds of HTML5 topics is the HTML5Rocks.com Web site.

Identifying the Code to Use to Meet Requirements

When creating applications in a business environment, it's highly important to interview the customer and learn about the customer's environment and needs. A project checklist and design document should be a part of every development project. The customer should be contacted for feedback and approval throughout the development process to ensure a successful project.

Designing and developing applications for an organization always requires planning before any code is written. An organization might not want to allocate in-house resources for design and development for various reasons, but might want to be able to modify applications quickly when needed. The organization might also have a lot of time, money, and training invested in a specific platform or language. In those types of cases, you must find out as much as you can about the customer's needs and environment before approaching details about how the application should look and function.

It's helpful to prepare a detailed project checklist that helps you gather customer information. The checklist should be general in nature to apply to nearly any customer you work with. (Remember, a customer can be a department or group even within your own organization.)

The checklist would include the phases of the software development life cycle, modified slightly for your business. The first phase involves concept determination, where the general nature of the application is established and what it will do (at a high level). During this phase, you should interview key customer stakeholders, develop assumptions about the application, and determine the technology (framework, language) that seems to fit the needs of the customer and the application. Following this phase you should create a design document that begins to spell out details about the application and the proposed development process.

CERTIFICATION READY
How do you ensure that you select the proper code to meet customer and application requirements?
3.5

The remainder of the checklist would include a succession of categories that bring the app through design and development, testing, and finalization. You should get customer feedback and approval at various points throughout the process to ensure that the final product will be successful.

SKILL SUMMARY

IN THIS LESSON YOU LEARNED:

- Silverlight for Windows Phone is a version of the Microsoft Silverlight framework. Silverlight uses XAML to create user interfaces, and it uses code created in C# or VB to make applications run.
- Silverlight applications use an event-driven model, whereas XNA applications use a game loop and polling. With Silverlight, you can integrate video and other multimedia elements into applications, but XNA can render 3D video games. HTML5 is a platform-independent markup language used to create HTML documents and Web applications. HTML5 is also regarded as a family of technologies that include HTML, CSS3, and JavaScript.
- You can use Silverlight for event-driven applications, especially business-type applications, and games that display a lot of text, use the software keyboard, and that access Windows Phone controls. XNA framework is designed for multi-screen 2D and 3D games. HTML5 is still emerging but is used to provide some features, such as audio, video, and canvas graphics, in browser-based applications.
- Silverlight for Windows Phone uses most of the same controls, which are visible elements that comprise the user interface, as are found in Silverlight. Some controls enable a user to interact with the application, whereas others display data or images, provide hyperlinks, or act as containers for other controls.
- HTML5 is used mainly for Web applications accessed from a mobile device, but the trend is for HTML5 to eventually rival or replace Silverlight as a mobile application development solution.
- C#, VB, and XAML are at the heart of most Windows Phone applications today, and HTML5 is the newcomer that's beginning to gain traction. It's essential to know the high-level differences between these technologies, and to understand the customer's environment and needs, to be able to make good planning decisions and meet requirements.
- The programming languages most often associated with Windows Phone applications are XAML for the UI and C# and VB for defining an application. Microsoft supports only C# for XNA framework apps. C# and VB are both object-oriented programming languages and share similar feature sets and functionality. HTML5 is a markup language that requires JavaScript for user interactivity.
- When creating applications in a business environment, it's highly important to interview the customer and learn about the customer's environment and needs. A project checklist and design document should be a part of every development project. The customer should be contacted for feedback and approval throughout the development process to ensure a successful project.

Knowledge Assessment

Fill in the Blank

Complete the following sentences by writing the correct word or words in the blanks provided.

1. _____ is a Web application framework that enables you to create Rich Internet Applications (RIAs). It provides many user interface controls and uses an event-driven execution model.

2. _____ is the latest draft specification of Hypertext Markup Language (HTML), the language of the Web. It is also a family of new HTML markup tags, CSS, JavaScript, and other related technologies.

3. _____ is a scripting language that adds interactivity to Web pages.

4. In Windows Phone, the _____ control displays content horizontally, extending beyond the edges of the display.

5. Silverlight generally uses _____ or _____ as the code behind the UI, which makes the application run. This is referred to as managed code.

6. The visible elements that make up a user interface are called _____, and examples include `Button`, `MediaElement`, and `WebBrowser` among many others.

7. _____ defines styles for HTML, usually in a separate file so you can easily change fonts, font sizes, and other attributes.

8. The _____ is a set of Visual Studio libraries designed primarily for multi-screen 2D and 3D game development.

9. _____ files mainly handle events from application controls, like the `Button`, `TextBox`, and `TextBlock` controls used in Windows Phone applications.

10. _____ _____ are code workarounds that simply add a keyword surrounded by dashes to the front of a CSS3 property name.

Multiple Choice

Circle the letter that corresponds to the best answer.

1. C# and VB are examples of which of the following? (Choose all that apply.)
   a. Object-oriented programming languages
   b. Mobile application development platforms
   c. Scripting languages
   d. Managed code

2. Which technology is the best choice for an event-driven business application?
   a. Silverlight
   b. XNA
   c. HTML5
   d. JavaScript

3. Which technology is the best choice for a 3D game that will include sprites and textures?
   a. Silverlight
   b. XNA
   c. HTML5
   d. JavaScript

4. Which of the following languages is most similar to C#?
   a. VB
   b. JavaScript
   c. C++
   d. Python

5. Which Windows Phone control displays Bing maps?
   a. `TextBlock`
   b. `Image`
   c. `Map`
   d. `MediaElement`

6. Which of the following uses a `doctype` declaration?
   a. HTML5
   b. C#
   c. VB
   d. XAML

7. What does the X in XAML refer to?
   a. Extra
   b. Extensible
   c. XL
   d. Excellent

8. Which of the following are most important to be shared and discussed with a customer at or near the beginning of an application development project? (Choose all that apply.)
   a. Project checklist
   b. Design document
   c. Detailed development process chart
   d. Icon choice for the app store

9. Which of the following is used to enable user interactivity in an HTML5 document?
   a. C#
   b. CSS
   c. JavaScript
   d. VB

10. Which methods does the XNA framework use?
    a. `Manipulate` and `Update`
    b. `Draw` and `Loop`
    c. `Update` and `Draw`
    d. `Update`, `Draw`, and all methods used in Silverlight

True/False

Circle T if the statement is true or F if the statement is false.

T F 1. The Windows Phone Pivot control switches between different views of an application or data.

T F 2. You can separate Silverlight from XAML much like you separate HTML from CSS.

T F 3. XNA uses a game loop model.

T F 4. All available controls appear in the Visual Studio IDE Toolbox by default.

T F 5. C# and VB have similar feature sets and functionality but use different syntax.

■ Competency Assessment

Scenario 5-1: Describe the Differences between Silverlight and Silverlight for Windows Phone

Lester is your workout buddy and has gotten very interested in mobile app development because of the enthusiasm you seem to bring to your projects. He is experimenting with the Windows Phone SDK tools and wants to know the difference between Silverlight and Silverlight for Windows Phone. What do you tell him?

Scenario 5-2: Design a Mobile Web Application

The manager of the local donut shop you and Lester visit after every workout has asked you to develop an app that customers can use to create their favorite donut. He wants the application to run on his Web site and be accessible by PCs and mobile devices. Which technologies do you consider for this project, and why?

■ Proficiency Assessment

Scenario 5-3: Understand the Software Development Life Cycle

Shakita was just promoted to client representative at BoxTwelve Mobile. Her responsibilities will include working directly with client stakeholders on development projects and walking them through the development process. She asked for tips on preparing for her first client meeting. What do you tell her?

Scenario 5-4: Understand Application Requirements

Your sister Kellie is working on a school group project in which the task is to create a mobile app game that uses sprites, textures, and sounds when certain tasks are achieved. The game must include access to the software keyboard available on Windows Phones for users to enter their names, which will be displayed along with their scores. What technology or technologies so you recommend she consider for the project?

Understanding Mobile App Development Concepts and Working with APIs

EXAM OBJECTIVE MATRIX

SKILLS/CONCEPTS	MTA EXAM OBJECTIVE	MTA EXAM OBJECTIVE NUMBER
Developing Mobile Applications	Manage the application life cycle.	4.1
Understanding Mobile Device APIs	Understand mobile device APIs.	4.2

KEY TERMS

Activated **event**

application state

audio **element**

Closing **event**

Data Protection API (DPAPI)

Deactivated **event**

dormant application

Launching **event**

Location API

ManipulationCompleted **event**

ManipulationDelta **event**

ManipulationStarted **event**

NavigationService **class**

page state

splash screen

tombstoning

video element

Windows Phone application life cycle

You've learned a lot about the Windows Phone operating system as an entry-level application developer at BoxTwelve Mobile. Your manager has asked you to create and deliver a presentation about the Windows Phone application life cycle to summer interns. She would also like you to address tips for creating responsive applications and conserving battery life.

■ Developing Mobile Applications

> **↓ THE BOTTOM LINE**
>
> An important part of developing mobile applications for Windows Phone devices is to understand the phases an application goes through. This is referred to the Windows Phone application life cycle. You must also know how to create applications that are responsive, conserve energy, provide feedback to users in the form of messages and status bars, and store passwords securely.

This lesson dives into all kinds of topics related to mobile app development. You'll begin by covering the Windows Phone application life cycle, which includes how application state information is preserved when an application is activated and deactivated.

You'll also pick up tips and best practices for balancing code between battery usage and performance, and for creating more responsive applications. The last part of the section focuses on managing visible status for long-running operations, storing passwords on devices, and creating a custom splash screen.

Managing the Application Life Cycle

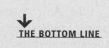

TAKE NOTE*

An application terminates when a user closes it or when another process closes it.

> To create a good user experience and manage memory efficiently, the Windows Phone operating system allows only one application to run in the foreground at a time. An application's life cycle begins after the application launches. From there, the application can be in one of three states: running, dormant, or tombstoned. An application terminates when the user or some process closes it.

When you launch a Windows Phone application, it opens to its initial page. Because most applications have multiple pages, the user can navigate to those pages using controls you provide in the application. The user can press the hardware Back button on the phone to return to the previous page. Once the user reaches the first page of the application and presses the Back button, the application terminates. From launch to termination, the application goes through several common events and states.

CERTIFICATION READY

What are the three primary states in the Windows Phone application life cycle?

4.1

The Windows Phone Execution model describes the *Windows Phone application life cycle*, which is the series of events and states that dictate how every Windows Phone application must operate to provide a consistent and responsive user experience. The general application life cycle of a Windows Phone OS 7.01 mobile app is shown in Figure 6-1. The life cycle

Figure 6-1

The general Windows Phone OS 7.01 application life cycle

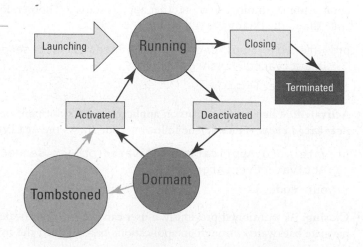

begins when the application launches. From there, the application can be in one of three states: running, dormant, or tombstoned. Being able to transition between these states helps to conserve a device's memory and battery power.

To create a good user experience and manage memory efficiently, the Windows Phone operating system allows only one application to run in the foreground at a time. Any other application that's open is deactivated and put into a dormant state. A *dormant application* is still in memory but is not executing. It may be activated to run in the foreground again, forcing the current active app to be deactivated. (Windows Phone OS 7.1 uses the dormant state, Windows Phone 7.0 does not.)

Several apps can be in a dormant state at the same time. If a new application launches that requires more memory than is available, the operating system tombstones one or more dormant applications. *Tombstoning* terminates an application but saves its state so it can be activated and resume where it left off.

TAKE NOTE *

You should *not* provide a mechanism, such as a button, for a user to quit or exit a Windows Phone application.

A running application continues to run until an action closes the application, such as when:

- The user navigates away from the current application, such as by launching a different application from a Tile on the Start screen
- The user presses the hardware Button repeatedly to navigate backwards to the first page of the application, and then presses the hardware Back button again

Some applications generate data that should be available after an application terminates and is eventually launched again. You'll learn later in this lesson how to save data before an application terminates. First, let's look at some of the events that occur during the application life cycle.

Exploring Windows Phone Application Life Cycle Events

Four primary events occur during the application life cycle, which move an application from one state to another: launching, deactivated, activated, and closing:

- **Launching:** When an application starts from the Start screen, the *Launching event* is raised and a new instance of the application runs. The following code shows the Launching event. Because the Launching event is for new instances, the code doesn't execute when an application reactivates:

```
private void Application_Launching(object sender,
    LaunchingEventArgs e)
{ your code }
```

- **Deactivated:** When a user navigates away from an application, the *Deactivated event* is raised. This occurs when the user presses the Start button or takes a phone call while an application is running, starts another app, or starts a Chooser, for example. The following code shows the Deactivated event:

```
private void Application_Deactivated(object sender,
    DeactivatedEventArgs e)
{ your code }
```

- **Activated:** When a user revisits an application that's dormant or tombstoned, the *Activated event* is raised. The following code shows the Activated event:

```
private void Application_Activated(object sender,
    ActivatedEventArgs e)
{ your code }
```

- **Closing:** As mentioned previously, a user can press the hardware Back button to navigate backwards through an application's pages. When the first page of an application is reached and the Back button is pressed again, the ***Closing event*** is raised and the application terminates. Here is the Closing event code:

```
private void Application_Closing(object sender,
    ClosingEventArgs e)
{ your code }
```

The Visual Studio IDE provides handler stubs (starter code) for the Launching Deactivated, Activated, and Closing events in the App.xaml.cs or App.xaml.vb file of Windows Phone project templates. You simply add code in these event handlers to manage the application state.

 LEARN ABOUT LIFE CYCLE EVENT HANDLERS

GET READY. To learn about life cycle event handlers in a Windows Phone application, per-form the following steps:

1. In the Visual Studio IDE, start a new project using the **Windows Phone Application** template. You don't have to name the project because we'll only view code in the template for this exercise.

2. Expand **App.xaml** in Solution Explorer, and then double-click **App.xaml.cs** or **App.xaml.vb**.

3. Scroll down to locate the Launching event handler stub, shown below:

```
private void Application_Launching(object sender,
    LaunchingEventArgs e)
        {
        }
```

4. Notice that code for the Activated, Deactivated, and Closing events follow, as shown in Figure 6-2.

Figure 6-2

Code stubs for the Launching, Activated, Deactivated, and Closing events

```
// Code to execute when the application is launching (eg, from Start)
// This code will not execute when the application is reactivated
private void Application_Launching(object sender, LaunchingEventArgs e)
{
}

// Code to execute when the application is activated (brought to foreground)
// This code will not execute when the application is first launched
private void Application_Activated(object sender, ActivatedEventArgs e)
{
}

// Code to execute when the application is deactivated (sent to background)
// This code will not execute when the application is closing
private void Application_Deactivated(object sender, DeactivatedEventArgs e)
{
}

// Code to execute when the application is closing (eg, user hit Back)
// This code will not execute when the application is deactivated
private void Application_Closing(object sender, ClosingEventArgs e)
{
}
```

5. Read the comments before each handler. The `Launching` event comments indicate that the event will not execute when the application is reactivated. The `Activated` event will not execute when the application is first launched. The `Deactivated` event will not execute when the application is closing, and the `Closing` event will not execute when the application is deactivated. Knowing what you do about the four events and the application life cycle, explain the comments.

6. Close the project file and leave the Visual Studio IDE open if you plan to complete the next exercise during this session.

Preserving Application State Information and Handling Activate/Deactivate Functions

CERTIFICATION READY
What is the difference between a page state and an application state?
4.1

A **page state** is information about a particular page in an application, like data entered into `TextBox` and `TextBlock` controls, for example. (The concept of a "page" is covered in detail later in this lesson in the "Working with the NavigationService Class" section.) An **application state** is a set of information about an application and includes data used by multiple pages in the application, such as Web service data or a user interface theme.

The Windows Phone operating system provides different ways to save state information on the device: using state dictionaries and isolated storage. Saving state information is what makes it possible to navigate away from a page and then return to the same page as you left it, or to resume an application after it was deactivated and tombstoned.

CROSS REFERENCE *
For more information about isolated storage, see Lesson 2.

Application state data is stored and retrieved through the `PhoneApplicationService.State` property. The `Deactivated` event stores data through the property, whereas the `Activated` event retrieves data. The `IsApplicationInstancePreserved` property of `ActivatedEventArgs` indicates whether the application is returning from a dormant state or if it was tombstoned.

Page data is accessed during or after the page's `OnNavigatedTo` method has been called and during or before the page's `OnNavigatedFrom` method has been called. The `OnNavigatedTo` method is called whenever the user navigates to a page, whether during normal navigation, at launch, or at activation. The `OnNavigatedFrom` method is called whenever the user navigates away from a page, and when the application is deactivated.

TAKE NOTE *

During activation, an application must complete the event handlers and page navigation methods in less than 10 seconds or the application terminates. In practice, this step should be completed as soon as possible. Ten seconds is actually a lot of time, and users might find anything beyond 5 or 6 seconds to be intolerable.

You can store persistent data to isolated storage on your device rather than a state dictionary using the `IsolatedStorageSettings.ApplicationSettings` property. However, loading data from isolated storage can take several seconds depending on the amount or type of data. Microsoft recommends that you use isolated storage for data that will be stored long term.

➡ EXPLORE WINDOWS PHONE STATES

GET READY. To learn about Windows Phone states, perform the following steps:

1. Using a Web browser, go to the "Execution Model Overview for Windows Phone" Web page at http://bit.ly/nMYLLh.

2. Browse the content on the Web page.

3. State dictionaries are mentioned in the Terminology section. Research the term "serializable" to determine its meaning.

4. Search for **PhoneApplicationService.State** on Microsoft.com. What are the exceptions that may be thrown when using the `PhoneApplicationService.State` method?

5. Search for **IsApplicationInstancePreserved** on Microsoft.com. Which namespace does this property belong to?

6. Go to the "How to: Preserve and Restore Page State for Windows Phone" Web page at http://bit.ly/c88DzxAn.

7. Browse the content on the Web page.

8. Locate the **OnNavigatedFrom** and **OnNavigatedTo** methods and examine the code.

9. Close the Web browser.

More on Tombstoning

A tombstoned application has been deactivated but the state information is stored. If a user navigates back to a tombstoned application, it activates. As mentioned in the previous section, the `IsApplicationInstancePreserved` property of `ActivatedEventArgs` indicates whether the application is returning from a dormant state or if it was tombstoned. `IsApplicationInstancePreserved` takes on boolean values: true means the application was dormant, false means the application was tombstoned.

Up to five applications can be tombstoned at a time. Once that maximum is reached, launching another app results in termination of a tombstoned application.

Because you don't know if the user will return to a tombstoned application or not, you should save the data to persistent storage during the Deactivated event.

> **➕ MORE INFORMATION**
>
> The "How to: Preserve and Restore Application State for Windows Phone" Web page at http://bit.ly/rkptDh explores application state handling.

Balancing Code between Battery Usage and Performance

The Windows Phone application life cycle prevents third-party applications from running in the background, by design. Doing so conserves battery life and helps the current active application run as responsively as possible. Windows Phone OS 7.1 introduces some new features that allow an application to perform actions in the background while another app is active and running. A few of the new features are:

- **Background audio:** Windows Phone can play an audio application when another application is executing. The audio application has to register an AudioPlayerAgent that runs in the background.

- **Fast Application Switching:** When a user navigates away from an application in Windows Phone OS 7.1, the application goes into the dormant state. Fast Application Switching is built in to the operating system and enables the user to resume a dormant application very quickly. This feature is similar in principle to Fast User Switching or program switching in the Windows operating system.

- **Scheduled tasks:** Background agents enable you to supply code that the operating system runs periodically, even when the associated application isn't running.

The ability for a native application to run in the background is referred to as multitasking.

EXPLORE BACKGROUND AUDIO

GET READY. To see how the `BackgroundAudioPlayer` agent and `AudioPlayerAgent` work, perform the following steps:

1. In the Visual Studio IDE, go to the Start page, and click **Code Samples for Windows Phone** in the Learning Resources section.

2. Download and install the C# version of **Background Audio Player Sample** to your Projects folder. (If you're not sure how to access this code sample, refer to the Download a Code Sample exercise in Lesson 1.) This code sample implements the `AudioPlayerAgent`.

3. Open the project in your Visual Studio IDE. Notice that two projects are listed in Solution Explorer: the application project and the background agent project. See Figure 6-3.

Figure 6-3

This solution includes an application project and a background agent project

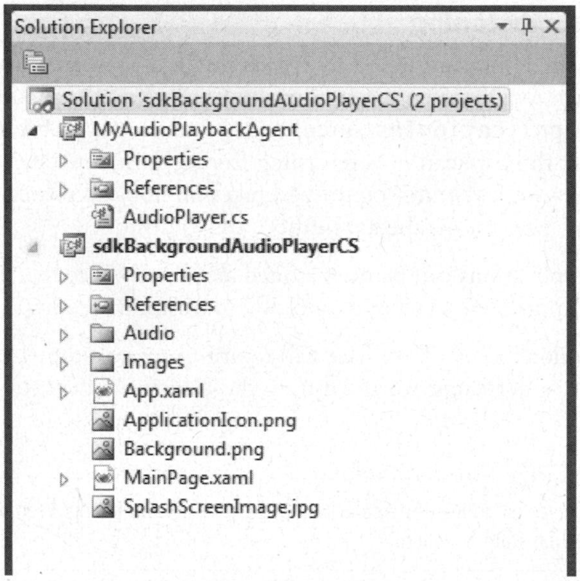

4. Click the **Start Debugging** button on the toolbar or press **F5** to launch the application in Windows Phone Emulator.

5. In the emulator, click the **Play** button (the middle button).

6. When the music begins to play, click the **Start** button at the bottom of the emulator, and then click the **Internet Explorer** tile. Notice that the audio continues to play even though the browser is now the active foreground application.

7. Close the emulator and then click **OK** in the Visual Studio IDE.

8. Let's examine the code that applies to multitasking. In Solution Explorer, right-click **App.xaml**. In Code Editor, notice that the following using statements are included in this code sample:

```
using System.IO.IsolatedStorage;
using System.Windows.Resources;
using System.Windows.Navigation;
using Microsoft.Phone.BackgroundAudio;
```

9. Scroll down to the CopyToIsolatedStorage method, as shown in Figure 6-4. The BackgroundAudioPlayer agent plays files from isolated storage or from a remote Uniform Resource Identifier (URI). The files array lists the names of the audio files pulled from storage. There's a call to this method near the beginning of the App class section.

Figure 6-4

The CopyToIsolatedStorage method

```
/// <summary>
/// Copies the files from the application data to isolated storage.
/// </summary>
private void CopyToIsolatedStorage()
{
    using (IsolatedStorageFile storage = IsolatedStorageFile.GetUserStoreForApplication())
    {
        // Copy audio files to isolated storage
        string[] files = new string[] { "Ring01.wma", "Ring02.wma", "Ring03.wma" };

        foreach (var _fileName in files)
        {
            if (!storage.FileExists(_fileName))
            {
                string _filePath = "Audio/" + _fileName;
                StreamResourceInfo resource = Application.GetResourceStream(new Uri(_filePath, UriKind.Relative));

                using (IsolatedStorageFileStream file = storage.CreateFile(_fileName))
                {
                    int chunkSize = 4096;
                    byte[] bytes = new byte[chunkSize];
                    int byteCount;

                    while ((byteCount = resource.Stream.Read(bytes, 0, chunkSize)) > 0)
                    {
                        file.Write(bytes, 0, byteCount);
                    }
                }
            }
        }
    }
}
```

10. The AudioPlayerAgent runs in the background when you switch to a different foreground application, such as when you launched Internet Explore in the emulator. The agent is implemented in the AudioPlayer.cs file. Double-click the **AudioPlayer.cs** file to view it in Code Editor and browse the code. Play state changes are handled by the OnPlayStateChanged method, as shown in Figure 6-5.

Figure 6-5

The OnPlayState-Changed method

```
/// </summary>
/// <param name="player">The BackgroundAudioPlayer</param>
/// <param name="track">The track playing at the time the playstate changed</param>
/// <param name="playState">The new playstate of the player</param>
/// <remarks>
/// Play State changes cannot be cancelled. They are raised even if the application
/// caused the state change itself, assuming the application has opted-in to the callback.
///
/// Notable playstate events:
/// (a) TrackEnded: invoked when the player has no current track. The agent can set the next track.
/// (b) TrackReady: an audio track has been set and it is now ready for playack.
///
/// Call NotifyComplete() only once, after the agent request has been completed, including async callbacks.
/// </remarks>
protected override void OnPlayStateChanged(BackgroundAudioPlayer player, AudioTrack track, PlayState playState)
{
    switch (playState)
    {
        case PlayState.TrackEnded:
            PlayNextTrack(player);
            break;

        case PlayState.TrackReady:
            // The track to play is set in the PlayTrack method.
            player.Play();
            break;
    }

    NotifyComplete();
}
```

11. Close the code sample file and leave Visual Studio 2010 Express open if you continue to the next exercise during this session.

➕ **MORE INFORMATION**

Visit the "Multitasking for Windows Phone" Web page at http://bit.ly/phuCRK for details about background applications.

CERTIFICATION READY
When an application throws an exception, what does Microsoft require applications to provide to users?
4.1

Providing User Feedback and Visible Status for Applications

Microsoft requires that Windows Phone applications provide a user-friendly message when handling exceptions. In addition, an application must display a visual progress bar or busy indicator if an application appears unresponsive for more than three seconds due to a time-intensive operation such as a large file download.

If you decide not to use a progress bar, you should provide a button or other control that enables the user to cancel the operation if they choose.

CERTIFICATION READY
What is an example of a visible status for a long-running operation?
4.1

As noted in Lesson 5, you can use the progress and message controls to provide feedback to users. The `ProgressBar` control displays a visual status of a time-intensive operation, like downloading data across a network connection. The `Popup` control displays a message, such as an alert or an error message, on top of content currently displayed. Figure 6-6 shows a progress bar that's part of the Custom Indeterminate Progress Bar code sample.

Figure 6-6

A progress bar that displays red dots across the screen

Microsoft also requires that applications display some kind of feedback to users within a few seconds of launching an app. The easiest method is to use a *splash screen*, which is generally a JPG file that displays as soon as a user launches an application and continues to display until the application loads.

Windows Phone templates in the Visual Studio IDE include a default splash screen named SplashScreenImage.jpg. The file has an icon of a clock against a black background.

CERTIFICATION READY
What are the requirements for creating your own splash screen?
4.1

You can create your own splash screen using any image you want. Many developers use the splash screen to provide branding for their apps. The splash screen file must be 480 pixels wide by 800 pixels tall and named SplashScreenImage.jpg. The `Build Action` property must be set to `Content`.

You can also create an animated splash screen that indicates progress if your app takes a while to load. The easiest animation would be to use the Performance Progress Bar in the Silverlight toolkit.

CREATE A SPLASH SCREEN

GET READY. To create a splash screen, perform the following steps:

1. In a graphics program such as Microsoft Paint, create a JPG that's 480 x 800 pixels in size. To open Paint, click Start, type **paint** in the Start menu **Search programs and files** text box, and click **Paint** in the results list.

2. In Paint, click the menu button in the upper-left corner of the window and select **Properties** in the resulting menu.

3. In the Image Properties dialog box, change the Width setting to **480** and the Height setting to **800.** Click **OK.**

4. To create a colored background, click the **Color 1** button on the toolbar, click the background color swatch of your choice in the color palette, click the **Fill with color** button on the toolbar (which looks like a paint bucket), and then click anywhere in the drawing canvas.

5. To add text, click the **Color 1** button again, and then click the **white** color in the color palette.

6. Click the **Text** button on the toolbar (the Text button looks like a capital "A"), drag to create a text box in the upper half of the drawing canvas as shown in Figure 6-7, and then type **MyFirstApp** in the text box.

Figure 6-7

Adding text to the splash screen

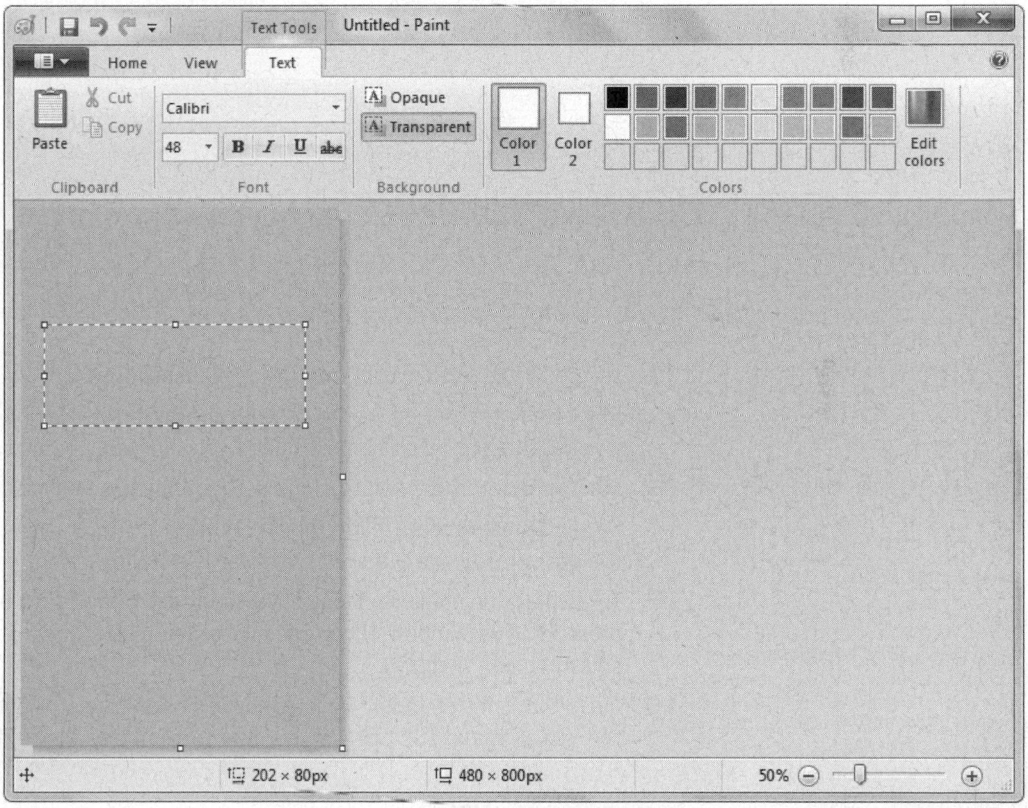

7. Highlight the text and select the font and font size of your choice.

8. Center the text on the canvas by hovering your mouse pointer over an edge of the text box until the pointer changes to a four-arrow cross, click and hold the left mouse button, and then move the box until it looks centered.

9. Create another text box in the lower half of the drawing canvas and type **Loading . . .** in the text box. Center the box if necessary.

10. Click the menu button in the upper-left corner of the window, select **Save**, navigate to the Windows desktop, enter **SplashScreenImage** in the File name text box, select JPEG from the File type drop-down list, and click **Save**. Your splash screen should look similar to Figure 6-8.

Figure 6-8

A custom splash screen

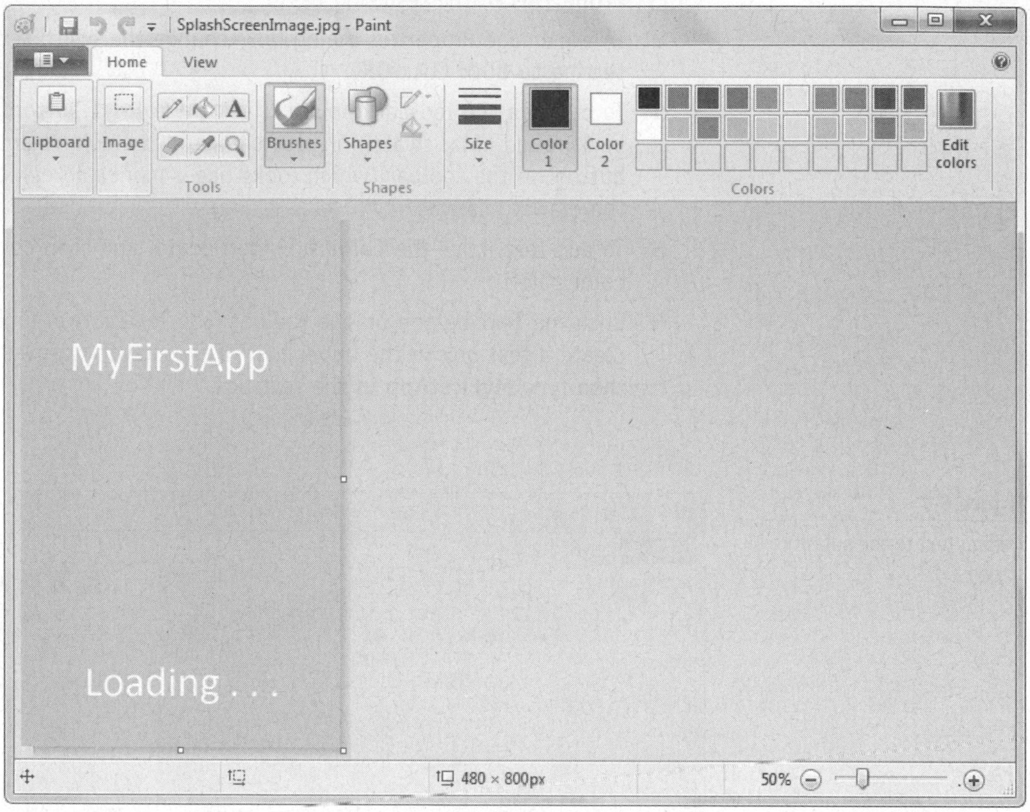

11. In the Visual Studio IDE, open the MyFirstApp project you created in Lesson 3.

12. Right-click the project name in Solution Explorer, select **Add**, select **Existing Item**, navigate to the **SplashScreenImage.jpg** file you created, select it, and then click **Add**.

13. When prompted to replace the existing SplashScreenImage.jpg file, click **Yes**.

14. Select **SplashScreenImage.jpg** in Solution Explorer. Display the Properties window if it's not already available. Ensure that the Build Action value is set to **Content**.

15. To display the splash screen, click the **Start Debugging** button on the toolbar or press **F5**. The Windows Phone Emulator launches. Once the code begins to load, the splash screen displays.

16. Close the Paint program. Close Windows Phone Emulator and the project file, but leave the Visual Studio IDE open if you plan to complete the next exercise during this session.

Storing Passwords

In order to safely store passwords, PINs, and other private data on a device, you must encrypt the data. Windows 7.1 OS provides the *Data Protection API (DPAPI)* for this purpose. You use the ProtectedData class and the Protect and Unprotect methods to encrypt and decrypt data, respectively. ProtectedData provides a mechanism for encrypting byte arrays and then decrypting them to return them to their original state. The ProtectedData class is in the System.Security.Cryptography namespace.

CERTIFICATION READY
Which API can you use to store passwords securely on a Windows Phone?
4.1

In the following code sample from the Microsoft site for an application that protects PINs on a device, the PIN is first converted and then encrypted using the Protect method. The Protect method uses the data to be encrypted as parameters. The null byte array means the complexity of the encryption is not being increased. Finally, the encrypted PIN is stored in isolated storage.

```
private void BtnStore_Click(object sender, RoutedEventArgs e)
{
    // Convert PIN to a byte[]
    byte[] PinByte = Encoding.UTF8.GetBytes(TBPin.Text);

    // Encrypt PIN using Protect() method
    byte[] ProtectedPinByte = ProtectedData.Protect(PinByte, null);

    // Store encrypted PIN in isolated storage
    this.WritePinToFile(ProtectedPinByte);

    TBPin.Text = "";
}
```

The Unprotect method uses the encrypted data as parameters.

 EXPLORE DATA ENCRYPTION

GET READY. To learn more about data encryption in Windows Phone OS 7.1, perform the following steps:

1. Using a Web browser, visit the "How to: Encrypt Data in a Windows Phone Application" Web page at http://msdn.microsoft.com/en-us/library/hh487164(v=VS.92).aspx.

2. Read the page and then follow the steps to create the PIN encryption application.

3. Test the program in the Windows Phone Emulator to test the interface. Although the encryption may require a physical device, the exercise helps you become familiar with the code required to encrypt data.

4. Close the project file, but leave the Visual Studio IDE open if you plan to complete the next exercise during this session.

Understanding Mobile Device APIs

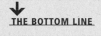
↓
THE BOTTOM LINE

The NavigationService class enables users to navigate two or more pages in an application. The Location API gathers location information from a Windows Phone device. The Bing Maps Silverlight Control for Windows Phone displays maps in applications based on user input. HTML5 provides the forms, canvas, and audio and video features, which can be created with minimal code. Manipulation events include tap, double tap, drag, pinch, and flick, and the last three are controlled by the ManipulationStarted, ManipulationDelta, and ManipulationCompleted methods.

This section covers several Windows Phone APIs. You'll begin by exploring the NavigationService class for moving between pages of an application. Then you'll see how location information is gathered from a Windows Phone device and used in applications, and learn how to incorporate dynamic maps in applications. Next, you'll learn how to create forms and canvas drawings, and deliver audio and video from an HTML5 perspective. Finally, you'll discover how to incorporate manipulation (touch) methods into your applications.

Working with the NavigationService Class

The `NavigationService` class is responsible for enabling movement between pages of a Windows Phone application, similar to how a user moves from one Web page to another on a Web site.

CERTIFICATION READY
What is the purpose of the `NavigationService` class?
4.2

Windows Phone applications use a navigation model similar to how Web page browsing works. As a user moves from one page to another, the application keeps track of pages and allows the user to view previous pages using the phone's hardware Back button. This functionality is provided by the ***NavigationService class***.

The Windows Phone navigation model is based on `PhoneApplicationFrame` controls, which is what enables users to navigate through pages. A frame is a kind of container that contains one or more pages. A page is a Silverlight page that contains content, and may include links and/or buttons. A link or button lets the user move to another page. Figure 6-9 shows an example of a page within a frame. You've seen this concept in all of the Windows Phone Emulator examples throughout the book.

Figure 6-9

A page within a frame

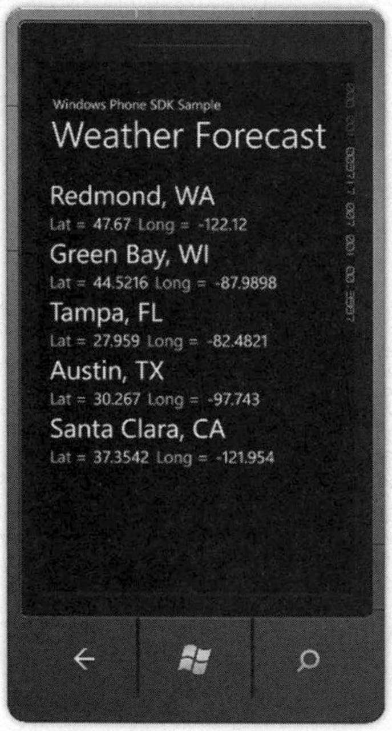

It's important to note moving from a splash screen or a login screen to the Start screen isn't considered to be navigation, rather, it's referred to as a transition. In Windows Phone, moving between two pages is considered navigation.

To use the `NavigationService` class to move between pages of a two-page application, use a hyperlink or a button and code it with the `NavigationService.Navigate` method to navigate to the another page.

ADD NAVIGATION TO MOVE TO A SECOND PAGE

GET READY. To create an app with two pages and provide a hyperlink from one page to another, perform the following steps:

1. In the Visual Studio IDE, create a new project based on the Windows Phone Application C# template.
2. Name it **MyNavigation**. This application has a single page.

3. To add a second page to the application, right-click the **MyNavigation** project in Solution Explorer and select **Add > New Item**.

4. In the Add New Item dialog box, select **Windows Phone Portrait Page**.

5. In the Name textbox at the bottom of the dialog box, enter **SecondPage.xaml** and click **Add**.

6. In Solution Explorer, double-click **MainPage.xaml**.

7. In the design surface, select the My Application box. This highlights the appropriate TextBox control in Code Editor. In Code Editor, change the Text property to **My Navigation**.

8. In Solution Explorer, double-click **SecondPage.xaml**.

9. In the design surface, select the **My Application** box and change the Text property in Code Editor to **My Navigation**.

10. In the design surface, click the Page Name box. Change Text="page name" to **Text="Page 2"** in Code Editor. See Figure 6-10.

Figure 6-10

Modifications made to SecondPage.xaml

```
<!--TitlePanel contains the name of the application and page title-->
<StackPanel x:Name="TitlePanel" Grid.Row="0" Margin="12,17,0,28">
    <TextBlock x:Name="ApplicationTitle" Text="MY NAVIGATION" Style="{StaticResource PhoneTextNormalStyle}"/>
    <TextBlock x:Name="PageTitle" Text="Page 2" Margin="9,-7,0,0" Style="{StaticResource PhoneTextTitle1Style}"/>
</StackPanel>
```

11. In Solution Explorer, double-click **MainPage.xaml**.

12. Open the Toolbox, if necessary, and drag the **HyperlinkButton** control from the Toolbox onto the design surface and drop it below the Page 1 box.

13. Double-click the **HyperlinkButton** control. The MainPage.xaml.cs file opens in Code Editor showing a new OnClick event handler stub.

14. In the hyperlinkButton1_Click method add the following code between the curly brackets, as shown in Figure 6-11:

```
NavigationService.Navigate(new Uri("/SecondPage.xaml",
    UriKind.RelativeOrAbsolute));
```

This code uses the NavigationService.Navigate method to navigate to the second page in the application.

Figure 6-11

Adding the NavigationService.Navigate method

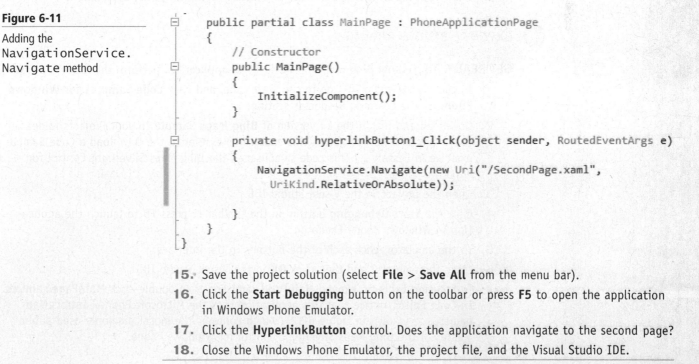

```
public partial class MainPage : PhoneApplicationPage
{
    // Constructor
    public MainPage()
    {
        InitializeComponent();
    }

    private void hyperlinkButton1_Click(object sender, RoutedEventArgs e)
    {
        NavigationService.Navigate(new Uri("/SecondPage.xaml",
            UriKind.RelativeOrAbsolute));

    }
}
```

15. Save the project solution (select **File > Save All** from the menu bar).

16. Click the **Start Debugging** button on the toolbar or press **F5** to open the application in Windows Phone Emulator.

17. Click the **HyperlinkButton** control. Does the application navigate to the second page?

18. Close the Windows Phone Emulator, the project file, and the Visual Studio IDE.

➕ MORE INFORMATION

The "Frame and Page Navigation Overview for Windows Phone" at http://bit.ly/M9EIHw. The NavigationService class is detailed at http://bit.ly/N303BS.

Using Mapping and GeoLocation APIs

Windows Phone devices have built-in GPS hardware you can use to determine the device's latitude and longitude. The Location API works with the hardware and the Microsoft Location Service to provide location information to applications. The Bing Maps Silverlight Control for Windows Phone enables you to provide dynamic maps in applications.

Windows Phone devices have built-in GPS hardware to detect the geographic positioning of the device. Geolocation works with a device's Accelerometer, Compass, and Gyroscope features. A Windows Phone can also use Wi-Fi and cellular connections to determine geolocation. GPS is more accurate but consumes more battery power, so it's best to use GPS only when high accuracy is needed.

Geolocation is handy not only for knowing your current longitude and latitude coordinates, but can be used in applications for geo-tagging Twitter tweets, discovering services nearby, and sharing your location with co-workers and friends.

The Windows Phone 7 *Location API* allows you to determine the current position and movement of the device, expressed in latitude and longitude. Applications can determine a device's geographic location by using the Microsoft Location Service, a Microsoft-hosted Web service. This service collects data from the device and looks up the information in its databases.

Developers creating any location-aware applications must keep user privacy in mind. Therefore, you should build in a prompt that runs when the application first opens that enables users to give consent for the application to use their location.

Another way to provide location information in applications is to incorporate mapping using Bing Maps. You need to use the Bing Maps Silverlight Control for Windows Phone and sign up for a key from the Bing Maps service, which lets you authorize the application.

CERTIFICATION READY
Which API can you use to create location-aware applications?
4.2

➡ EXPLORE BING MAPPING

GET READY. To see how Bing mapping works in an application, perform the following steps:

1. In the Visual Studio IDE, go to the Start page, and click **Code Samples for Windows Phone** in the Learning Resources section.

2. Download and install the C# version of **Bing Maps Sample** to your Projects folder. (If you're not sure how to access this code sample, refer to the Download a Code Sample exercise in Lesson 1.) This code sample uses the Bing Maps Silverlight Control for Windows Phone.

3. Open the project in the Visual Studio IDE.

4. Click the **Start Debugging** button on the toolbar or press **F5** to launch the application in Windows Phone Emulator.

5. In the emulator, click each of the buttons in the interface.

6. Close the emulator and then click **OK** in the Visual Studio IDE.

7. In Solution Explorer, expand **MainPage.xaml** and then double-click **MainPage.xaml.cs**. In Code Editor, notice that this application uses the Microsoft.Phone.Controls.Maps namespace (shown in Figure 6-12), which contains the most commonly used public classes of the Bing Maps Silverlight Control for Windows Phone.

Figure 6-12

The Bing Maps Sample
MainPage.xaml.cs file

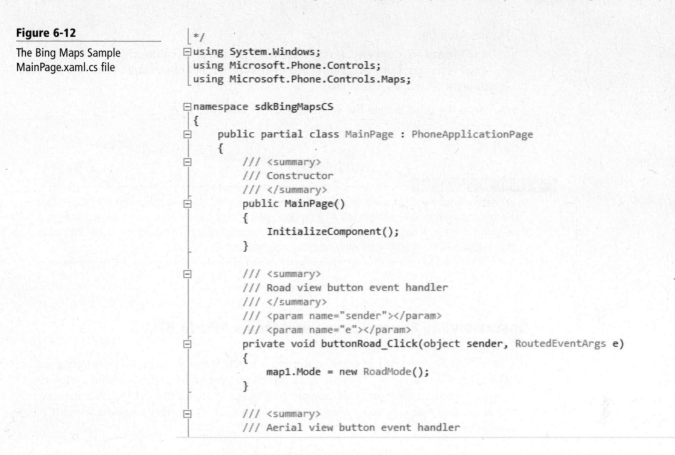

```csharp
*/
using System.Windows;
using Microsoft.Phone.Controls;
using Microsoft.Phone.Controls.Maps;

namespace sdkBingMapsCS
{
    public partial class MainPage : PhoneApplicationPage
    {
        /// <summary>
        /// Constructor
        /// </summary>
        public MainPage()
        {
            InitializeComponent();
        }

        /// <summary>
        /// Road view button event handler
        /// </summary>
        /// <param name="sender"></param>
        /// <param name="e"></param>
        private void buttonRoad_Click(object sender, RoutedEventArgs e)
        {
            map1.Mode = new RoadMode();
        }

        /// <summary>
        /// Aerial view button event handler
```

8. In Solution Explorer, expand App.xaml and then double-click **App.xaml.cs**. Browse the code in Code Editor. You'll see that some code, such as `Application.Current.Host.Settings.EnableRedrawRegions = true`, is commented out. (See Figure 6-13.) A live version of this app is available through the Windows Marketplace and is fully functioning.

Figure 6-13

The `OnPlayState-Changed` method

```csharp
public App()
{
    // Global handler for uncaught exceptions.
    UnhandledException += Application_UnhandledException;

    // Standard Silverlight initialization
    InitializeComponent();

    // Phone-specific initialization
    InitializePhoneApplication();

    // Show graphics profiling information while debugging.
    if (System.Diagnostics.Debugger.IsAttached)
    {
        // Display the current frame rate counters.
        Application.Current.Host.Settings.EnableFrameRateCounter = false;

        // Show the areas of the app that are being redrawn in each frame.
        //Application.Current.Host.Settings.EnableRedrawRegions = true;

        // Enable non-production analysis visualization mode,
        // which shows areas of a page that are handed off to GPU with a colored overlay.
        //Application.Current.Host.Settings.EnableCacheVisualization = true;

        // Disable the application idle detection by setting the UserIdleDetectionMode property of the
        // application's PhoneApplicationService object to Disabled.
        // Caution:- Use this under debug mode only. Application that disables user idle detection will continue to run
        // and consume battery power when the user is not using the phone.
        PhoneApplicationService.Current.UserIdleDetectionMode = IdleDetectionMode.Disabled;
    }
}
```

9. Research the

   `Application.Current.Host.Settings.EnableRedrawRegions` and
   `Application.Current.Host.Settings.EnableCacheVisualization` methods
   to learn what they accomplish.

10. Close the code sample file and the Visual Studio IDE.

➕ MORE INFORMATION

To get details about the Location API, go to the Microsoft "Location API" Web site at http://bit.ly/M9DQVV. The "How to: Get Data from the Location Service for Windows Phone" Web page at http://bit.ly/rc6MzG provides steps for creating a location-aware app. Visit the "Bing Maps Silverlight Control for Windows Phone" Web page at http://bit.ly/cDUWAQ to learn more about mapping in mobile devices.

Understanding Forms, Canvas, and Media APIs in HTML5

The HTML5 Forms API lets you create simple input forms to gather data from mobile Web users. Canvas is a drawing program that creates dynamic graphics within a browser based on calculations rather than having to reference static images. Media APIs include the audio and video element, which enable you to stream or embed multimedia with a minimum of code.

HTML5 provides several new application programming interfaces (APIs) that you can use to develop or enhance mobile Web applications. They include the Forms API for capturing input from users, Canvas for creating drawings on the fly, and GeoLocation for determining a device's location.

Forms

A Web form is a Web page that provides input fields for a user to enter data, which is sent to a server for processing. From there, the information is stored in a database or forwarded to a recipient. HTML5 introduces several new form and input element attributes, such as `url` for entering a single Web address, `email` for a single email address or a list of email addresses, and `search` to prompt users to enter text they want to search for. The new attributes make form development much easier than in the past. What used to take a lot of scripting can be accomplished by HTML5 tags.

On the flip side, many of the new attributes are not yet supported by all of the major browsers. However, if you use a new element or attribute that isn't yet supported, the browser "falls back" to an alternate display, a different form of input, or what have you.

To create a form, use the `<form>` start and end tags. All of the form's content and fields go between the two `<form>` tags. Most forms also include the `id` attribute in the start tag, as follows:

```
<form id="keyword">
    <content and fields>
</form>
```

The `fieldset` element is used with many forms to group related elements. The `<fieldset>` tag draws a box around individual elements and/or around the entire form, as shown in Figure 6-14.

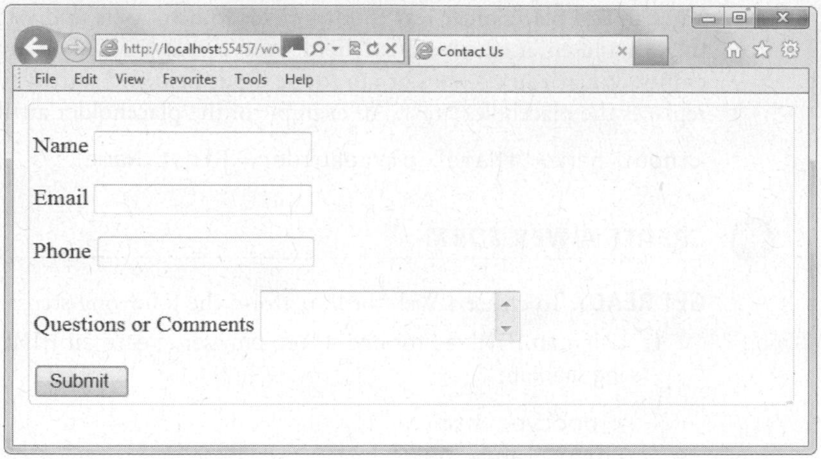

Figure 6-14

The `fieldset` element groups related elements in a form and adds a border

If the form is included in an HTML document with other items, you can use the `<div>` tag at the beginning and end of the form to separate it from other content. Using the `<div>` tag also lets you include inline formatting, if the form is short and simple and you don't want to create a CSS style sheet. The `<div>` tag uses the `id` attribute and appears before the first `<form>` tag. The `label` element displays the label for each field.

An example of the markup for a very simple form is:

```
<div id="contact-form"
  style="font-family:'Arial Narrow','Nimbus Sans L',sans-
  serif;">
    <form id="contact" method="post" action="">
      <fieldset>
        <label for="name">Name</label>
        <input type="text" name="name" />
      </fieldset>
      <fieldset>
        <label for="email">Email</label>
        <input type="email" name="email" />
      </fieldset>
    </form>
</div> <!-- end of contact-form -->
```

The form is shown in Figure 6-15.

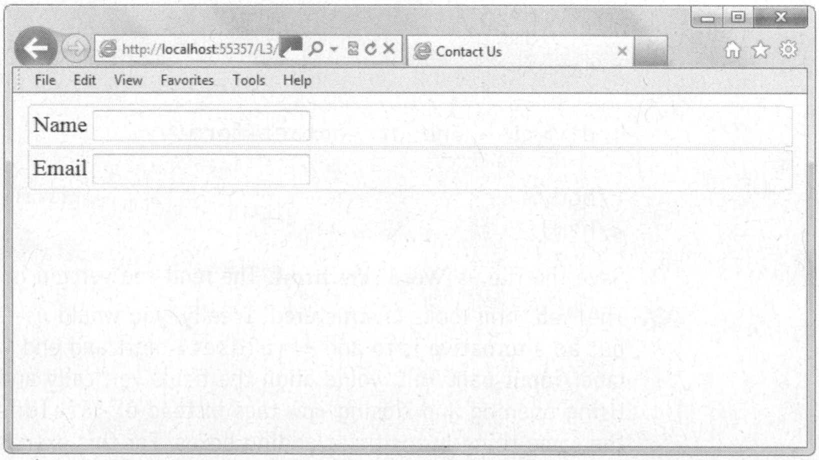

Figure 6-15

A very simple form

You can add placeholder text to form fields to help users understand the type of information they should enter or select. Placeholder text displays inside an input field when the field is empty. When you click on or tab to the input field and start typing, the newly entered text replaces the placeholder text. An example of the placeholder attribute is:

```
<input name="fName" placeholder="First Name" />
```

 CREATE A WEB FORM

GET READY. To create a Web form, perform the following steps:

1. Using an HTML editor and a Web browser, create an HTML document with the following markup:

```
<!doctype html>
<html lang="en">
<head>
<meta charset="utf-8">
<title>Contact Us</title>
</head>
<body>
  <div id="contact-form">

  <form id="contact" method="post" action="">
  <fieldset>

  <label for="custname">Name</label>
  <input type="text" id="custname" />

  <label for="email">Email</label>
  <input type="email" id="email" />

  <label for="phone">Phone</label>
  <input type="text" id="phone" />

  <label for="message">Questions or
    Comments</label>
  <textarea name="message"></textarea>

  <input type="submit" name="submit" id="submit"
    value="Submit" />

</fieldset>
</form>

</div><!-- End of contact-form -->

</body>
</html>
```

2. Save the file as **WebForm.html**. The rendered version is shown in Figure 6-16.

3. The Web form looks unstructured. Ideally, you would use CSS to apply alignment, but an alternative is to add <fieldset> start and end tags around each label/input pair. This would align the fields vertically and add boxes around them. Using opening and closing <p> tags instead of <fieldset> tags would accomplish the same thing but without adding boxes. For this exercise, use the <p> tags.

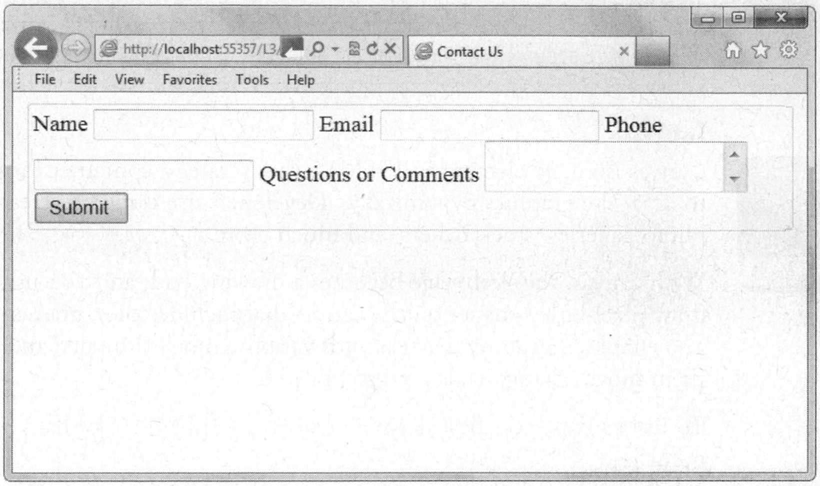

Figure 6-16

The beginning of a Web form

Figure 6-17 shows the same Web form with <p> tags around the label/input pairs, including the comments field.

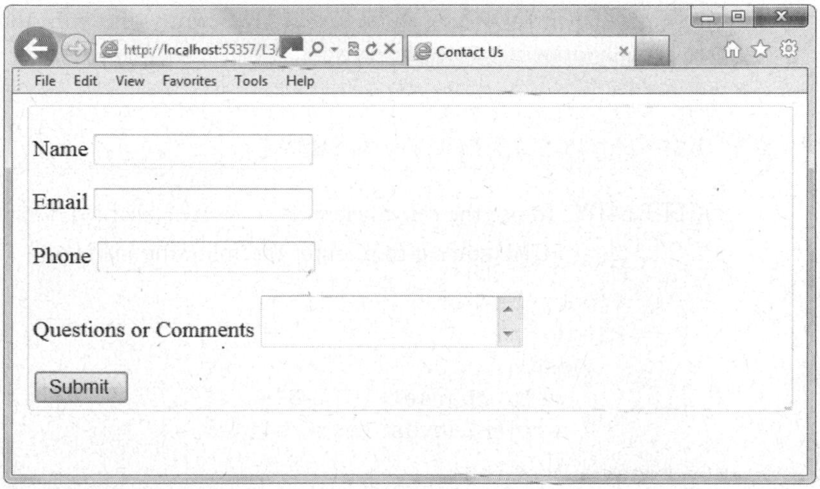

Figure 6-17

A Web form using <p> tags to align fields vertically

4. Add placeholder text to all fields. The result should look similar to Figure 6-18.

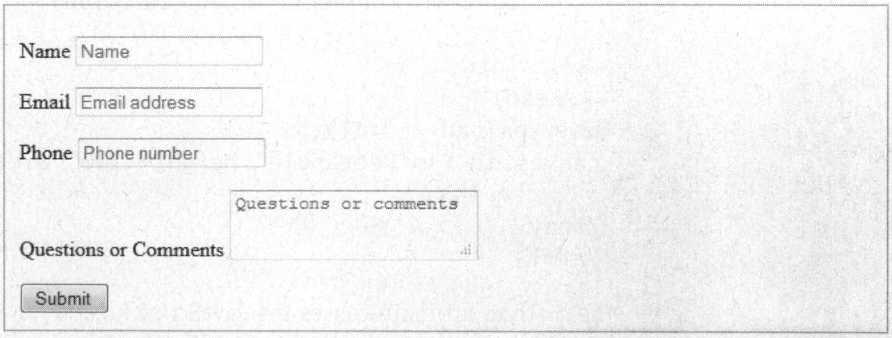

Figure 6-18

A Web form with placeholders added to each field

5. Resave the file.
6. Close the file but leave the HTML editing tool and Web browser open if you continue to the next exercise during this session.

➕ MORE INFORMATION

To learn more about HTML5 input element attributes, go to the W3c.org Web site at http://bit.ly/I1PW3P.

Canvas

CERTIFICATION READY
What is canvas in HTML5?
4.2

Canvas is a new element in HTML5 that creates a container for graphics and uses JavaScript to draw the graphics dynamically. Developers use canvas to create online games, rotating photo galleries, stock tickers, and much more.

With canvas, the Web page becomes a drawing pad, and you use JavaScript commands to draw pixel-based shapes on the canvas that include color, gradients, and pattern fills. Canvas also enables you to render text with various embellishments, and animate objects by making them move, change scale, and so on.

To use canvas, you first define a canvas in HTML. The basic syntax for the canvas element is:

```
<canvas id="smlRectangle" height="100" width="200"></canvas>
```

This element creates your drawing pad. The canvas element requires the **id** attribute to reference the canvas in JavaScript. You should also specify the dimensions of the canvas—the height and width—which are in pixels. JavaScript works with the two-dimensional (2D) API to actually draw items on the canvas.

➡ USE CANVAS TO CREATE A SHAPE

GET READY. To use the canvas element to create a shape, perform the following steps:

1. In an HTML editing tool, enter the following markup:

```
<!doctype html>
<html>
  <head>
    <meta charset="UTF-8">
    <title>Canvas Test</title>
<script>
    function f1() {
       var canvas =
         document.getElementById("smlRectangle");
       context = canvas.getContext("2d");
       context.fillStyle = "rgb(0,0,255)";
       context.fillRect(10, 20, 200, 100);
    }
  </script>
  </head>
<body onload = "f1();">
<canvas id="smlRectangle" height="100" width="200 ">
   </canvas>
</body>
</html>
```

TAKE NOTE *

You can include JavaScripts inside the head element of your HTML document, or in an external file.

The **onload** attribute causes the JavaScript function in the script to run. This script first finds the element with the id smlRectangle:

```
var canvas = document.getElementById("smlRectangle");
```

The **context.fillStyle** property sets the style that fills the rectangle to the color blue using the RGB values 0, 0, 255. The **context.fillRect** method creates a

200-pixel wide × 100-pixel tall rectangle, positioned 10 pixels down and 20 pixels over from the upper-left corner of the canvas and fills it using the color specified by `fillStyle`.

2. Save the file as **canvas.html** and view it in a browser. The shape should appear as shown in Figure 6-19.

Figure 6-19

The Web page with a canvas shape

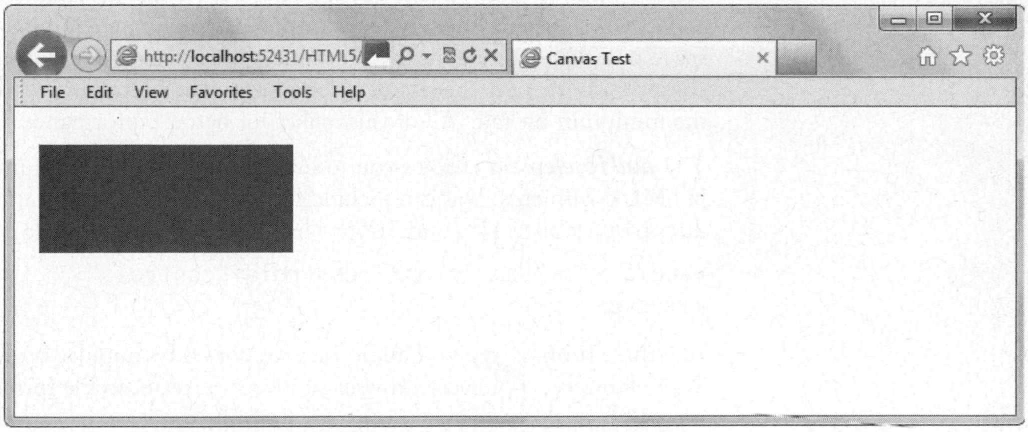

3. If a blue rectangle doesn't appear, go to the W3C Markup Validation Service Web page at **http://validator.w3.org**. Upload **canvas.html** and click **Check** to have the service check it. Fix any errors reported by the checker. Save the file again and view it in a browser.

4. Close the file but leave the HTML editing tool and Web browser open if you continue to the next exercise during this session.

Audio and Video

The HTML5 audio element and video element enable you to provide multimedia from a Web browser without the need for plug-ins, such as those for Microsoft Windows Media Player, Microsoft Silverlight, Adobe Flash, and Apple QuickTime. You use the `<video>` and `<audio>` tags in HTML documents to incorporate multimedia.

The *video element* enables you to incorporate videos in HTML documents using minimal code. The following is an example of the markup for embedding an MP4 file to a Web page:

```
<video src="video.mp4" width="400" height="300">
</video>
```

The `src` attribute points to the name of the video file (in this case, video.mp4) to be played. The height and width attributes specify the size of window in which the video will display.

Other attributes are available that you can add for control of the video:

- **poster:** Displays a static image file before the video loads
- **autoplay:** Start playing the video automatically upon page load
- **controls:** Displays a set of controls for playing, pausing, and stopping the video, and controlling the volume
- **loop:** Repeats the video

Using all of the aforementioned control attributes, the markup would look similar to this:

```
<video src="video.mp4"
    width="400" height="300
    poster="splash.jpg"
```

```
      autoplay="autoplay"
      controls="controls"
      loop="loop">
</video>
```

Notice that this markup refers to an MP4 video file. Other popular Web video formats also include H.264, OGG, and WebM. Along with a video format, you should also specify the codec, which is a technology used for compressing data. Compression reduces the amount of space needed to store a file, and it reduces the bandwidth needed to transmit the file. Video compression reduces the size of video images while retaining the highest quality video with the minimum bit rate. All of this makes for better performance.

The **_audio element_** enables you to incorporate audio, such as music and other sounds, in HTML documents. You can include the same control-related attributes as the video element: `autoplay`, `controls`, and `loop`. This example shows just the controls attribute included:

```
<audio src="sample.mp3" controls="controls">
</audio>
```

The three primary types of audio files supported by popular browsers are OGG, MP3, and WAV. However, not every browser supports every audio file format, at least not today. For the most part, MP3 is the best choice for multiple browser compatibility.

To help ensure your audio plays on the majority of browsers and devices, use the `source` attribute to include multiple formats in your markup. This example shows the same audio file available in two formats:

```
<audio controls="controls">
  <source src="sample.ogg" type="audio/ogg" />
  <source src="sample.mp3" type="audio/mp3" />
</audio>
```

You can find a lot of free audio files, which are also royalty and copyright free, at http://flashkit.com. This is a good resource for learners, and for developers who may need a sound effect for a project. Another source is the Public Domain Sherpa Web site at http://www.public domainsherpa.com/public-domain-recordings.html. You can also make your own recordings using your computer and recording software. Windows includes the Sound Recorder, which lets you save audio files in WAV format.

→ WORK WITH THE VIDEO ELEMENT

GET READY. To work with the HTML5 `video` element, perform the following steps:

1. Create a folder on your computer named **HTML5**.

2. Locate an MP4 video clip. If you don't have a video clip on your computer, search for a public domain MP4 file on the Web and download it. Save the video file to your HTML5 folder.

3. In your HTML editing tool, create an HTML file with the following markup. Replace **sample.mp4** with the name of your video file.

```
<!doctype html>
<html>
  <head>
    <meta charset="UTF-8">
    <title>Video Example</title>
  </head>
<body>
  <video
    width="400" height="300"
```

```
        autoplay="autoplay"
        controls="controls">
        <source src="sample.mp4" type="video/mp4" />
    </video>
  </body>
</html>
```

4. Save your file as **video.html**.

5. Go to the W3C Markup Validation Service Web page at **http://validator.w3.org**. Upload **video.html** and click **Check** to have the service check it. Fix any errors reported by the checker that relate to missing tags or typos, if any.

6. Open the HTML file in a Web browser. Does the video play automatically? Do the controls appear? You should open the video.html file in a few different Web browsers as a test. The major Web browsers are Internet Explorer, Mozilla Firefox, Opera, Apple Safari, and Google Chrome.

7. Close the file, the editing tool, and the Web browser.

➕ MORE INFORMATION

For more information on incorporating multimedia into HTML5 mobile Web pages, go to http://bit.ly/M3aLfU.

Understanding Manipulation Events

> Windows Phone devices have a four-point multi-touch screen for capturing gestures as input. Standard gestures include tap, double tap, drag, flick, and pinch. The `System.Windows.Input.Touch.FrameReported` event, which is in the `System.Windows.Input.Touch` class, is called when a user creates individual touch contact points like tap, double tap, and hold. The `ManipulationStarted`, `ManipulationDelta`, and `ManipulationCompleted` events control more complicated gestures such as drag, pinch, and flick.

Windows Phone applications can use touch events, mouse events, and manipulation events for user input. You learned in Lesson 1 that Windows Phone devices have a four-point multi-touch screen for capturing gestures. Standard gestures include tap, double tap, drag, flick, and pinch.

You can use Silverlight mouse events, such as `MouseLeftButtonDown` and `MouseLeftButtonUp`, to handle touch events that don't involve direction or continuous motion, like tap and double tap. The standard `Button Click` event also corresponds to a tap gesture.

However, Microsoft recommends using touch events instead. You can also use the `Tap`, `DoubleTap`, and `Hold` events on any elements that are created using user interface controls. The `System.Windows.Input.Touch.FrameReported` event, which is in the `System.Windows.Input.Touch` class, is called when a user creates individual touch contact points like tap, double tap, and hold.

For more complicated gestures that use continuous motion, such as drag, flick, and pinch, three primary manipulation events are used in Silverlight for Windows Phone:

- *ManipulationStarted event* is raised when the user initially touches the screen.
- *ManipulationDelta event* is raised repeatedly as a finger moves on the screen's surface.
- *ManipulationCompleted event* is raised when the user removes a finger from the screen.

You can also use manipulation events for individual touch points if your application includes both individual and multi-touch points.

CERTIFICATION READY
What is the purpose of the `ManipulationStarted` and `ManipulationDelta` events?
4.2

➔ CREATE A TOUCH APPLICATION

GET READY. To create a touch application, perform the following steps:

1. Using a Web browser, visit the "How to: Handle Manipulation Events" Web page at http://bit.ly/M9WMUH.

2. Read the page and then follow the steps to create a touch-enabled application.

3. Open the application in Windows Phone Emulator. A blue box should appear. You can test the app if you have a computer with a touch screen. You'll learn how to build test apps and test them on actual devices in Lesson 8.

4. Close the project file and the Visual Studio IDE.

➕ **MORE INFORMATION**

Visit the "How to: Handle Manipulation Events" Web page at http://bit.ly/M9WMUH to learn more about manipulation events in Windows Phone applications.

SKILL SUMMARY

IN THIS LESSON YOU LEARNED:

- An important part of developing mobile applications for Windows Phone devices is to understand the phases an application goes through. This is referred to the Windows Phone application life cycle.

- You must also know how to create applications that are responsive, conserve energy, provide feedback to users in the form of messages and status bars, and store passwords securely.

- To create a good user experience and manage memory efficiently, the Windows Phone operating system allows only one application to run in the foreground at a time.

- A Windows Phone application's life cycle begins after the application launches. From there, the application can be in one of three states: running, dormant, or tombstoned. An application terminates when the user or some process closes it.

- Four primary events occur during the Windows Phone application life cycle, which move an application from one state to another: launching, deactivated, activated, and closing.

- The `NavigationService` class enables users to navigate two or more pages in an application. The Location API gathers location information from a Windows Phone device.

- The Bing Maps Silverlight Control for Windows Phone displays maps in applications based on user input.

- Windows Phone devices have built-in GPS hardware you can use to determine the device's latitude and longitude. The Location API works with the hardware and the Microsoft Location Service to provide location information to applications. The Bing Maps Silverlight Control for Windows Phone enables you to provide dynamic maps in applications.

- The HTML5 Forms API lets you create simple input forms to gather data from mobile Web users. Canvas is a drawing program that creates dynamic graphics within a browser based on calculations rather than having to reference static images. Media APIs include the audio and video element, which enable you to stream or embed multimedia with a minimum of code.

- Windows Phone devices have a four-point multi-touch screen for capturing gestures as input. Standard gestures include tap, double tap, drag, flick, and pinch.

- The `System.Windows.Input.Touch.FrameReported` event, which is in the `System.Windows.Input.Touch` class, is called when a user creates individual touch contact points like tap, double tap, and hold.

- The `ManipulationStarted`, `ManipulationDelta`, and `ManipulationCompleted` events control more complicated gestures such as drag, pinch, and flick.

Knowledge Assessment

Fill in the Blank

Complete the following sentences by writing the correct word or words in the blanks provided.

1. The _____ describes the Windows Phone application life cycle, which is the series of events and states that dictates how every Windows Phone application must operate to provide a consistent and responsive user experience.

2. _____ terminates an application but saves its state so it can be activated and resume where it left off.

3. When an application starts from the Start screen, the _____ event is raised and a new instance of the application runs.

4. When the first page of an application is reached and the Back button is pressed again, the _____ event is raised and the application terminates.

5. An _____ state is a set of information about an application and includes data used by multiple pages in the application, such as Web service data or a user interface theme.

6. A _____ is generally a JPG file that displays as soon as a user launches an application and continues to display until the application loads.

7. In order to safely store passwords, PINs, and other private data on a device, you must encrypt the data. Windows 7.1 OS provides the _____ for this purpose.

8. The Windows Phone 7 _____ API allows you to determine the current position and movement of the device, expressed in latitude and longitude.

9. _____ is a new element in HTML5 that creates a container for graphics, and uses JavaScript to draw the graphics dynamically.

10. The _____ event occurs when a user first touches the screen of a Windows Phone device.

Multiple Choice

Circle the letter that corresponds to the best answer.

1. Which event is raised when a user presses the Start button or takes a phone call while an application is running?
   a. Launching
   b. Deactivated
   c. Activated
   d. Closing

2. Which of the following is not a requirement for a splash screen?
   a. Includes a progress bar
   b. 480 pixels wide by 800 pixels tall
   c. Named SplashScreenImage.jpg
   d. Build Action property set to Content

3. Which method accesses page data?
   a. `OnNavigatedTo`
   b. `PhoneApplicationService`.State
   c. `CopyToIsolatedStorage`
   d. `Closing`

4. Which of the following can an application do when it's dormant?
   a. Display new emails
   b. Gather mapping information

    c. Calculate a canvas drawing

    d. Play audio

5. Which of the following HTML5 features uses a fieldset tag?

    a. Canvas

    b. Forms

    c. Audio

    d. Video

6. Which gesture can be handled using a standard Silverlight mouse event?

    a. Pinch

    b. Flick

    c. Tap

    d. Drag

7. Which event is raised repeatedly as a finger moves on the screen's surface?

    a. `ManipulationStarted`

    b. `ManipulationDelta`

    c. `ManipulationPinch`

    d. `ManipulationCompleted`

8. When gathering location information, which of the following is likely to reduce battery life the fastest?

    a. Using cellular service

    b. Using Wi-Fi

    c. Using the device's built-in GPS hardware

    d. Using a Web service

9. Which class is used primarily when navigating between pages in a Windows Phone application?

    a. `ProtectedData`

    b. `PhoneApplicationPage` class

    c. `NavigationService.Navigate`

    d. `NavigationService`

10. Which technology does HTML5 canvas use to draw shapes?

    a. JavaScript

    b. CSS

    c. HTML

    d. None of the above

True/False

Circle T if the statement is true or F if the statement is false.

T F **1.** The difference between a dormant application and a tombstoned application is that a dormant application is still in memory and a tombstoned application is terminated.

T F **2.** When a user revisits an application that's dormant or tombstoned, the Activated event is raised.

T F **3.** `ManipulationDelta` occurs repeatedly as a finger moves while touching the screen.

T F **4.** You can use Silverlight mouse events, such as `MouseLeftButtonDown` and `MouseLeftButtonUp`, to handle touch events that don't involve direction or continuous motion, like tap and double tap.

T F **5.** You use the `ProtectedData` class and the `Protect` and `Unprotect` methods to encrypt and decrypt data, respectively.

■ Competency Assessment

Scenario 6-1: Understand the Windows Phone Application Life Cycle

Meredith is just learning about Windows Phone application development and has asked you to briefly explain the Windows Phone application life cycle. What do you tell her?

Scenario 6-2: Save State Information

You are tutoring Arthur, a high school student, to help him prepare for an upcoming exam. Arthur is struggling to understand the purpose of state information and how to save and access it. What do you tell him?

■ Proficiency Assessment

Scenario 6-3: Protect Passwords

Harriet is working on a Windows Phone application that requires a password. She created a user interface that prompts for a password and allows the user to enter a password in a box. She isn't sure how to deal with passwords from that point forward. How do you advise her?

Scenario 6-4: Choose the Proper Code for a Touch-Enabled Application

Jose is creating a touch-enabled picture game in Silverlight. He is confused as to which methods to use. His game will include a mix of touch and multitouch events. How do you advise him?

Using Mobile Device Controls and Creating User Interfaces

EXAM OBJECTIVE MATRIX

SKILLS/CONCEPTS	MTA EXAM OBJECTIVE	MTA EXAM OBJECTIVE NUMBER
Working with Mobile Device Controls	Understand Mobile Device Controls.	4.3
Creating the User Interface and Experience	Build the User Interface.	4.4

KEY TERMS

Application Tile	MediaElement control
Canvas	Panels
collection	Secondary Tile
custom control	StackPanel
data template	style
event handler	theme
Grid	Tile
Image control	user experience

The application development team at BoxTwelve Mobile has asked you to work on an app development project independently. You are to create a simple Twitter client application that retrieves the tweets of any Twitter user by entering the user name in a text box and clicking a button to retrieve the tweets. You must build the user interface, add the appropriate controls, and provide code that makes the application run.

■ Understanding Mobile Device Controls

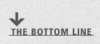
THE BOTTOM LINE

Windows Phone displays the elements users view or interact with in an application by using controls. The Windows Phone SDK comes with a standard set of controls like Button, Image, and WebBrowser. The Silverlight for Windows Phone Toolkit provides additional controls that help you enhance the user interface (UI).

This lesson covers Windows Phone controls and building the user interface for an application. Some of the information in this lesson will sound familiar to you—you've already used techniques like adding controls to an application and have worked with events. However, the information is worth repeating to reinforce the topics, and you'll learn some how-to details you didn't encounter in previous lessons. You'll also see how to create a simple application from beginning to end.

Working with Windows Phone Controls

You use controls to create the user interface in a Windows Phone app. Most controls allow you to modify their properties such as width, height, or foreground. When a user acts on a control, such as clicking a button or entering text into a text block, an event is raised. An event handler is a method you create in the code-behind file to handle the event.

Lesson 5 introduced various categories of Silverlight controls, such as those for navigation, buttons, text, lists, and progress bars. As you learned, you use controls to create the user interface (UI) in Windows Phone applications. The Toolbox in the Visual Studio IDE includes controls like `Button`, `TextBlock`, `TextBox`, and `WebBrowser`, among many others.

CERTIFICATION READY
How can you add a control to an application?
4.3

You can add a control to an application using three different techniques: drag a control from the Toolbox to the design surface in the Visual Studio IDE, edit the XAML file, or edit the code-behind file.

When you drag and drop a control onto the design surface, the Visual Studio IDE creates an entry in the XAML file for you (see Figure 7-1).

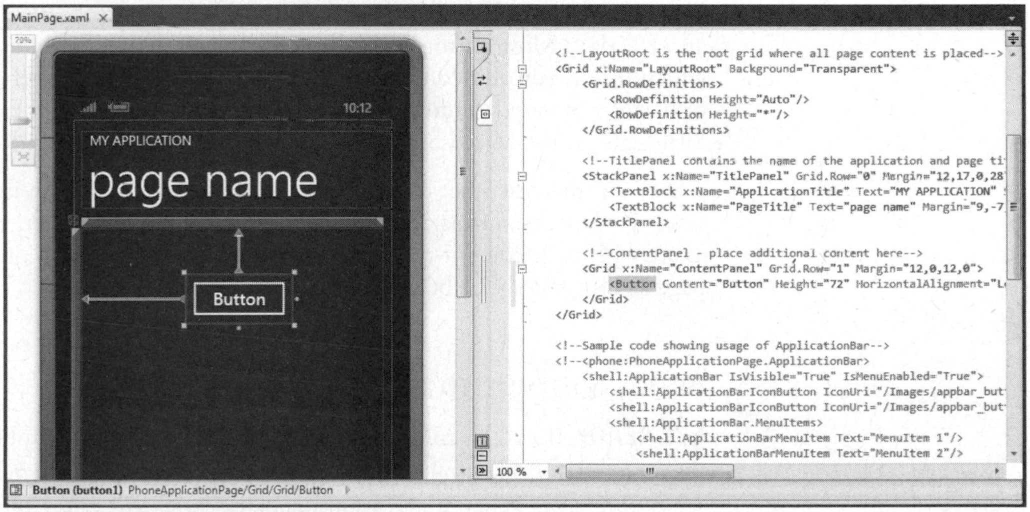

Figure 7-1

A new control added to an application and its corresponding XAML file entry

When adding a control manually in XAML or the code-behind file, you might need to add a reference to the assembly and add a namespace mapping. When adding a control using XAML, you "declare" the control. The following XAML code declares a button, names it, and sets its content, height, and width.

```
<Button Height="50" Width="100" Content="Find" x:Name="button1"/>
```

To add a control directly to the code-behind file, you add code that creates and names the control, sets its content (often, the text that displays on the control as a prompt for the user), and adds it to the visual tree so it displays in the application. The following is code you could add to the code-behind file for the Button control:

```
Button button1 = new Button();
button1.Height = 50;
button1.Width = 100;
button1.Content = "Find";
button1.Name = "button1";
this.LayoutRoot.Children.Add(button1);
```

As you can see, using the Visual Studio IDE Toolbox to add a control to an application is easy and is generally the preferred method by beginners. You're less likely to make a coding error and have to spend extra time debugging your application. As you become more comfortable with controls, move into manual coding.

+ MORE INFORMATION

Visit the "Getting Started with Controls" Web page at http://bit.ly/LiGkNl to learn more about controls.

Understanding Control Properties and Classes

Each Silverlight control derives from certain classes, and each class has many different properties you can configure for a control. The default button controls, for example, include Button and HyperlinkButton, and the selection controls are CheckBox, RadioButton, and Slider. Most button and selection controls derive from the ContentControl class, which means you add content to them with the Content property. The source of these controls is the System.Windows.Controls namespace in the .NET Framework Class Library for Silverlight or the Microsoft.Phone.Controls namespace in Windows Phone.

Other controls use other classes. The TextBlock control is an instance of the TextBlock class, the layout controls derive from the Panel class, and so on. For a long list of controls, along with their content type and content property, see the "Control Content Models" Web page at http://bit.ly/Oab6zp.

➡ ADD A CONTROL TO AN APPLICATION

GET READY. To add a control to an application, perform the following steps:

1. In the Visual Studio IDE, create a new project named **L7-Practice** using the C# Windows Phone Application template. To do so, select **File > New Project**, select **Silverlight for Windows Phone** under the Visual C# category in the left pane, select **Windows Phone Application** in the middle pane, and enter **L7-Practice** in the Name text box near the bottom of the window, as shown in Figure 7-2. Click **OK**.

2. Click **OK** in the New Windows Phone Application dialog box.

3. Open the Toolbox, drag the **Button** control to the design surface, and then close the Toolbox. The application should look similar to Figure 7-3.

4. Select **File > Save MainPage.xaml** to save the file.

5. Close the project file and leave the Visual Studio IDE open if you plan to complete the next exercise during this session.

Figure 7-2

Starting a new application

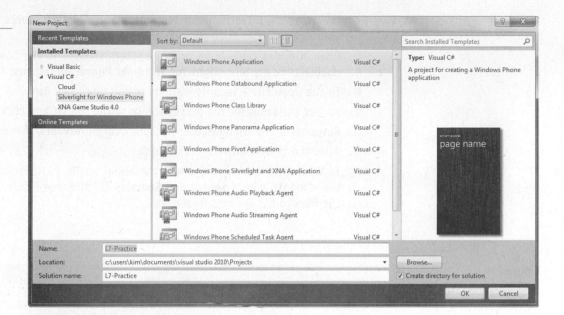

Figure 7-3

A Button control on the design surface

You can install the Silverlight for Windows Phone Toolkit to add more controls to the Visual Studio IDE. The current toolkit contains the `AutoCompleteBox`, `ListPicker`, `LongListSelector`, `ContextMenu`, `DatePicker`, `TimePicker`, `ToggleSwitch`, and `WrapPanel` controls.

You don't need these controls to work through exercises in this lesson; however, you will need the toolkit installed to explore design templates in a later exercise. Either way, it's good to know how to install the toolkit so the controls are available when you have time to explore them.

 INSTALL AND EXPLORE SILVERLIGHT FOR WINDOWS PHONE TOOLKIT

GET READY. To install Silverlight for Windows Phone Toolkit and find out about controls it provides, perform the following steps:

1. Make sure all programs on your computer are closed.

2. Open a Web browser and go to the Microsoft Silverlight Toolkit CodePlex Web site at http://silverlight.codeplex.com/.

3. Download the latest version of the **Silverlight for Windows Phone Toolkit** MSI file to the Downloads folder on your computer.

4. Download the **Silverlight for Windows Phone Toolkit Source & Sample** ZIP file to your Visual Studio 2010\Projects folder.

5. Open Windows Explorer on your computer, navigate to the Downloads folder, and then double-click the **Silverlight for Windows Phone Toolkit.msi** file.

6. In the Open File - Security Warning dialog box, click **Run**.

7. Accept the terms for the public license of the toolkit and click **Install**.

8. Respond to any Windows User Account Control prompts, if necessary.

9. After the toolkit installs, click **Finish**.

10. In Windows Explorer, navigate to the Visual Studio 2010\Projects folder, double-click the **<month year> Source and Samples** ZIP file (see Figure 7-4), and then extract the files to the Projects folder.

Figure 7-4

The Source and Samples ZIP file

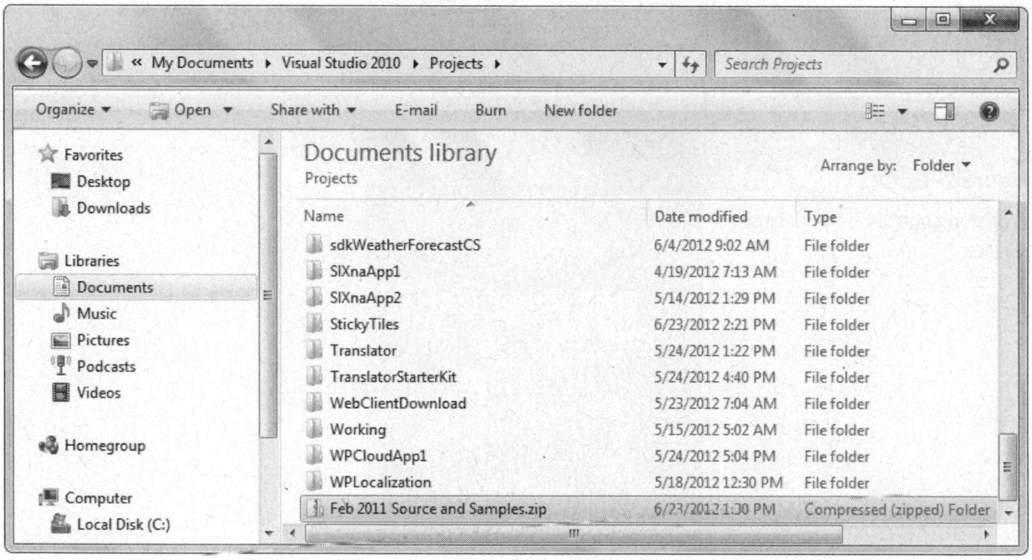

11. Close Windows Explorer.

12. Open the Visual Studio IDE.

13. To see the new controls, open the Toolbox, right-click within the Toolbox, and select **Choose Items**. Scroll the list of controls. If you see a control you want to add to the Toolbox, check the control's checkbox and click **OK**.

14. To see how the Silverlight for Windows Phone Toolkit controls work, open the sample app. To do so, select **File > Open Project**, scroll through the list of applications to locate the sample app, which is in a folder named <month year> Source and Samples. Double-click the folder, and then double-click the subfolder named **WindowsPhone7**. Select **PhoneToolkit.sln** and click **Open**.

15. If the security warning dialog box displays, click **OK**.

16. Select **PhoneToolkitSample** in Solution Explorer and start the Windows Emulator (click **Start Debugging** on the toolbar or press **F5**). Figure 7-5 shows the main page of the sample application.

17. Click each control sample on the main page and try it.

18. Close the project file and leave the Visual Studio IDE open if you plan to complete the next exercise during this session.

Figure 7-5

The Phone Toolkit Sample app in Windows Phone Emulator

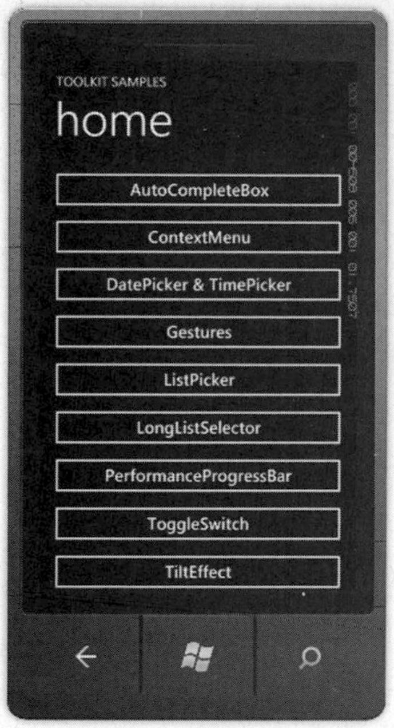

Modifying a Control Name and Properties

CERTIFICATION READY
Which techniques can you use to modify the properties of a control?
4.3

You change the appearance of a control by setting control properties. Much like adding a control, you can modify a control's properties by setting properties using different techniques: in the Properties window, manually in the XAML files, or manually in code. You can also resize controls in the design surface by selecting the control and then dragging a resizing handle up, down, or to the left or right. See Figure 7-6.

Figure 7-6

Resizing handles on a control

The Properties window lets you configure the specific height and width of a control, in addition to changing its name, background color, and many other properties.

MODIFY A CONTROL'S PROPERTIES

GET READY. To modify a control's properties, perform the following steps:

1. In the Visual Studio IDE, open the **L7-Practice.sln** project file. To do so, select **File > Open Project,** navigate to the **Projects** folder, locate and double-click the **L7-Practice** folder, and then double-click the **L7-Practice.sln** file.

2. On the design surface, click and hold your left mouse button over the word **Button**, and then drag the control to the right side of the page as shown in Figure 7-7.

Figure 7-7

Repositioning a control in the design surface

3. Right-click the control and then select **Properties** from the shortcut menu. Drag the left side of the Properties window further to the left, if necessary, to be able to read the window's contents more easily.

4. In the Properties window, locate the Height and Width properties and notice their values. You can quickly find a property by entering its name in the Search text box at the top of the Properties window.

5. In the MainPage.xaml file in Code Editor, locate the Button declaration and compare the information to the properties in the Properties window.

6. Change the Height property in the Properties window to **80** and press enter. Notice that the button's Height property changes in Code Editor automatically, as shown in Figure 7-8.

Figure 7-8

Comparing the properties in the Property window against the MainPage.xaml file

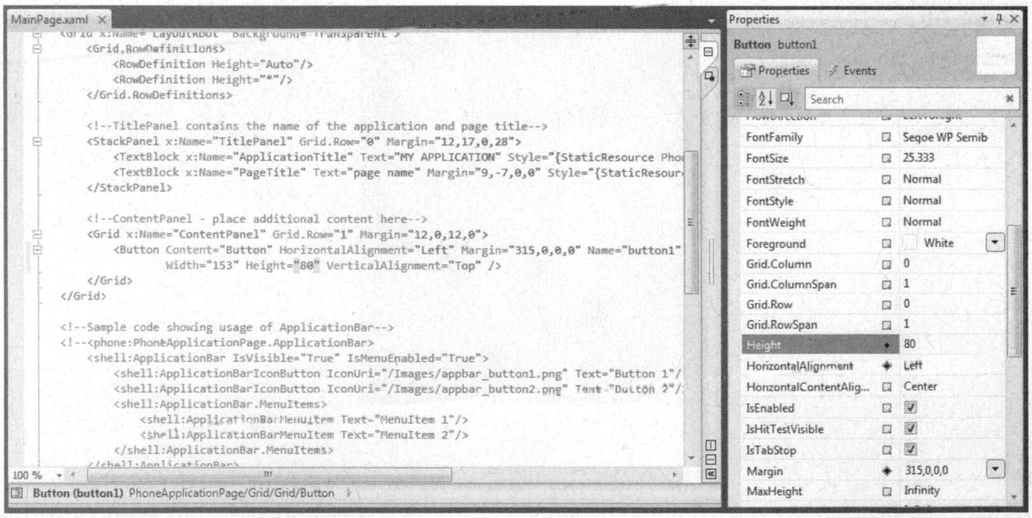

7. In Code Editor, scroll to the right to locate the Width property and change it to **200**. Scroll down the Properties window and notice that the value for the Width property is now 200.

8. In Design view, the Button control now bleeds off the right side of the screen, as shown in Figure 7-9. Grab the Button control with your mouse pointer and drag it to the left so you can once again see the entire control.

Figure 7-9

Adjusting the height and width of the Button control caused an alignment problem

9. Change the foreground color of the Button control, which changes the font color of the button's label, by locating the Foreground property in the Properties window. Click the down arrow to the right of the Foreground value. A color picker displays, as shown in Figure 7-10. Change the button's `Foreground` property value by moving the slider bars. The color change displays automatically in the design surface.

Figure 7-10

A color picker to change the foreground color of a button

Properties	▼ ⟊ ✕
Button button1	

Properties   ⚡ Events

Search   ✕

ContentTemplate	☐	Resource...
Cursor	☐	
DataContext	☐	Binding...
FlowDirection	☐	LeftToRight
FontFamily	☐	Seqoe WP Semibold
FontSize	☐	25.333
FontStretch	☐	Normal
FontStyle	☐	Normal
FontWeight	☐	Normal
Foreground	◆	☐ White

| ☑ ■ ☐ ▨ |
R	255
G	255
B	255
A	255
☐ White	🖊

10. Select **File > Save** to save the file.

11. Leave the project file open in the Visual Studio IDE. You'll use the same file in the next exercise.

Adding an Event Handler

When a user acts on a control, such as clicking a button or entering text into a text block, an event is raised. An *event handler* is a method you create to handle the event. You create event handlers by double-clicking a control in the design surface and adding code in the code-behind file that displays in Code Editor. You can also create an event handler using the Properties window.

To create an event handler using the Properties window, select a control in the design surface, open the Properties window, and click the Events tab. The events you can apply to the control display. For example, Figure 7-11 shows a partial list of events for the `ListBox` control. Just double-click the event you want to associate with the control, and the code-behind file displays in Code Editor with a new event handler created. You must add code that produces an action when the event is raised.

Figure 7-11

The Events tab for the `ListBox` control

Properties	▼ 廿 ×
ListBox listBox1	
📑 Properties ⚡ Events	
Search	✕
BindingValidationError ☑	
DoubleTap ☑	
GotFocus ☑	
Hold ☑	
IsEnabledChanged ☑	
KeyDown ☑	
KeyUp ☑	
LayoutUpdated ☑	
Loaded ☑	
LostFocus ☑	
LostMouseCapture ☑	
ManipulationCompleted ☑	
ManipulationDelta ☑	
ManipulationStarted ☑	
MouseEnter ☑	
MouseLeave ☑	
MouseLeftButtonDown ☑	
MouseLeftButtonUp ☑	

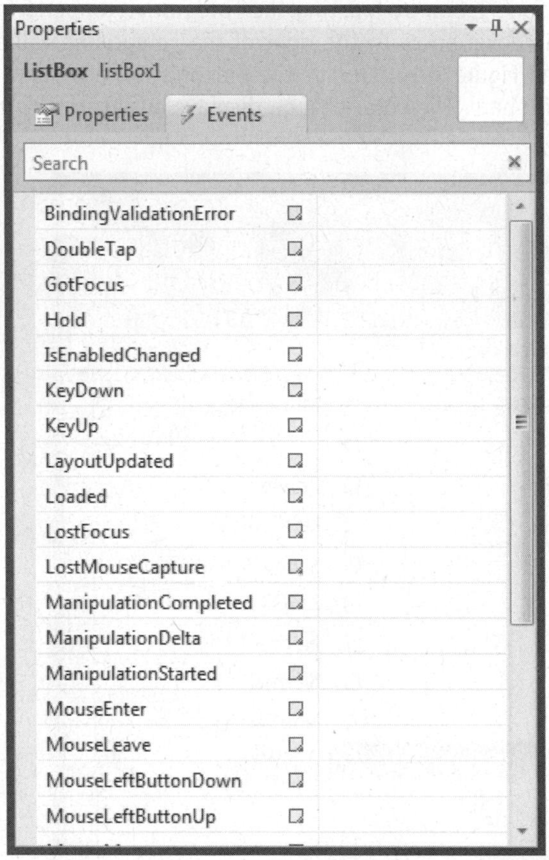

When you create an event using the Properties window in a C# project, the Visual Studio IDE automatically adds an attribute that specifies the event handler to the XAML file. If you're working on a VB project, the code is added to the end of the event handler in the code-behind file.

 ADD AN EVENT TO AN APP

GET READY. To add an event to an app, perform the following steps:

1. In the Visual Studio IDE, in the L7-Practice.sln project file, right-click the **Button** control and select **Properties** from the shortcut menu. The Properties window opens.
2. Click the **Events** tab. The events for the Button control display.

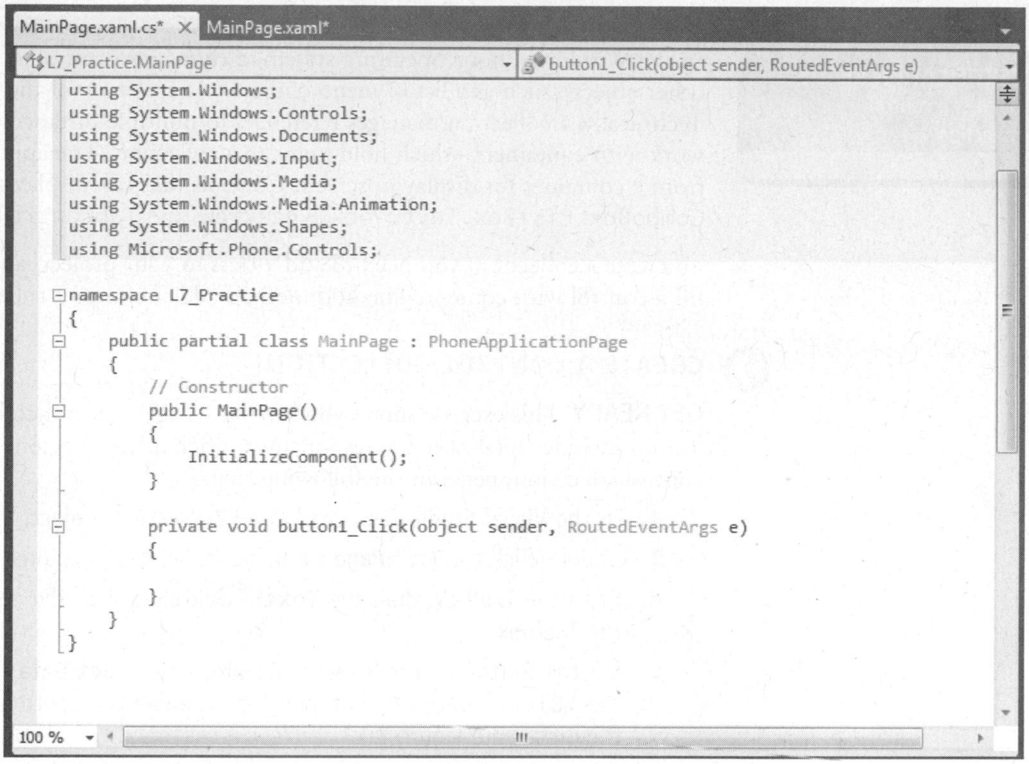
MainPage.xaml.cs* MainPage.xaml*
L7_Practice.MainPage
button1_Click(object sender, RoutedEventArgs e)
using System.Windows;
using System.Windows.Controls;
using System.Windows.Documents;
using System.Windows.Input;
using System.Windows.Media;
using System.Windows.Media.Animation;
using System.Windows.Shapes;
using Microsoft.Phone.Controls;

namespace L7_Practice
{
    public partial class MainPage : PhoneApplicationPage
    {
        // Constructor
        public MainPage()
        {
            InitializeComponent();
        }

        private void button1_Click(object sender, RoutedEventArgs e)
        {

        }
    }
}
100 %

Figure 7-12

The code-behind file for the `Click` event

3. Double-click the **`Click`** event. The code-behind file displays with an event handler, as shown in Figure 7-12. You would add code to this event handler to take some action in response to a user clicking the button.
4. Select **File** > **Save** to save the file.
5. Close the project file and leave the Visual Studio IDE open if you plan to complete the next exercise during this session.

MORE INFORMATION

For more information on adding events to a control, visit the "Getting Started with Controls" Web page at http://bit.ly/LiGkNl.

Building Custom Controls

CERTIFICATION READY
What is a Windows Phone custom control?
4.3

In addition to using and modifying controls that are built in to the Visual Studio IDE, you can create a custom control. A ***custom control*** is essentially a new control based on, or derived from, an existing control. Once you create the new control, you just modify its functionality. For example, you can use the Button or `TextBlock` control, modify its functionality and rename it, and you've created a custom control.

The following are some key points you should know about custom controls:

- They're reusable. To use a custom control, you must load the control's assembly into your project.
- They can contain a collection of items. (You'll learn about collections in the next section.)
- They can allow the user to select items.
- They can allow automatic sorting and filtering based on criteria you or the user provides.

A custom control can be difficult to create and usually requires a deep understanding of the Silverlight user interface model. Therefore, it's best to build one when you know you'll use the control repeatedly in an application or in other applications.

Displaying Collections of Items

In the Windows Phone operating system, a *collection* is an object that can keep track of other objects, such as a list of menu choices or a tree view of the folders in a file system. Technically, a collection manages references to multiple instances of other classes. Collections work with containers, which hold items in a collection. The application can retrieve an item from a container for display onscreen. Controls that can display a collection of objects include ComboBox, ListBox, TextBlock, TreeView, and TabControl.

To create a collection, you need to add a class to your project, and then use item properties to fill a control with content. The Add method adds items to a collection.

CREATE A CONTROL COLLECTION

GET READY. This exercise shows you how to set up a control collection. The example collection includes total sales figures for three different sales regions for a company. To create a control collection, perform the following steps:

1. In the Visual Studio IDE, open the **L7-Practice** project.
2. Double-click the **MainPage.xaml** file in Solution Explorer.
3. Open the Toolbox, drag the **TextBlock** control to the design surface, and then close the Toolbox.
4. Set the Button control's Content property to **Get Data**, and delete the value for the TextBlock control's Text property. Arrange the controls on the design surface so they resemble Figure 7-13.

Figure 7-13

The application thus far

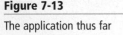

5. You need to add a new class to the project. To do so, right-click **L7-Practice** in Solution Explorer, select **Add**, select **New Item**, select **Class**, and then type **Sales** in the Name text box at the bottom of the window. (See Figure 7-14.) Click **Add**. The Sales.cs file opens.
6. Insert the following properties into public class Sales:

```
public string Region { get; set; }
public string Total { get; set; }
```

7. Double-click the **MainPage.xaml.cs** file in Solution Explorer and add three instances of the Sales class inside the click event handler:

```
Sales sales1 = new Sales();
sales1.Region = "East Coast";
sales1.Total = "$10,000";
```

Figure 7-14

Adding a class

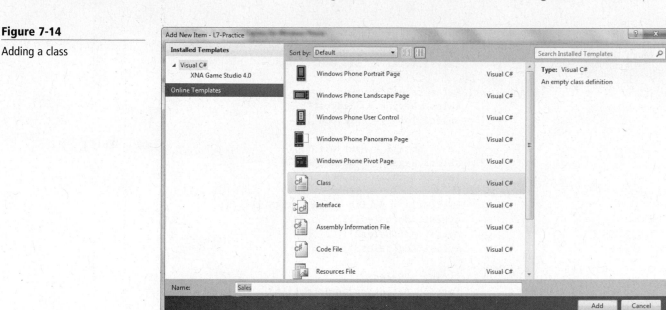

```
Sales sales2 = new Sales();
sales2.Region = "Midwest";
sales2.Total = "$12,000";

Sales sales3 = new Sales();
sales3.Region = "West Coast";
sales3.Total = "$8,000";
```

Three different objects of the Sales class are created—`sales1`, `sales2`, and `sales3`—along with their attributes.

8. Add the following code in the same handler (not under the closing brackets) in the MainPage.xaml.cs file:

```
List<Sales> myList = new List<Sales>();
        myList.Add(sales1);
        myList.Add(sales2);
        myList.Add(sales3);

        string mySales = "";
        foreach (Sales sales in myList)
        {
                mySales += sales.Region + "-" + sales.Total +
Environment.NewLine;
        }

        textBlock1.Text = mySales;
```

This code creates a collection in the form of a list called `myList` that can hold references to objects of the `Sales` class. The `Add()` method adds objects to the list. The `foreach` statement works with collections, iterating through the list and retrieving the region and total dollar amount for each region. Each object's attributes are stored in a string variable `mySales`. The Enviornment.NewLine inserts a new line. The code should look like Figure 7-15.

9. Click the **Start Debugging** button on the toolbar or press **F5** to open the application in the Windows Phone Emulator. Click the **Get Data** button. The list data displays.

Figure 7-15

The MainPage.xaml.cs code

```
Sales sales1 = new Sales();
sales1.Region = "East Coast";
sales1.Total = "$10,000";

Sales sales2 = new Sales();
sales2.Region = "Midwest";
sales2.Total = "$12,000";

Sales sales3 = new Sales();
sales3.Region = "West Coast";
sales3.Total = "$8,000";

List<Sales> myList = new List<Sales>();
myList.Add(sales1);
myList.Add(sales2);
myList.Add(sales3);

string mySales = "";
foreach (Sales sales in myList)
{
    mySales += sales.Region + "-" + sales.Total + Environment.NewLine;
}

textBlock1.Text = mySales;
        }
    }
```

10. Close the emulator.

11. Select **File > Save All** to save the project.

12. Close the project file and leave the Visual Studio IDE open if you plan to complete the next exercise during this session.

➕ **MORE INFORMATION**

For more details about Windows Phone control collections, see the "Controls that display a collection of items" section of the "Control Content Models" Web page at http://bit.ly/KHmK29.

Using a Data Template to Display Items in a Control

Many Windows Phone applications display data retrieved from the Web or some other remote source, and display the data in controls. The data might be a Twitter feed, Facebook posts, stock quotes, or news headlines, for example.

A *data template* enables you to bind data items to list items and customize how list items are displayed on a Windows Phone device. A common scenario in which you use a data template is when you retrieve data from a URI, which is most often in XML format, and then parse the data and present it in a list box. You can use DataTemplate as a property to ItemTemplate in a XAML file to present bound data in a list box.

The next exercise has you build an application named Get The Tweets that retrieves tweets from any Twitter user. The exercise uses familiar controls and a data template.

➡ **BUILD THE GET THE TWEETS APP**

GET READY. This exercise is a simplified version of the Twitter client sample application at http://bit.ly/Lca2pb. To build an application named Get The Tweets, perform the following steps:

1. In the Visual Studio IDE, create a new project named **GetTheTweets** using the C# Windows Phone Application template.

2. Double-click the **MainPage.xaml** file in Solution Explorer. The file opens in Code Editor. Near the beginning of the code, change the SupportedOrientations property to **PortraitOrLandscape**, as follows:

   SupportedOrientations="PortraitOrLandscape" Orientation="Portrait"

3. In the TitlePanel section, locate the TextBlock named ApplicationTitle. Change the Text property from MY APPLICATION to **GET THE TWEETS**.

4. Change the PageTitle TextBlock's Text property to **Enter Tweeter**.

5. Open the Toolbox and drag the **TextBox** control to the design surface, just under Enter Tweeter. Pull the TextBox control to the left margin of the page. Resize the width of the TextBox control so it take up about two-thirds of the width of the page by dragging its right resizing handle. Delete the **Text** property of the TextBox control in Code Editor. Change the Name property to **txtUserName**.

6. From the Toolbox, drag the **Button** control to the design surface and drop it to the right of the TextBox control. Drag the Button control into place (toward the TextBox control) so it doesn't bleed off the right side of the page but doesn't touch the TextBox control. Change the Content property of the Button control to **Fetch** in Code Editor or the Properties window.

7. Double-click the **Button** control in the design surface to create an event handler in the code-behind file.

8. Click the **MainPage.xaml** tab above Code Editor to switch back to that file.

9. From the Toolbox, drag the **ListBox** control to the design surface and drop it under the TextBox and Button controls. Close the Toolbox. Resize the ListBox control to take up the remaining space on the page. You will code the ListBox to display the tweeter's profile image and tweets so name the ListBox **lstTwitter**. The application should look similar to Figure 7-16.

Figure 7-16

The arrangement of the Get The Tweets controls on the design surface

10. In the application, when the user clicks the Fetch button, the app uses a Twitter API and WebClient networking to download tweets from a specific tweeter. The data returned from the Twitter call will be in XML format which must be parsed for display. This app will use LINQ to XML in the System.Xml.Linq library to parse the data.

To add code that will connect to a URI, grab data for display in the application, and parse it, switch to the code-behind file (**MainPage.xaml.cs**) and enter the following code in the button click event handler. The handler code and starting and ending curly brackets are included below for reference but you do not need to repeat them; simply start with "Webclient twitter . . . ."

```csharp
private void button1_Click(object sender, RoutedEventArgs e)
{
    WebClient twitter = new WebClient();

    twitter.DownloadStringCompleted += new
DownloadStringCompletedEventHandler(twitter_DownloadString
Completed);

    twitter.DownloadStringAsync(new
Uri("http://api.twitter.com/1/statuses/user_timeline.
xml?screen_name=" + txtUserName.Text));
}


void twitter_DownloadStringCompleted(object sender,
    DownloadStringCompletedEventArgs e)
{
    if (e.Error != null)
        return;

    XElement xmlTweets = XElement.Parse(e.Result);

    lstTwitter.ItemsSource = from tweet in
xmlTweets.Descendants("status")
                                select new
TwitterItem
                                {
                                    ImageSource =
tweet.Element("user").Element("profile_image_url").Value,
                                    Message =
tweet.Element("text").Value
                                };
}
```

The code should look like Figure 7-17.

Figure 7-17

The code for retrieving tweets and parsing the data

```csharp
public MainPage()
{
    InitializeComponent();
}

private void button1_Click(object sender, RoutedEventArgs e)
{
    WebClient twitter = new WebClient();
        twitter.DownloadStringCompleted += new DownloadStringCompletedEventHandler(twitter_DownloadStringCompleted);
        twitter.DownloadStringAsync(new Uri("http://api.twitter.com/1/statuses/user_timeline.xml?screen_name=" + txtUserName.Text));
}

void twitter_DownloadStringCompleted(object sender, DownloadStringCompletedEventArgs e)
{
    if (e.Error != null)
        return;

    XElement xmlTweets = XElement.Parse(e.Result);

    lstTwitter.ItemsSource = from tweet in xmlTweets.Descendants("status")
                select new TwitterItem
                {
                    ImageSource = tweet.Element("user").Element("profile_image_url").Value,
                    Message = tweet.Element("text").Value
                };
    }
}
```

11. Select **File** > **Save All** to save the project at this point.

12. You need to add a reference to the System.Xml.Linq library and then create a new class called TwitterItem. To add a reference to the System.Xml.Linq library, right-click **References** in Solution Explorer, select **Add Reference**, scroll down and locate **System.Xml.Linq**, select it, and click **OK**.

13. Add **using System.Xml.Linq;** to the end of the using statements list at the top of the MainPage.xaml.cs code-behind file.

14. The TwitterItem class will contain two items—ImageSource and Message—which will be used to display the tweeter's profile image and tweets. To add a new class that contains the Twitter items, right-click the project name in Solution Explorer, select **Add**, select **Class** in the dialog box that displays, name the class **TwitterItem**, and click **Add**.

15. Double-click **TwitterItem.cs** in Solution Explorer and add the following two string code statements to the TwitterItem class:

```
public class TwitterItem
{
    public string ImageSource { get; set; }
    public string Message { get; set; }
}
```

The code should look like Figure 7-18. ·

Figure 7-18

Adding string code to the TwitterItem class

```
using System;
using System.Net;
using System.Windows;
using System.Windows.Controls;
using System.Windows.Documents;
using System.Windows.Ink;
using System.Windows.Input;
using System.Windows.Media;
using System.Windows.Media.Animation;
using System.Windows.Shapes;

namespace GetTheTweets
{
    public class TwitterItem
    {
        public string ImageSource { get; set; }
        public string Message { get; set; }
    }
}
```

16. In the MainPage.xaml file, add an ItemTemplate to the ListBox control, which determines the layout of each item in the list. The ItemTemplate uses DataTemplate as its property. The DataTemplate binds parsed data to the UI elements (ImageSource and Message) that display the data. First, replace the ListBox code in Main.xaml with the following:

```
<ListBox Name="lstTwitter" Grid.Row="1" Margin="10, 10, 10, 10">
```

17. Insert the following code after the `ListBox` code:

```xml
<ListBox.ItemTemplate>
    <DataTemplate>
        <StackPanel Orientation="Horizontal"
Height="110" Margin="-10,-10,-10,-10">

            <Image Source="{Binding ImageSource}"
Height="73" Width="73" VerticalAlignment="Top"
Margin="10,10,8,10"/>
            <TextBlock Text="{Binding Message}"
Margin="10" TextWrapping="Wrap" FontSize="18"
Width="350" />
        </StackPanel>
    </DataTemplate>
</ListBox.ItemTemplate>
</ListBox>
```

The code should look like Figure 7-19.

Figure 7-19

Adding the `ItemTemplate` and `DataTemplate` code

```xml
<!--TitlePanel contains the name of the application and page title-->
<StackPanel x:Name="TitlePanel" Grid.Row="0" Margin="12,17,0,28">
    <TextBlock x:Name="ApplicationTitle" Text="GET THE TWEETS" Style="{StaticResource PhoneTextNormalStyle}"/>
    <TextBlock x:Name="PageTitle" Text="Enter Tweeter" Margin="9,-7,0,0" Style="{StaticResource PhoneTextTitle1Style}"/>
</StackPanel>

<!--ContentPanel - place additional content here-->
<Grid x:Name="ContentPanel" Grid.Row="1" Margin="12,0,12,0">
    <TextBox Height="72" HorizontalAlignment="Left" Name="txtUserName" VerticalAlignment="Top" Width="300" />
    <Button Content="Fetch" Height="72" HorizontalAlignment="Left" Margin="308,0,0,0" Name="button1" VerticalAlignment="Top"
        Width="160" Click="button1_Click" />
    <ListBox Name="lstTwitter" Grid.Row="1" Margin="10, 10, 10, 10">
        <ListBox.ItemTemplate>
            <DataTemplate>
                <StackPanel Orientation="Horizontal" Height="110" Margin="-10,-10,-10,-10">
                    <Image Source="{Binding ImageSource}" Height="73" Width="73" VerticalAlignment="Top" Margin="10,10,8,10"/>
                    <TextBlock Text="{Binding Message}" Margin="10" TextWrapping="Wrap" FontSize="18" Width="350" />
                </StackPanel>
            </DataTemplate>
        </ListBox.ItemTemplate>
    </ListBox>
</Grid>
</Grid>
```

18. Select **File > Save All** to save the project.

19. Click the **Start Debugging** button on the toolbar or press **F5** to open the Windows Phone Emulator. When the application loads, click in the text box. The built-in keyboard displays. Click the **&123** button, click the **@** symbol, and then click the buttons to enter **windowsphone**. Click **Fetch**. The @WindowsPhone tweets should display.

20. Close the emulator.

21. Leave the project file open in the Visual Studio IDE if you plan to complete the next exercise during this session.

TAKE NOTE*

If you are unable to click in the `TextBox` control in Windows Phone Emulator, close the emulator and in the design surface, check whether the `ListBox` control needs to be moved down to uncover the `TextBox` control.

Arranging Content with Panels

You use Panels to lay out controls in Windows Phone applications. The Grid panel uses columns and rows, the `StackPanel` lays out controls in a vertical or horizontal line, and the Canvas panel specifies a precise location for a control.

CERTIFICATION READY

Which panel element enables you to lay out controls in rows and columns?

4.3

Panels enable you to define how controls are laid out in a Windows Phone application. The three Panel elements are `Grid`, `StackPanel`, and `Canvas`.

The ***Grid*** is a panel that uses columns and rows similar to a spreadsheet; the intersection of a column and row is a cell. You can place controls in a cell within the `Grid`, which can shrink and grow depending on the `Height` and `Width` property values you assign. When you create a new project, the `Grid` container is automatically created by default. The following is an example of `Grid` code:

```
<Grid>
    <Grid.RowDefinitions>
        <RowDefinition Height="Auto"/>
        <RowDefinition Height="100"/>
    </Grid.RowDefinitions>
    <Grid.ColumnDefinitions>
        <ColumnDefinition Width="Auto"/>
        <ColumnDefinition Width="100"/>
    </Grid.ColumnDefinitions>
    <TextBlock Text="Text1" Grid.Row="0" Grid.Column="0"/>
    <TextBlock Text="Text2" Grid.Row="0" Grid.Column="1"/>
    <Button Content="Button1" Grid.Row="1" Grid.Column="0"/>
    <Button Content="Button2" Grid.Row="1" Grid.Column="1"/>
</Grid>
```

Grid row and column numbering start at 0, so the first row is row 0 and the first column is column 0. Notice that the rows and columns use a mix of fixed and auto height and width values. A fixed value specifies the exact height or width, whereas the Auto value allows the row or column to resize depending on the content in the Grid. You can also use an asterisk (*) alone or with a number to indicate proportional sizing. A number with an asterisk, such as 2*, indicates a relative proportion. If you don't include the `Height` or `Width` property, they default to a proportional value of 1*, which is the same as *.

The **StackPanel** is a panel that arranges controls in either a vertical line (the default) or a horizontal line. `StackPanel`s are most often contained within a Grid. The following is an example of `StackPanel` code:

```
<StackPanel Background="Blue">
    <TextBlock Text="Text1"/>
    <TextBlock Text="Text2"/>
    <Button Content="Button1"/>
    <Button Content="Button2"/>
</StackPanel>
```

CERTIFICATION READY
Which panel element lets you locate a control using x and y coordinates?
4.3

The **Canvas** is a panel that lets you locate controls in a specific location using x and y coordinates in pixels. The following is an example of `Canvas` code:

```
<Canvas Width="300" Height="300" Background="Blue">
    <TextBlock Text="Text" Canvas.Left="100" Canvas.Top="100"/>
</Canvas>
```

Because Canvas specifies a precise location, it isn't used as often as `Grid` and `StackPanel` because they work dynamically. A dynamically changeable interface is best for device orientation changes.

➜ EXPLORE THE GET THE TWEETS APP GRID

GET READY. To modify the grid for the Get The Tweets app, perform the following steps:

1. In the Visual Studio IDE, open the **GetTheTweets.sln** project file if it's not already open.
2. Open **MainPage.xaml** in Code Editor. Notice that this app uses a Grid for aligning the tweeter's image horizontally alongside the tweet.

3. Using the information you learned about Grid rows and columns, which controls are located in the first Grid row?

4. Which controls are located in the second Grid row?

5. Which row is the ListBox control located in?

6. Close the project file and leave the Visual Studio IDE open if you plan to complete the next exercise during this session.

➕ MORE INFORMATION

To learn more about Panels and layout, see the "layout on the screen" Web page at http://bit.ly/LnOHJo.

Working with Tiles

> Push notifications include toast, Tile, and raw. An application uses two types of Tiles: an Application Tile and secondary Tiles.

Lesson 4 covered push notifications. You learned that push notifications allow a Web service to send data to a Windows Phone device. The three types of push notifications are toast, Tile, and raw:

- Toast notifications display at the top of the screen, often in text format similar to a short text message.

- Tile notifications can update Tiles on the device's Start screen. A Tile notification can alert the user to some type of event, like an impending storm in the area or receipt of an email, by changing the icon, strings, and/or the Tile's background.

- Raw notifications occur only when the associated app is running. Raw notifications enable you to safely push custom data to an application, such as updated stock quotes or weather data, without notifying the user.

This section focuses on Tiles and understanding the difference between the two primary types of Tiles used by applications: Application Tiles and secondary Tiles.

A *Tile* is a link to an application that's displayed on the Windows Phone Start page. Tiles are part of the Metro style and usually contain an icon and two strings.

The *Application Tile* launches applications from the Start page. As applications are added to a device, the operating system lists them in an applications list. A user can pin an application to the Start page by pressing and holding an application title in the applications list. The pinned application is represented by an Application Tile.

Windows Phone 7.1 introduced *Secondary Tiles*, which are additional tiles on the Start page that link to unique information generated by an app, such as flight delays and cancellations or the weather for a particular city.

A fun thing about Tiles in Windows Phone 7.1 is their ability to flip, enabling you to use both sides of the Tile to display information. Properties for the front side of a Tile are Title, BackgroundImage, and Count. The title displays over the background image, which may be a solid color or an icon. The count (also known as a badge) is a number that displays on the Tile if the value is 1 to 99. A Count value of 0 does not display a number.

The properties for the back of a Tile are BackTitle, BackBackgroundImage, and BackContent. The back title is a character string that displays at the bottom of the tile, over the back background image. The back content is a character string of 39 characters or less that displays in the body of the back of a Tile.

⊕ **EXPLORE AN APPLICATION TILE**

GET READY. To learn about properties of an Application Tile, perform the following steps:

1. In the Visual Studio IDE, go to the Start page, and click **Code Samples for Windows Phone** in the Learning Resources section.

2. Download and install the C# version of **Tile Sample** to your Projects folder. (If you're not sure how to access this code sample, refer to the Download a Code Sample exercise in Lesson 1.) This code sample enables you to update an Application Tile, and to create, update, and delete secondary Tiles.

3. Open the project in the Visual Studio IDE.

4. Click the **Start Debugging** button on the toolbar or press **F5** to open the application in the Windows Phone Emulator. The application displays, as shown in Figure 7-20.

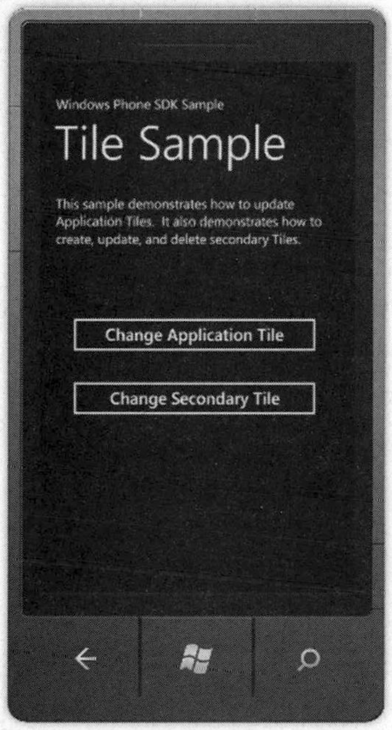

Figure 7-20

The main page of the Tile Sample application

5. Click the **Change Application Tile** button.

6. Click in the **Title** text box and type **app title**.

7. Click in the **Background Image** text box. Use the following settings to update the BackgroundImage and remaining text boxes:

   - BackgroundImage: green.jpg

   - Count: 2

   - BackTitle: back of tile

   - BackBackgroundImage: blue.jpg

   - BackContent: hi there!

8. Click the **Set Application Tile Properties** button.

9. To see the results of the modifications, click the **Start** button in the emulator, click the right-facing arrow to display the application list, click and hold **sdkTilesCS**, and then select **pin to Start**. The Application Tile is shown in Figure 7-21. Hover your mouse pointer over the Tile until it flips over.

Figure 7-21

The configured Application Tile

Front   Back

10. (Optional) Click the **Back** button to return to the main page. Click the **Change Secondary Tile** button. Use the following settings to update the secondary Tile, clicking the appropriate button to set each property:

    • Title: secondary tile

    • Background: red.jpg

    • Count: 8

    • Back title: back of tile

    • Back background: green.jpg

    • Back content: I'm back

11. Click the **Start** button in the emulator to see the changes.

12. Close the emulator and the project file but leave the Visual Studio IDE open if you plan to complete the next exercise during this session.

➕ MORE INFORMATION

For more information about Tiles, visit the "Tiles Overview for Windows Phone" Web page at http://msdn.microsoft.com/en-us/library/hh202948(v=VS.92).aspx.

Using Tasks and Choosers to Enhance Application Functionality

A Chooser is an API that triggers a task outside of the current application and can return information to the application. A Launcher also triggers a task but does not return information to the application.

Lesson 2 introduced you to Choosers and Launchers. As a refresher, Launchers and Choosers are APIs that are called from within an original application, temporarily use built-in applications on a device, and then return the user to the original application. A Chooser can return information to the original application, such as letting the user select an email address from a contact list or save a phone number, but a Launcher cannot. You code tasks into your applications that are triggered by a Chooser or a Launcher.

Some Choosers and Launchers are very simple to code. A common Launcher opens Bing Maps and retrieves driving directions from a starting point to an ending point. Another Bing Maps Launcher opens a map to a specific location, or pinpoints the locations of a search term you provide such as "hotel" or "airport."

 CONFIGURE A LAUNCHER

GET READY. To configure a launcher that opens a map in Bing Maps to a specific location, perform the following steps:

1. In the Visual Studio IDE, open the **L7-Practice** project.

2. Double-click the **MainPage.xaml** file in Solution Explorer.

3. Open the Toolbox, drag the **Button** control to the design surface and drop it under the existing controls. Close the Toolbox.

4. Set the new button's Content property to **Get Map**.

5. Add a reference to System.Device to your project. To do so, right-click the project name in Solution Explorer and select **Add Reference**. Scroll down to locate **System. Device**, select it, and click **OK**.

6. Add the following statements to the end of the using statements near the beginning of the code-behind file:

```
using Microsoft.Phone.Tasks;
using System.Device.Location;
```

7. Double-click the **Get Map** Button control on the design surface. In the code-behind file, add the following code to the button click event:

```
BingMapsTask bingMapsTask = new BingMapsTask();
bingMapsTask.SearchTerm = "Grand Canyon";
bingMapsTask.Show();
```

The code should look like Figure 7-22.

Figure 7-22

Code for the Get Map button

```
        string mySales = "";
        foreach (Sales sales in myList)
        {
            mySales += sales.Region + "-" + sales.Total + Environment.NewLine;
        }

        textBlock1.Text = mySales;
    }

    private void button2_Click(object sender, RoutedEventArgs e)
    {
        BingMapsTask bingMapsTask = new BingMapsTask();
        bingMapsTask.SearchTerm = "Grand Canyon";
        bingMapsTask.Show();
    }
}
```

8. Click the **Start Debugging** button on the toolbar or press **F5** to open the application in the Windows Phone Emulator. Click the **Get Map** button. Click **allow** when prompted for permission to use location data. The map displays with the Grand Canyon indicated, as shown in Figure 7-23.

Figure 7-23

The map showing the location
of the Grand Canyon

9. Close the emulator.

10. Select **File > Save All** to save the project.

11. Close the emulator and the project file but leave the Visual Studio IDE open if you plan to complete the next exercise during this session.

✚ MORE INFORMATION

The "Choosers for Windows Phone" Web page at http://bit.ly/aZH2jr and the "Launchers for Windows Phone" Web page at http://bit.ly/wZeKhP offer details on Choosers and Launchers.

■ Creating the User Interface and Experience

↓ THE BOTTOM LINE

The UI is more than just controls with event handlers or tasks that run outside of the original application. Microsoft requires that Windows Phone applications have a uniform look and feel that's achievable by following detailed UI design guidelines. A few key features that contribute to a uniform UI are styles and themes.

Now that you've learned the nuts and bolts about what goes into the UI, and had some practice creating a working application, you're ready to dive into the intricacies of what exactly creates the Windows Phone user experience.

The following sections walk you through design guidelines you need to know about to create applications that will pass Marketplace submission requirements and produce consistent and appealing applications.

Creating the User Experience

The *user experience* is everything the user sees and interacts with in a Windows Phone application. Designers and developers must follow the User Experience Design Guidelines for Windows Phone to create the kind of user experience required by Microsoft.

The Metro style defines the look and feel of Windows Phone applications. A Metro style application is clean and focused, without cluttering the interface with unnecessary controls, text, or decorations. Buttons and other controls should be intuitive and easy to use.

Microsoft provides the User Experience Design Guidelines for Windows Phone at http://bit.ly/lvMuSW, which help designers and developers create a proper and consistent user experience in Windows Phone applications. Although the guidelines span many pages, it's important to become as familiar as possible with the content before creating applications that you intend to share with others. You can also expect to see user experience design questions on the MTA 98-373 exam.

Some of the highlights of the guidelines include the following:

- Applications must be simple, readable, and minimalistic.
- To ensure readability by a large audience, you should use a minimum font size of 15 points in your applications.
- Touch targets, such as buttons, should be at least 9 mm square to ensure usability.
- Controls should be separated by space rather than directly next to each other.
- Button labels should not be more than two words.

Design Templates for Windows Phone 7

Microsoft provides a collection of Adobe Photoshop template files you can use to create application layouts. They are not actual templates you can open in the Visual Studio IDE, rather, they show different ways of using controls in a user interface, which can inspire your development projects. The controls are those included in the Windows Phone SDK and the Silverlight for Windows Phone Toolkit.

The ZIP file that contains the Photoshop design templates also includes a Design Template for Windows Phone 7.pdf document that illustrates each design template. The PDF is handy for developers who don't have Photoshop. There is also a Font.zip file included that contains the SegoeWP True Type font files used in Metro style applications.

 WORK WITH WINDOWS PHONE 7 DESIGN TEMPLATES AND UI STANDARDS

GET READY. To get the Windows Phone 7 design templates, perform the following steps:

1. Using a Web browser, go to "Design Resources for Windows Phone" Web page at http://bit.ly/hnrXaY.
2. Click the **Design Templates for Windows Phone 7** link.
3. Save the Design Templates for Windows Phone 7.zip file to your Visual Studio IDE Projects folder or another folder you use to hold app development files.
4. In Windows Explorer, navigate to the ZIP file, double-click it, and then extract the files.
5. Open the **Design Templates for Windows Phone 7.pdf** file. Browse its contents. Close the file when you're finished.
6. To work with a design templates project and see how pages are laid out using the Windows Phone UI Design standards, go to http://wp7designtemplates.codeplex.com/.
7. Click the **download** button and then download the WindowsPhone7UXGuide.zip file to your Visual Studio IDE Projects folder.
8. In Windows Explorer, navigate to the ZIP file, double-click it, and then extract the files.
9. In the Visual Studio IDE, open the **WindowsPhone7UXGuide.sln** project file.
10. In Solution Explorer, open the **Pages** folder.
11. Double-click each XAML page file to view it in Design view.
12. Close the project file and leave the Visual Studio IDE open if you plan to complete the next exercise during this session.

Creating Layout with Styles

A style provides an easy way to apply consistent formatting to controls of the same type. You define a style in XAML, and the TargetType property indicates which control is affected throughout the app. Styles use Setter elements to define each element of a style, such as height, font size, and so on.

A Windows Phone *style* is a collection of control property settings that you can apply to multiple controls of the same type. Let's say your application includes several TextBlock controls that you want to look the same. You can create property attributes in XAML that will affect all TextBlock controls in your application, rather than having to format each control one by one. When you want to change an attribute, making the change once affects all TextBlocks. The concept is similar to how Cascading Style Sheets (CSS) work with HTML documents.

In XAML, you create a Style section and set the TargetType property to the type of control you want to affect. You use Setter elements to apply specific style attributes like FontSize, Height, and so on. You can also assign a key to the style using the x:Key attribute and reference it by name when you declare a type.

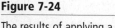 **APPLY A STYLE TO A CONTROL**

GET READY. To apply a style to a control using the TargetType property, perform the following steps:

1. In the Visual Studio IDE, open the **L7-Practice** project.

2. Double-click the **App.xaml** file in Solution Explorer.

3. Add the following Style code within the <Application.Resources> tags in the Application Resources section:

```
<Style TargetType="TextBlock">
    <Setter Property="Foreground" Value="SkyBlue" />
</Style>
```

4. Click the **Start Debugging** button on the toolbar or press **F5** to open the application in the Windows Phone Emulator. Click the **Get Data** button. The list data displays, this time in a skyblue font color.

Figure 7-24

The results of applying a style

5. Close the emulator.

6. Select **File** > **Save All** to save the project.

7. Close the project file and leave the Visual Studio IDE open if you plan to complete the next exercise during this session.

Understanding Themes, Accent Color, and Orientation

Themes apply a uniform look and feel to an application's background, and to the controls and other UI elements. Accent colors are part of a theme and apply only to controls and UI elements.

CERTIFICATION READY
What is a Windows
Phone theme?
4.4

A Windows Phone *theme* is a set of resources used to create a uniform style across all of the controls and UI elements on a Windows Phone device. By applying a theme, you can achieve a consistent look throughout an application. One common use for themes is to apply an organization's branding (color scheme) to an application.

The style properties of a theme include background colors and accent colors. The background color is the color of the background, which can be Dark or Light. Accent colors apply to controls and other UI elements, and you can choose from 10 standard colors as shown in Table 7-1.

Table 7-1

Common HTML tags
Windows Phone Theme
Accent Colors

COLOR	HEXADECIMAL (HEX) CODE
Blue	1BA1E2
Brown	996600
Green	339933
Lime	8CBF26
Magenta	FF0097
Orange	F09609
Pink	FF0097
Purple	A200FF
Red	E51400
Teal	00ABA9

Theme resources, such as styles, brushes, and control colors, are specified in ThemeResources.xaml. Each combination of accent and background has a different resource file.

Themes are applied by drawing from resources and resource dictionaries when an application launches. You apply themes using the Properties window for controls or in the XAML using the {StaticResource} markup extension.

Layering Graphical Elements

The Windows Phone operating system allows you to layer some controls to create visual effects in the interface. The order in which elements are displayed is referred to as z-order. Overlapping is handy for applying a border or background to a control.

In Windows Phone, you can layer elements in the interface. Silverlight draws (or displays) controls and other UI elements in the order in which they appear in XAML code, which means two controls can share the same area of a page, overlapping partially or completely. The order in which elements are displayed is referred to as z-order.

Overlapping is handy for applying a border or background to a control. You use the Border control to create a border and/or background for UI elements. The Opacity property affects the amount of transparency of a UI element, so you can control how much of an underlying element shows through the element on top.

CERTIFICATION READY
Which property controls the amount of transparency when an element is drawn in the UI?
4.4

Integrating Images and Media in an Application

You can add images and media to Windows Phone applications using the Image control and the MediaElement control, respectively.

CERTIFICATION READY
Which control is used to insert audio and video into an application?
4.4

Incorporating images and media in a Windows Phone application requires two controls: the *Image control* for images and the *MediaElement control* for video and audio.

To use the Image control, drag the Image control from the Toolbox to the design surface and then open the Properties window and specify a file path and file name where the image file is located in the Source property. The image displays in the user interface. The file path is referred to as the URI, but it can be a located on the Web or on your computer disk.

You can also drag the MediaElement control from the Toolbox to the design surface. The following code is automatically added to MainPage.xaml:

```
<MediaElement Height="120" HorizontalAlignment="Left"
Margin="265,286,0,0" Name="mediaElement1" VerticalAlignment="Top"
Width="160" />
```

To start playing the media, create a button with the following code in the button1_Click event handler:

```
private void button1_Click(object sender,
RoutedEventArgs e)
{
    mediaElement1.Stop();

    mediaElement1.Source = new
Uri("media/soundfile.mp3", UriKind.Relative);
}
```

Insert this code for the mediaElement1_MediaOpened event handler:

```
private void mediaElement1_MediaOpened(object sender, RoutedEventArgs e)
{
    MediaElement m = (MediaElement)sender;
    m.Play();
}
```

The Stop call ensures that the MediaElement is in the "stopped" state, the code for the Source property opens the media file, and the Play method plays the media file.

➡ INSERT AN IMAGE INTO AN APPLICATION

GET READY. To insert an image into an application and then change it to a different image, perform the following steps:

1. In Windows Explorer, create a subfolder in the Projects folder named **images**.
2. Create a simple drawing in Microsoft Paint with a solid background. The dimensions should be 173 × 173. Save the file as **image1.png** in the images subfolder.

3. In the Visual Studio IDE, create a new project named **Image-Practice** using the C# Windows Phone Application template.

4. Open the Toolbox and drag the **Image** control to the design surface.

5. Right-click the **Image** control and select **Properties** to open the Properties window.

6. In the Source property, click the ellipsis (three dots) to open the Add dialog box. Click the **Add** button, navigate to the **/Projects/images** folder, select **image1.png**, and click **OK**. The image displays on the design surface as shown in Figure 7-25.

7. Save and close the project file, close the Visual Studio IDE.

Figure 7-25

The Image control displaying an image

SKILL SUMMARY

IN THIS LESSON YOU LEARNED:

- Windows Phone displays the elements users view or interact in an application by using controls. The Windows Phone SDK comes with a standard set of controls like Button, Image, and WebBrowser. The Silverlight for Windows Phone Toolkit provides additional controls that help you enhance the user interface (UI).

- Controls are used to create the user interface in a Windows Phone app. Most controls allow you to modify their properties such as width, height, or foreground. When a user acts on a control, such as clicking a button or entering text into a text block, an event is raised. An event handler is a method you create in the code-behind file to handle the event.

- You use Panels to lay out controls in Windows Phone applications. The Grid panel uses columns and rows, the StackPanel lays out controls in a vertical or horizontal line, and the Canvas panel specifies a precise location for a control.

- Push notifications include toast, Tile, and raw. An application uses two types of Tiles: an Application Tile and secondary Tiles.

- A Chooser is an API that triggers a task outside of the current application and can return information to the application. A Launcher also triggers a task but does not return information to the application.

- The UI is more than just controls with event handlers or tasks that run outside of the original application. Microsoft requires that Windows Phone applications have a uniform look and feel that's achievable by following detailed UI design guidelines. A few key features that contribute to a uniform UI are styles and themes.

- The user experience is everything the user sees and interacts with in a Windows Phone application. Designers and developers must follow the User Experience Design Guidelines for Windows Phone to create the kind of user experience required by Microsoft.
- A style provides an easy way to apply consistent formatting to controls of the same type. You define a style in XAML, and the `TargetType` property indicates which control is affected throughout the app. Styles use Setter elements to define each element of a style, such as height, font size, and so on.
- Themes apply a uniform look and feel to an application's background, and to the controls and other UI elements. Accent colors are part of a theme and apply only to controls and UI elements.
- The Windows Phone operating system allows you to layer some controls to create visual effects in the interface. The order in which elements are displayed is referred to as z-order. Overlapping is handy for applying a border or background to a control.
- You can add images and media to Windows Phone applications using the Image control and the `MediaElement` control, respectively.

■ Knowledge Assessment

Fill in the Blank

Complete the following sentences by writing the correct word or words in the blanks provided.

1. An _____ is a method you create to handle an event.

2. A _____ is essentially a new control based on, or derived from, an existing control.

3. A _____ enables you to bind data items to list items and customize how list items are displayed on a Windows Phone device.

4. _____, which include Grid, StackPanel, and Canvas, enable you to define how controls are laid out in a Windows Phone application.

5. A _____ is a link to an application that's displayed on the Windows Phone Start page.

6. The _____ is everything the user sees and interacts with in a Windows Phone application.

7. A Windows Phone _____ is a collection of control property settings that you can apply to multiple controls of the same type.

8. _____ are additional tiles on the Start page that link to unique information generated by an app.

9. A Windows Phone _____ is a set of resources used to create a uniform style across all of the controls and UI elements on a Windows Phone device.

10. You use the _____ control to incorporate audio and video into a Windows Phone application.

Multiple Choice

Circle the letter that corresponds to the best answer.

1. Which techniques can be used to add a control to an application in the Visual Studio IDE? (Choose all that apply.)
   a. Right-click an existing control in the design surface and select Add.
   b. Drag a control from the Toolbox to the design surface.
   c. Edit the XAML file.
   d. Edit the code-behind file.

2. Most button and selection controls derive from which of the following classes?
   a. `TextBlock`
   b. `ContentControl`
   c. `Panel`
   d. `ItemsSource`

3. When populating a collection, which method is most commonly used?
   a. `Get`
   b. `Put`
   c. `List`
   d. `Add`

4. Which of the following lets you locate controls in a specific location using x and y coordinates in pixels?
   a. Grid
   b. StackPanel
   c. Canvas
   d. TextBlock

5. Which property is a character string that displays at the bottom of the back of a Tile and is 39 characters or less?
   a. `Title`
   b. `BackTitle`
   c. `BackContent`
   d. `BackBackgroundImage`

6. To ensure readability by a large audience, what is the minimum font size you should use in Windows Phone applications?
   a. 10 point
   b. 15 point
   c. 18 point
   d. 20 point

7. Which of the following is similar in concept to CSS?
   a. Styles
   b. StackPanels
   c. Data templates
   d. Collections

8. The style properties of a theme include which of the following? (Choose all that apply.)
   a. Font size
   b. Grid layout
   c. Background color
   d. Accent color

9. Which colors can you use as accent colors in a theme? (Choose all that apply.)
   a. Brown
   b. Skyblue
   c. Green
   d. Orange

10. Which of the following is *not* true of design templates for Windows Phone 7?
    a. They are Adobe Photoshop files.
    b. They are actual templates you can open in the Visual Studio IDE.
    c. They showcase controls from the Windows Phone SDK and the Silverlight for Windows Phone Toolkit.
    d. They use the Metro style.

True/False

Circle T if the statement is true or F if the statement is false.

T   F   **1.** The StackPanel is a panel that uses columns and rows similar to a spreadsheet.

T   F   **2.** You should add space between controls in the user interface.

T   F   **3.** A Chooser can return information to the original application but a Launcher cannot.

T   F   **4.** The background color of a theme may be one of 10 colors.

T   F   **5.** The order in which elements are displayed in the interface is referred to as the i-order.

■ Competency Assessment

Scenario 7-1: Create an Event Handler

Amit is a brand-new application developer. He's creating his first app that includes a TextBox control and a Button control. He wants the button to perform an action when clicked or tapped by the user, but doesn't know how to do that in the XAML file. To save himself some research time, he asks you for pointers. What do you tell him?

Scenario 7-2: Add Tasks to an Application

Lizzie is a consultant who is developing an application for sales people who travel across the United States. The application helps the sales people book flights and hotel rooms. She wants her application to include a way for users to locate hotels and restaurants in certain locations. She has asked you for advice as to the more efficient way to incorporate this functionality. What do you tell her?

■ Proficiency Assessment

Scenario 7-3: Understand Tiles

Dexter is a graphic design student who is learning about mobile app development to expand his skills. He has created an application and now wants to include Tiles for the app on the Start page. He doesn't understand the difference between an Application Tile versus secondary Tiles. What do you tell him?

Scenario 7-4: Ensure a Consistent User Interface

Sondra is a project manager overseeing a complex user interface development project by a team of developers. Although the team will meet weekly and have constant access to each other through instant messaging and screen sharing, each developer will work more or less independently. What can Sondra do to ensure that all developers create a consistent user interface?

Testing, Debugging, and Deploying a Mobile App

EXAM OBJECTIVE MATRIX

SKILLS/CONCEPTS	MTA EXAM OBJECTIVE	MTA EXAM OBJECTIVE NUMBER
Understanding Windows Phone Marketplace Submission Rules and Requirements	Understand design for mobile devices.	3.1
Setting Up a Test Environment	Work with Developer Tools.	3.4
Packaging and Deploying an Application	Work with Developer Tools.	3.4
Testing and Debugging Mobile Applications	Work with Developer Tools.	3.4
	Understand Code for Mobile Applications.	3.5

KEY TERMS

compile

metadata

non-transparent PNG file

side-loading

Windows Phone Developer Registration tool

Windows Phone Emulator

Windows Phone Marketplace

XAP file

You have created the Twitter client application as requested by the BoxTwelve Mobile application development team. Now it's time to test the app, debug the app, and prepare it for submission to the Windows Phone Marketplace.

■ Understanding Windows Phone Marketplace Submission Rules and Requirements

THE BOTTOM LINE

Windows Phone apps are distributed through the Windows Phone Marketplace, whether the apps are free or for a fee. You must have an App Hub membership to submit apps to the Marketplace. Microsoft requires that all apps go through a stringent testing and certification process before being accepted for Marketplace listing.

The *Windows Phone Marketplace* is an online store where developers can sell apps or give them away for free. All apps must pass Microsoft certification requirements to be listed in the Marketplace.

Recall from Lesson 1 that you must first sign up and pay for an annual membership at App Hub (http://create.msdn.com/en-US/); memberships cost $99 per year. Students registered at Microsoft DreamSpark can get an App Hub membership for free by completing the signup form on the DreamSpark Web site at https://www.dreamspark.com/.

App Hub membership allows you to deploy, test, and debug your applications on a physical device you acquire, and to publish and distribute your app through the Marketplace. During the App Hub membership signup process, you'll receive an Authenticode certificate that will be used by Microsoft to digitally sign apps you develop that pass certification requirements.

Microsoft publishes its detailed application submission requirements at http://bit.ly/IGDYqo and the same information is provided by App Hub. You must become highly familiar with the requirements before attempting to submit an app through App Hub for Marketplace consideration. Some of the highlights of the submission requirements are:

TAKE NOTE*

You must have a registered Windows Phone device to download apps from the Marketplace.

- Develop apps using documented APIs for the Windows Phone operating system version your app targets.
- Localize your app in at least one of the languages supported by Windows Phone.
- Submit an icon for use in the Windows Phone Marketplace catalog listing for your app.
- Submit one to eight screen shots of key screens of your app.
- Do not submit an XAP package (which is the package you build and actually upload to Microsoft) that exceeds 225 megabytes (MB). The app package must include a valid Windows Phone application manifest file named WMAppManifest.xml, a valid .NET application manifest file named AppManifest.xml, the assembly files for your app, and required artwork.

CERTIFICATION READY
What is the maximum file size of the XAP package you submit for Marketplace approval?
3.1

Note that submission requirements may change over time, so you should check them occasionally if you're developing a complex application that takes several weeks or months to complete.

The general Windows Phone application submission and certification process, shown in Figure 8-1, is summarized as follows:

- **Submit your app for certification:** Once you've developed and thoroughly tested a mobile app or game, you can submit it to the Windows Phone Marketplace for certification and approval. You must sign in to your App Hub account, create a submission application, and upload the application's XAP file.
- **Add metadata:** You must enter *metadata* for your app, which includes the application's title, description, the category it should appear in, and the icons that will accompany the app. You must also choose which countries your app may be distributed in and set the pricing for your app.

- **Validate:** Microsoft validates the XAP file while you enter metadata. You can select an option to publish the app right after certification if your app passes validation or choose to publish at a later date.

- **Test and certify:** Microsoft tests all apps to ensure they meet all policies and requirements, run properly, are reliable, and are free of malicious content. The company certifies apps that pass testing. During the testing and certification process, Microsoft repackages your application's XAP file and deploys it to a device. Microsoft provides a checklist to help you prepare for certification at http://bit.ly/9mWNla.

- **Sign:** Microsoft code-signs applications that meet all Windows Phone Marketplace requirements using the Authenticode certificate you obtained when you signed up for App Hub membership.

- **List in Marketplace:** Upon approval, your app may be published immediately or at a later date on the Windows Phone Marketplace Web site and will appear in the Windows Phone Marketplace catalog.

Figure 8-1

The Windows Phone Marketplace app submission and certification process

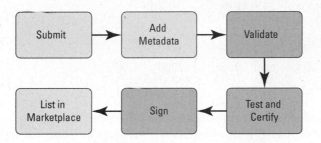

If your app does not pass certification testing you'll receive a failure report. You must fix any problems noted in the failure report, thoroughly retest the app, repackage the app, and submit it again for validation and certification testing.

REVIEW WINDOWS PHONE MARKETPLACE APPLICATION SUBMISSION AND CERTIFICATION REQUIREMENTS

GET READY. To ensure you understand the Marketplace submission and certification requirements, perform the following steps:

1. Using a Web browser, visit the "Application Submission Requirements" Web page at http://bit.ly/IGDYqo.

2. Read the contents of the Web page.

3. Take notes regarding any steps you need to take or items you must create before you can submit your app for testing and certification. For example, do you have the required artwork for your app? If not, can you create it yourself or do you need to consult with a graphic artist?

4. Close the Web browser.

➕ **MORE INFORMATION**

As noted previously, the "Application Submission Requirements" Web page at http://bit.ly/IGDYqo provides details on requirements for submitting apps for testing and certification. You should also browse the linked pages on the "Windows Phone Marketplace FAQ" Web page at http://bit.ly/iQpU6P.

Understanding Artwork Specifications

> Images and icons in a Windows Phone application include must meet Microsoft size specifications as shown in Table 8-1, and icons must be non-transparent PNG files. A **_non-transparent PNG file_** has 100 percent opacity, which means you can't see through the PNG file to view anything that's behind it.

The application's Tile on the Start page and the small icon alongside the application name in the applications list are considered part of the package imagery, in addition to any other images used in the app. Image files are generally located in your application's project folder unless you specify a different folder, such as an images subfolder, when adding them to your application.

Table 8-1

Windows Phone app image size specifications

IMAGES AND ICONS	PIXEL SIZE	FORMAT
Application (that appears in application list)	62 × 62	PNG
Application Tile	173 × 173	PNG
General application images	2000 × 2000 maximum	JPG or PNG

CERTIFICATION READY
What are the dimensions for the Application Tile as specified by Microsoft?
3.1

In addition, Microsoft requires that you submit one icon to appear in your application's Marketplace listing, which is what users see when browsing for apps. This icon should match or closely match the Application Tile icon in your application.

The following are required pieces of artwork for an app's Windows Phone Marketplace catalog listing, which must be in PNG format:

- A mobile app tile icon that measures 99 × 99 pixels in size
- A large PC app tile icon that measures 200 × 200 pixels in size

The following are optional pieces of artwork, which must be in PNG format:

- A large mobile app tile icon that measures 173 × 173 pixels in size for an app's Windows Phone Marketplace catalog listing
- Background art for the Background panorama that measures 1000 × 800 pixels in size; you must provide this background art if your app is selected as a featured app in the Marketplace catalog

Finally, you must submit one to eight screen shots of screens in your app, which are used in the Details page of the Marketplace catalog for your listing. This is a marketing tool of sorts, because users browse the details page to decide if they want to buy your app.

The screen shots must be 480 × 800 pixels in PNG format. In addition, the screen shots must show app graphics only, and may not include the Windows Phone Emulator chrome (the sides of the emulator that resemble an actual device), frame rate counters, or debugging information.

The next exercise has you review the artwork for your application, and offers a tip for creating icons if you still need them.

⊖ CHECK YOUR APPLICATION'S ARTWORK

GET READY. To check your application's artwork, perform the following steps:

1. Locate the icon files you already have for your application. They should be in your app's project folder unless you created a separate folder for them during development.

2. Confirm that the icons make sense for your application. Consider getting feedback from a trusted friend or associate.

3. Verify that the icons meet the Marketplace standards regarding size and format (non-transparent PNG). If not, replace the icons.

4. If you need icons, consider using Microsoft Expression Design or a similar program to create them. Expression Design provides tools for creating graphics. If you want to try creating icons for your app, consider downloading and installing a trial version of Expression Design from Microsoft.com (search for **Expression Design**), and then go through the Creating Windows Phone 7 Application and Marketplace Icons tutorial at http://bit.ly/9LLi8P. The tutorial is long, but the author provides a lot of details that walk you through each step.

5. Practice taking crisp, clear screen shots of your app in Windows Phone Emulator. The "How to: Create Screenshots for Windows Phone Marketplace" Web page at http://bit.ly/fSNp9y offers guidance. The Windows Phone Emulator has a built-in screen capture tool, which should be the tool of choice. However, you can also use the Windows Snipping Tool, which saves in PNG or JPG format, in addition to third-party screen capture utilities such as SnagIt, IrfanView, and many others.

+ MORE INFORMATION

For details about artwork specifications, visit the "Application Artwork" Web page at http://bit.ly/LPW6SH.

■ Setting Up a Test Environment

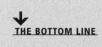

↓
THE BOTTOM LINE

Testing a Windows Phone application requires the *Windows Phone Emulator* and a physical Windows Phone device (at some point during development). You also need a set of utilities that come with the Windows Phone SDK and the Microsoft Zune software.

To test Windows Phone applications, you need the Windows Phone Emulator and a physical Windows Phone device. In addition, you need the following utilities:

- **Windows Phone Developer Registration tool:** To register a device with Microsoft through your App Hub account

- **Zune software:** For PC-to-device synchronization to test an app package on a device connected to your computer

- **Windows Phone Connect Tool:** To connect a Windows Phone device to a computer to test an app on the physical device

- **Application Deployment tool:** To deploy your app to a registered device

- **Windows Phone Capability Detection Tool:** To detect application capabilities for apps that target Windows Phone OS 7.0

- **Windows Phone Marketplace Test Kit:** To detect application capabilities for apps that target Windows Phone OS 7.1

- **Windows Phone Performance Analysis tool:** To analyze and improve the performance of an application

You'll revisit these tools throughout the remainder of this lesson.

By this point in the book you're familiar with the *Windows Phone Emulator*, a virtual device environment that's built in to the Visual Studio IDE. You've used the emulator throughout the lessons to view the user interface (UI) of applications and their functionality.

CERTIFICATION READY
Can you use the Application Deployment tool to deploy an app package to Windows Phone Emulator?

3.4

However, the emulator is limited as to what it can do. For example, you cannot directly use the camera, Compass, Gyroscope, Accelerometer, or GPS features in Windows Phone Emulator, although you can simulate Accelerometer and location-related apps. In addition, some networking features do not work in the emulator. Even so, the emulator is a good first step toward testing the UI and functionality of your apps during development.

At some point during development, you must use a physical Windows Phone device for testing purposes. Doing so ensures that the application will work in the real world. Many schools make devices available to students for use in the classroom. You can also use an old phone you're no longer using as long as it runs the Windows Phone operating system.

If you must acquire a device on your own, you can shop for phones through the Windows Phone Marketplace Buy Web page at http://bit.ly/qsKLnu. The links on the page direct you to service plan provider sites, where you can buy phones with or without a service contract. Various e-commerce sites sell phones that are unlocked and/or don't require a cellular service plan. You might be able to find a low-cost phone through channels such as Amazon, eBay, or Craigslist.

> **TAKE NOTE** *
>
> If you have only one Windows Phone device and use it as your personal phone, it is not recommended that you use the device for testing apps.

⊕ EXPLORE WINDOWS PHONE DEVICE AVAILABILITY

GET READY. To find out where to acquire Windows Phone devices for development and testing, perform the following steps:

1. Using a Web browser, search for **unlocked Windows Phone for developer**.

2. Use a word processor or spreadsheet to make notes as you research sources of Windows Phone devices. Keep track of which sites have devices available that would make a good addition to your development toolkit. Also note the prices.

3. Go to App Hub at http://create.msdn.com/en-US/ and search the forums for tips on acquiring test devices.

4. Visit Amazon.com, eBay.com, Craigslist.org, and a few similar Web sites and search for **Windows Phone**.

5. Save your notes in the word processor spreadsheet program, close the program, and close the Web browser.

> **⊕ MORE INFORMATION**
>
> Visit the "Troubleshooting Windows Phone Emulator" Web page at http://bit.ly/M3en1V for information on troubleshooting issues that arise when using Windows Phone Emulator.

Currently, Microsoft allows developers to register three devices per App Hub account tied a Windows Live ID. If you require more than three devices to develop apps, Microsoft will consider your circumstances and possibly allow you to register the additional devices.

To register a device, you must use the *Windows Phone Developer Registration tool*, which registers a Windows Phone device with Microsoft for development purposes. The tool was installed when you installed the Windows Phone SDK. Once you register your device, you can install, run, and test unsigned applications on the device.

⊕ REGISTER A WINDOWS PHONE DEVICE

GET READY. If you have a Windows Phone device for development and testing and want to register and unlock it, perform the following steps:

1. Connect your Windows Phone device to your PC with a USB cable. The Zune software you installed in Lesson 1 should start automatically. If not, select **Start**, type **Zune** in the **Search programs and files** text box, and then click **Zune** in the results list.

2. To open the Windows Phone Developer Registration tool, select **Start > All Programs > Windows Phone SDK version > Windows Phone Developer Registration**. The Windows Phone Developer Registration window displays, as shown in Figure 8-2.

Figure 8-2

The Windows Phone Developer Registration window

3. Type your Windows Live ID and account password in the text boxes, and then click **Register.** A status message displays, stating that your phone has been successfully registered.

4. Close the Windows Phone Developer Registration program.

5. In Zune, register your device with the Zune application if you haven't done so already. Follow the prompts to unlock your device.

6. Close the Zune software program.

■ Packaging and Deploying an Application

↓ **THE BOTTOM LINE**

Creating a release build of an application deployment package prepares the app to be run on a device. The build process, whether it's a debug or release build, creates a XAP file that contains the manifest files, assembly files, and graphics and any other resource files.

You can create two kinds of deployment builds using the Visual Studio IDE: a debug build and a release build. Recall from Lesson 3 that when you click the Start Debugging button on the toolbar or press F5 in the Visual Studio IDE, the program checks your application for errors and creates a debug build of your application. If no severe build errors are detected, your application opens in the Windows Phone Emulator, as long as you selected one of the emulator versions in the Select target for Windows Phone projects drop-down list to the right of the Start Debugging button on the toolbar.

When you want to test the app on a physical device, you need to create a release build of your application. You can create a release build in the Visual Studio IDE by selecting Debug > Build Solution from the menu bar or by pressing F6.

Creating a build *compiles* the application, which means to translate the programming language files into a format the device can read. The XAML and code files you've worked with in the Visual Studio IDE are compiled into a data link library (DLL) file, which is then compressed into a file with a .XAP extension. The *XAP file* contains all of the files, including graphic images and icons, needed to run and view the application on a device. The file is simply an archive file—you could change the extension to "zip" and open it like any other archive file.

CERTIFICATION READY
What does it mean to compile an application?
3.4

The XAP file is located in the project folder's \Bin\Debug subfolder, along with the files that are included in the XAP file.

The XAP file has at least one assembly related to the code in your app, additional assemblies (if any), the WMAppManifest.xml file, and the .NET AppManifest.xaml file. At a minimum, the following files are included:

CERTIFICATION READY
Which files are in a XAP file?
3.4

- WMAppManifest.xml
- AppManifest.xaml
- The assembly files specified in the AppManifest.xaml file

Figure 8-3 shows the files in the \Bin\Debug folder for the GetTheTweets application.

Figure 8-3

The XAP file along with the files it contains

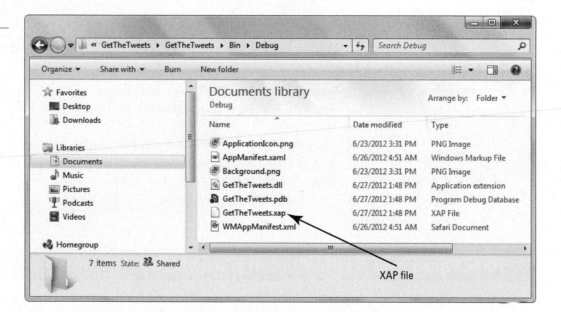

Once you generate a XAP file, you use the Application Development tool to copy the application to a physical device or to Windows Phone Emulator. The physical device must be registered and unlocked to be able to install apps for testing. Installing apps to a test device is referred to as *side-loading*.

TAKE NOTE*

The Zune software ordinarily runs in the background when you test an app on a physical device connected to your computer. However, for apps that include media APIs, Zune locks the local media database and prevents interaction between the APIs and your app. In this case, you should use the Windows Phone Connect Tool to connect your device and computer and then exit the Zune software.

⊕ CREATE A RELEASE BUILD AND DEPLOY TO A DEVICE

GET READY. To create a release build of an application and deploy to a physical device, perform the following steps:

1. In the Visual Studio IDE, open the project file for the application you want to deploy to a physical device, such as **GetTheTweets.**

2. Select **Debug** > **Build Solution** from the menu bar or press **F6.** If no errors are detected, the IDE creates the XAP package and then displays a Build succeeded message, as shown in Figure 8-4.

Figure 8-4

The Build succeeded message

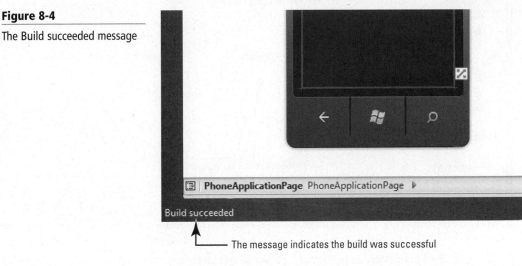

The message indicates the build was successful

3. Connect your device to your computer with a USB cable. The Zune software should start automatically; if not, start it manually.

4. Select **Start** > **All Programs** > **Windows Phone SDK version** > **Application Deployment.**

5. Select **Windows Phone Device** as the target device, as shown in Figure 8-5.

Figure 8-5

Selecting Windows Phone Device in the Application Deployment tool

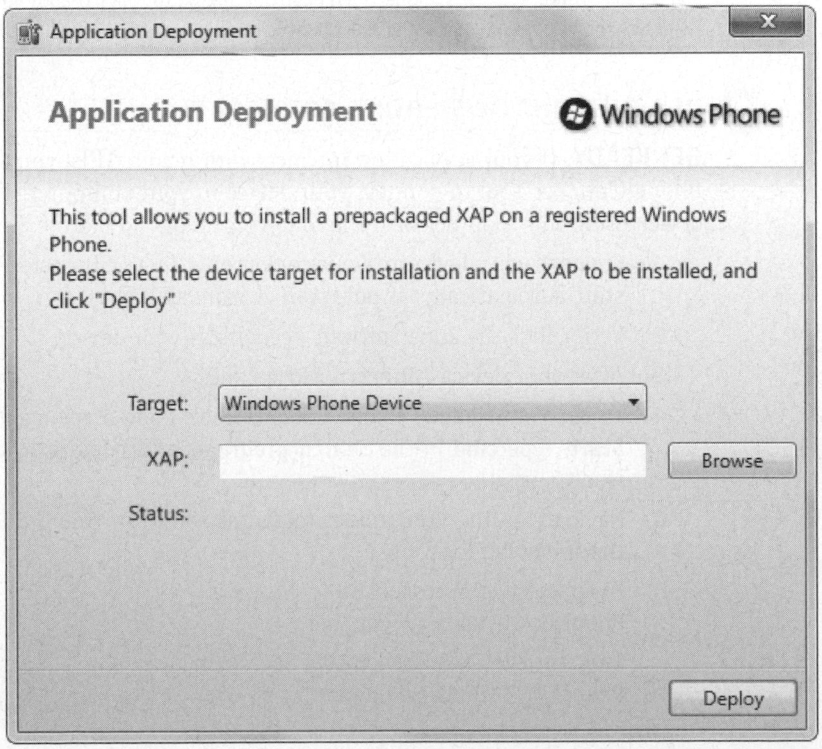

6. In the XAP field, browse for the application file you built in Step 1 (see Figure 8-6), select it, click **Open**, and then click the **Deploy** button. It can take a minute or two before the application is available in the application list on the device.

Figure 8-6

Selecting the XAP file

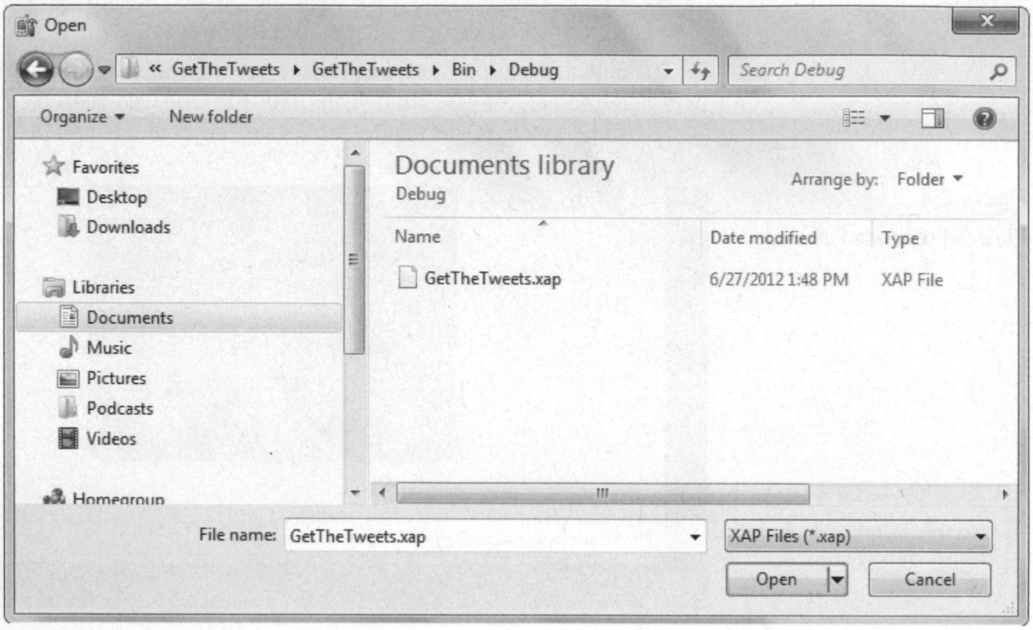

7. Use the application as you would normally and note any changes you need to make to the application's user interface and code, if any.

8. Close the application on the device and disconnect the device from the computer.

➕ MORE INFORMATION

For more information about creating an application package and deploying it to a device, visit the "Deploying and Testing on Your Windows Phone" Web page at http://bit.ly/h5hQYU and the "How to: Build and Deploy a Windows Phone Application Using Visual Studio" Web page at http://bit.ly/Lt6iOi.

USE THE WINDOWS PHONE CONNECT TOOL

GET READY. If your application interacts with media APIs, you'll need to use the Windows Phone Connect Tool to connect your device to your computer. To see how to connect to a device using this tool, perform the following steps:

1. Connect your device to your computer with a USB cable. The Zune software should start automatically; if not, start it manually.

2. Verify that the Zune software recognizes your device.

3. After your device connects, close Zune.

4. To use the Windows Phone Connect Tool, open a command prompt. To do so, select **Start**, type **cmd** in the **Search programs and files** text box, and click **cmd.exe** in the results list.

5. Navigate to the **WPConnect** folder, as shown in Figure 8-7. You can find it at one of the following locations:

Program Files\Microsoft SDKs\Windows Phone\v7.1\Tools\WPConnect

Program Files (x86)\Microsoft SDKs\Windows Phone\v7.1\Tools\WPConnect

Figure 8-7

The WPConnect folder

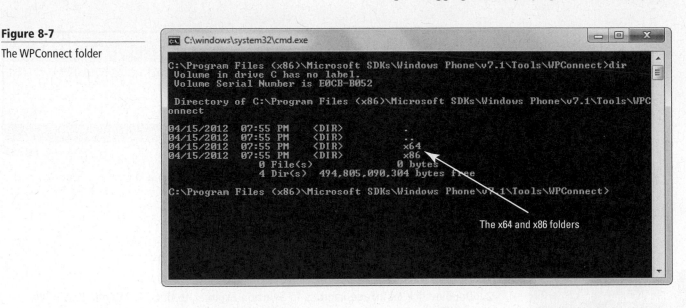

The x64 and x86 folders

6. Navigate to the **x86** or **x64** subfolder, depending on which version of the SDK you're running.

7. At the command prompt, enter **WPConnect.exe**.

8. A message appears confirming that your device is connected. You could now run the Application Deployment tool to test an application on the device, if necessary.

9. Disconnect the device and close the command prompt window.

■ Testing and Debugging Mobile Applications

↓ **THE BOTTOM LINE**

Testing an application in the Windows Phone Emulator and on a physical device helps you ensure that the UI works as expected and helps you detect any runtime errors.

When you prepare to use Windows Phone Emulator (by pressing the F5 key), the software detects any build errors. Those are the errors that prevent the code from being compiled and prevent you from opening the application in the emulator.

Runtime errors occur when an application is executing, and appear as unexpected or incorrect behaviors of the application. The only way to detect runtime errors is by testing an application on a physical device or in the emulator. You must note the odd behavior, return to the IDE, and attempt to fix the code or modify the UI. This process can be very easy if the glitch is obvious, but can also be very time-consuming if the issue requires a lot of code modification (and it can!).

Identifying Code Errors

CERTIFICATION READY
How does a build error differ from a runtime error?
3.4

A routine but sometimes frustrating part of creating and testing applications is to debug them and identify code errors. The Visual Studio IDE helps you identify code errors by displaying information in an Error List when build errors are detected.

A build error is often easier to resolve than a runtime error because the Visual Studio IDE opens an Error List window and presents information about build errors. An example of a build error is shown in Figure 8-8. The report clearly shows that the Zune software isn't running, so a release build cannot be created.

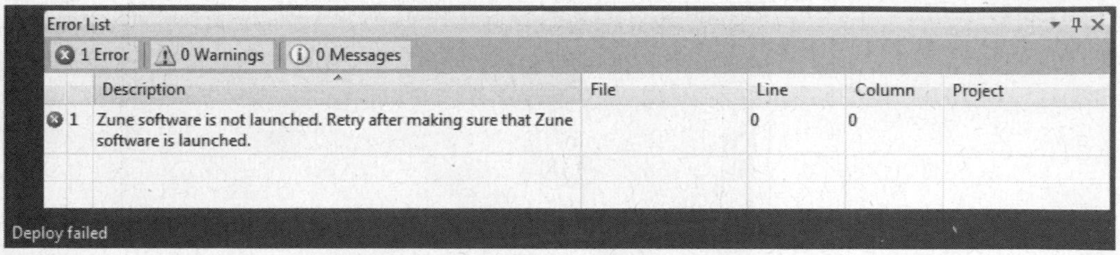

Figure 8-8

The Error List window indicates the build error that occurred

To resolve this issue, you would start the Zune software, verify your device is connected and recognized, and then try to build the solution again.

DEBUG AN APPLICATION AND IDENTIFY ERRORS

GET READY. To debug an application, perform the following steps:

CERTIFICATION READY

Which feature in the Visual Studio IDE helps you identify build errors?

3.5

1. In the Visual Studio IDE, open the **Scrolling Example** project.
2. Double-click **MainPage.xaml.cs** in Solution Explorer to open it in Code Editor. We'll modify some code so you can see an error appear in the Error List.
3. Scroll to the bottom of the code and delete the last curly bracket.
4. Select **File > Save All**.
5. Click the **Start Debugging** button on the menu bar or press **F5**.
6. The Errors List window displays in the Visual Studio IDE, as shown in Figure 8-9.

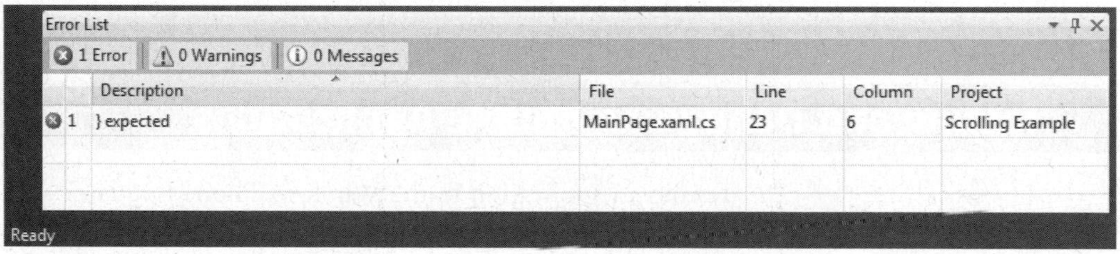

Figure 8-9

The Errors List after modifying code in MainPage.xaml.cs to throw an error

7. The error window shows a curly bracket is missing from a section of code in the MainPage.xaml.cs file of the Scrolling Example project. The report also indicates the code line and column where the bracket is missing. If you didn't already know what caused the error (but you do, because you deleted the bracket), the error window pinpoints the error for you.
8. Close the file without saving the changes but leave the Visual Studio IDE open.

Evaluating Code

You can use the Windows Phone Performance Analysis Tool and the Windows Phone Marketplace Test Kit to evaluate your code for Marketplace readiness. The Windows Phone Capability Detection tool can help you resolve any issues with your application manifest if your app is targeted to Windows Phone OS 7.0.

This section addresses how to evaluate code for readiness for the Windows Phone Marketplace. After testing an application and when you're ready to submit an application to the Marketplace, you should run the application through the Windows Phone Performance Analysis tool and the Windows Phone Marketplace Test Kit (or the Windows Phone Capability Detection Tool (for Windows Phone OS 7.0 apps).

The Windows Phone Performance Analysis tool checks the operating system and device resources your app consumes as it runs. It reports back to you on any bottlenecks or other issues you should address to improve the performance of your app.

The Windows Phone Marketplace Test Kit thoroughly examines your application, looking for any missing files. It will autodetect your app's capabilities if your app is targeted to Windows Phone OS 7.1.

Some of the things the Windows Phone Marketplace Kit will look for are the following, which are required for Marketplace submission:

- A valid Windows Phone application manifest file, named WMAppManifest.xml; the <Title> element in the WMAppManifest.xml file must contain the application title
- A valid .NET application manifest file, named AppManifest.xml
- An Application Tile
- The assembly files as specified in the AppManifest.xml file

If any issues are detected with the phone capabilities that are listed in the WMAppManifest. xml file for applications targeting Windows Phone OS 7.0, you can run the Windows Phone Capability Detection tool. It autodetects your app's capabilities and ensures your application manifest is correct. If you rebuild the application and still receive errors regarding the app manifest, your application might be using undocumented APIs.

CERTIFICATION READY
Which tool autodetects your application's capabilities and ensures your application manifest is correct?
3.5

RUN THE WINDOWS PHONE PERFORMANCE ANALYSIS

GET READY. To evaluate an application using the Windows Phone Performance Analysis, perform the following steps:

1. In the Visual Studio IDE, open the **GetMyTweets** project file.
2. Check the Build Action on each of the image files. Are all image files set to Content? If not, change the Build Action value.
3. Save the project file.
4. To run the Windows Phone Performance Analysis tool, you must first build the application by pressing **F6**.
5. When the build is complete, select **Debug > Start Windows Phone Performance Analysis**. Leave **Execution** selected in the window that displays, as shown in Figure 8-10. Click the **Launch Application** link. The tool connects to the Windows Phone Emulator.

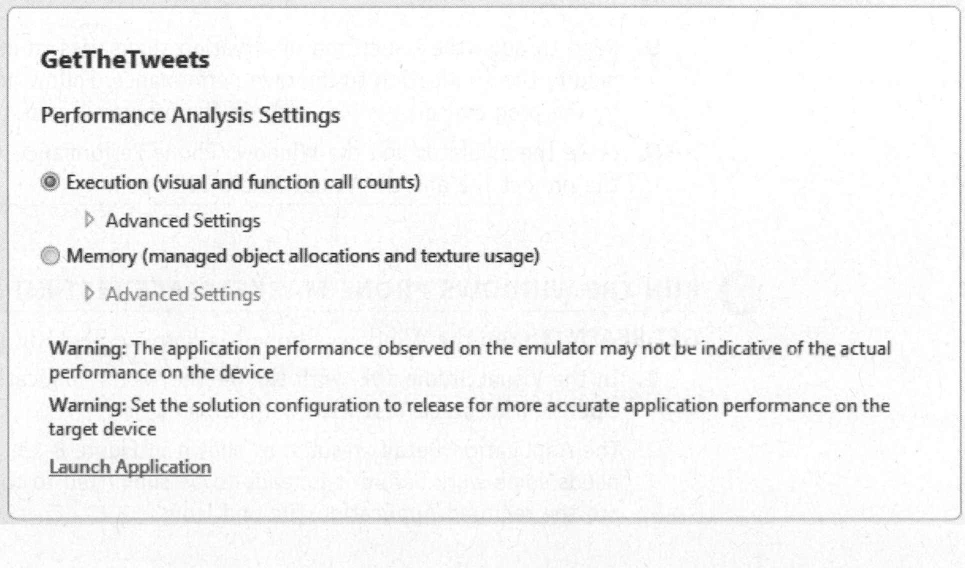

Figure 8-10

Selecting to profile execution performance data in the application

GetTheTweets

Performance Analysis Settings

◉ Execution (visual and function call counts)

▷ Advanced Settings

◯ Memory (managed object allocations and texture usage)

▷ Advanced Settings

Warning: The application performance observed on the emulator may not be indicative of the actual performance on the device

Warning: Set the solution configuration to release for more accurate application performance on the target device

Launch Application

6. Use the application to get tweets from the @WindowsPhone Twitter user.

7. Click the **Back** button in the emulator to stop the profiling. The performance data displays in chart form, as shown in Figure 8-11.

Figure 8-11

The results of the profiling

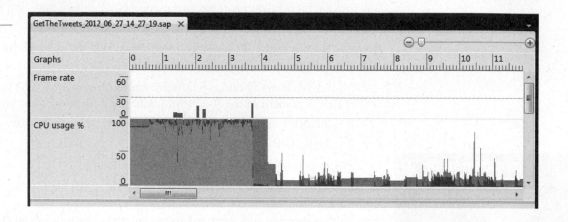

8. To get more information about a portion of the data, click and drag your mouse pointer over the timeline that corresponds to spikes or other unusual data points. The information displays below the chart, as shown in Figure 8-12.

Figure 8-12

More information about profiled performance data

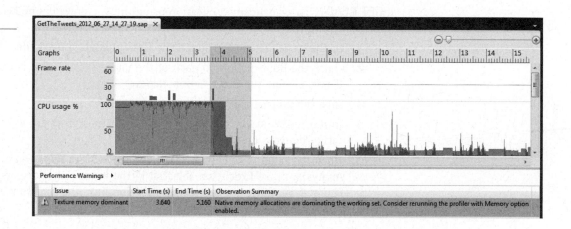

9. Read through the issues and observation summaries to determine if you need to modify the application to improve performance. Follow any recommendations offered by the program, if possible, and run the program again.

10. Close the emulator and the Windows Phone Performance Analysis window but leave the project file and the Visual Studio IDE open.

RUN THE WINDOWS PHONE MARKETPLACE TEST KIT

GET READY. To run the Windows Phone Marketplace Test Kit, perform the following steps:

1. In the Visual Studio IDE, with the GetTheTweets application open, select **Project > Open Marketplace Test Kit** from the menu bar.

2. The Application Details results, as shown in Figure 8-13, indicate that this application needs some work before it is ready to be submitted to the Marketplace, mainly to create the required Application Tile and icons.

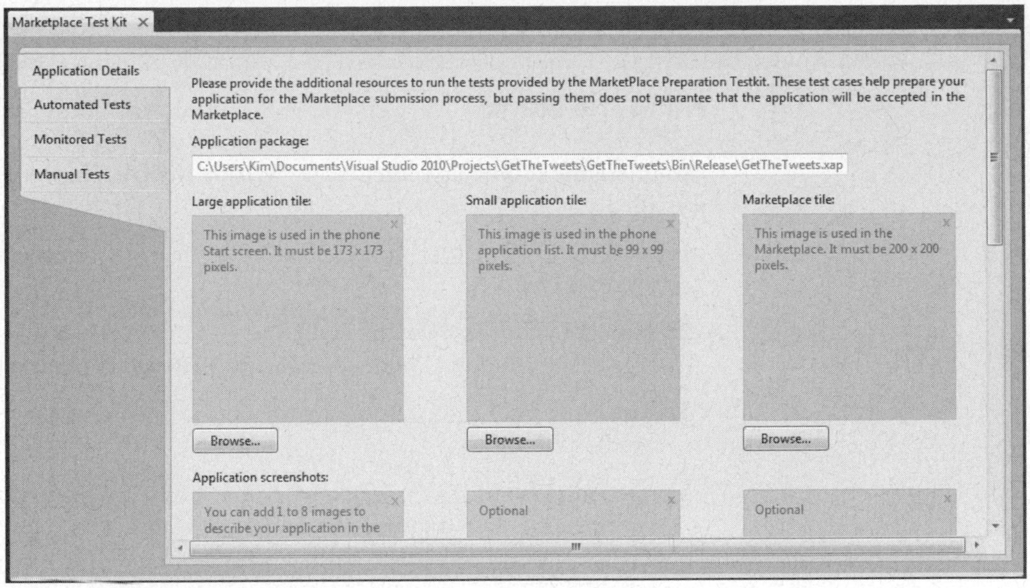

Figure 8-13

The Application Details results of the Windows Phone Marketplace Test Kit

3. Click the **Browse** button for each issue shown and read the information.
4. Click the **Automated Tests** tab on the left, and then click **Run Tests**. Browse the results of the tests.
5. Click the **Monitored Tests** tab on the left, and then click **Start Application**. Browse the results of the test.
6. Click the **Manual Tests** tab on the left, and browse the results of the tests.
7. Close the project file and the Visual Studio IDE.

SKILL SUMMARY

IN THIS LESSON YOU LEARNED:

- Windows Phone apps are distributed through the Windows Phone Marketplace, whether the apps are free or for a fee. You must have an App Hub membership to submit apps to the Marketplace. Microsoft requires that all apps go through a stringent testing and certification process before being accepted for Marketplace listing.
- Testing a Windows Phone application requires the Windows Phone Emulator and a physical Windows Phone device (at some point during development). You also need a set of utilities that come with the Windows Phone SDK and the Microsoft Zune software.
- Creating a release build of an application deployment package prepares the app to be run on a device. The build process, whether it's a debug or release build, creates a XAP file that contains the manifest files, assembly files, and graphics and any other resource files.
- Testing an application in the Windows Phone Emulator and on a physical device helps you ensure that the UI works as expected and helps you detect any runtime errors.
- A routine but sometimes frustrating part of creating and testing applications is to debug them and identify code errors. The Visual Studio IDE helps you identify code errors by displaying information in an Error List when build errors are detected.
- You can use the Windows Phone Performance Analysis Tool and the Windows Phone Marketplace Test Kit to evaluate your code for Marketplace readiness. The Windows Phone Capability Detection tool can help you resolve any issues with your application manifest.

Knowledge Assessment

Fill in the Blank

Complete the following sentences by writing the correct word or words in the blanks provided.

1. The _____ is an online store where developers can sell apps or give them away for free.

2. To register a device, you must use the _____ tool, which registers a Windows Phone device with Microsoft for development purposes.

3. The _____ is a virtual device environment that's built in to the Visual Studio IDE.

4. Creating a build _____ an application, which means to translate the programming language files into a format the device can read.

5. The _____ file contains all of the files, including graphic images and icons, needed to run and view the application on a device.

6. The XAML and code files are compiled into a _____ file, which is then compressed into a file with a .XAP extension.

7. The physical device must be registered and unlocked to be able to install apps for testing. Installing apps to a test device is referred to as _____.

8. Students registered at _____ can get an App Hub membership for free.

9. You must enter _____ for your app, which includes the application's title, description, the category it should appear in, and the icons that will accompany the app.

10. A _____ file has 100 percent opacity, which means you can't see through the image file to view anything that's behind it.

Multiple Choice

Circle the letter that corresponds to the best answer.

1. Which of the following is included in an App Hub membership? (Choose all that apply.)
   a. The ability to deploy, test, and debug your applications on a physical device
   b. The ability to publish your app to the Marketplace
   c. A free Windows Phone device for development purposes only
   d. A free Windows Phone device and one year of cellular service

2. Which of the following is not a requirement for Marketplace acceptance of your app?
   a. Use of documented APIs
   b. Localization of at least two languages supported by Windows Phone
   c. An icon for use in the Windows Phone Marketplace catalog listing
   d. One to eight screen shots of key screens of your app

3. What is the maximum size of an XAP package Microsoft will accept for consideration for Marketplace submission?
   a. 10 MB
   b. 25 MB
   c. 100 MB
   d. 225 MB

4. After you submit an application to Microsoft for submission to the Marketplace, which of the following does Microsoft handle? (Choose all that apply.)
   a. Add metadata
   b. Validate
   c. Test and certify
   d. Sign

5. After you submit an application to Microsoft for submission to the Marketplace, which of the following are you responsible for handling?
   a. Add metadata
   b. Validate
   c. Test and certify
   d. Sign

6. What is the required size of the Application Tile?
   a. 62 × 62
   b. 99 × 99
   c. 173 × 173
   d. 200 × 200

7. Which file holds all of the files needed for an app to run on a device?
   a. ZIP
   b. DLL
   c. XAP
   d. XAML

8. Which of the following would result in a build error?
   a. An image file that's much too big for the content in the screen
   b. An application manifest file that doesn't include all of the applications capabilities
   c. A missing Application Tile
   d. Missing code

9. Which of the following is most likely to result in a runtime error?
   a. An image file that's much too big for the content in the screen
   b. An application manifest file that doesn't include all of the applications capabilities
   c. A missing Application Tile
   d. Missing code

10. Which of the following must you use to be able to deploy and test an app that interacts with media APIs to a physical device?
   a. Windows Phone Marketplace Tool Kit
   b. Windows Phone Connect Tool
   c. Zune
   d. Windows Phone Capability Detection Tool

True/False

Circle T if the statement is true or F if the statement is false.

T   F   1. You must buy a Windows Phone through the Windows Phone Marketplace to use as a development tool.

T   F   2. The screen shots you take of various screens in your app for posting on the Details page of your app's Marketplace listing must be 200 × 200 pixels in size.

T   F   3. The AppManifest.xml file lists the assemblies in your application.

T   F   4. You can run a debug build of your app on a physical device.

T   F   5. Only students may be eligible for Microsoft DreamSpark membership.

■ Competency Assessment

Scenario 8-1: Locate Windows Phone Marketplace Submission Requirements

CiCi wants to learn about Windows Phone Marketplace submission requirements before she begins developing her first application. She is searching through the Help system in the Visual Studio IDE but can't locate the information she needs. How do you advise her?

Scenario 8-2: Understand Artwork Specifications

Maxwell is a crackerjack programmer but lacks graphic arts skills. She wants to create a few icons for her new game app but isn't having any luck using Microsoft Paint. What do you suggest she try?

■ Proficiency Assessment

Scenario 8-3: Prepare for Marketplace Submission

Walter is a rather experienced app developer who has developed a spectacular app. He's excited and ready to post it for the world to use. He wants to know if he really needs to take the time to run the Windows Phone Marketplace Tool Kit against his app. What do you tell him?

Scenario 8-4: Resolve Application Manifest Issues

Jamal is a freelance app developer whose specialty is apps for the iPhone. He created his first Windows Phone app targeted to Windows Phone OS 7.0 for a new client and it turned out very well. However, he keeps getting errors regarding his WMAppManifest.xml file. He's stumped and asks for your help. What do you tell him?

Exam Objective	Skill Number	Lesson Number
Work with Physical Devices		
Understand mobile device tools.	1.1	1
Understand physical capabilities of the mobile device.	1.2	1
Plan for physical interactions with the mobile device.	1.3	1
Use Data with Mobile Devices		
Work with networked data.	2.1	3
Use data stores.	2.2	3
Use a Mobile Application Development Environment		
Understand design for mobile devices.	3.1	2, 8
Network for mobile devices.	3.2	4
Understand Silverlight.	3.3	5
Work with developer tools.	3.4	2, 8
Code for mobile applications.	3.5	5, 8
Develop Mobile Applications		
Manage the application life cycle.	4.1	6
Understand mobile device APIs.	4.2	6
Understand mobile device controls.	4.3	7
Build the user interface.	4.4	7

Index